Law and Religion in American History

This book continues the dialogue on the separation of church and state with an approach that emphasizes intellectual history and the constitutional theory that underlies American society. McGarvie explains that the founding fathers of America considered the right of conscience to be an individual right to be protected against governmental interference. While the religion clauses enunciated this right, its true protection occurred in the creation of separate public and private spheres. Religion and the churches were placed in the private sector. Yet, politically active Christians have intermittently mounted challenges to this bifurcation in calling for a greater public role for Christian faith and morality in American society. Written for scholars in American law, history, and political science – as well as for any general reader interested in the separation of church and state – this book is an intellectual history of law and religion that contextualizes a 400-year-old ideological struggle in American society.

MARK DOUGLAS MCGARVIE, J.D., PhD, is a research scholar at the Institute of Bill of Rights Law at Marshall-Wythe School of Law at the College of William and Mary. For the 2015–16 school year, he taught at the University of Zagreb Law School in Croatia as a Fulbright Scholar. His publications include *One Nation Under Law: America's Early National Struggles to Separate Church and State* (2004) and contributions to *The Cambridge History of Law in America* (2011) and *No Establishment of Religion: America's Contribution to Religious Liberty* (2012) as well as various law reviews and history journals.

The priest had got upon his feet, toward the last, and now he stood there passing his hand back and forth across his forehead like a person who is dazed and troubled; then he turned and wandered toward the door of his little workroom, and as he passed through it I heard him murmur sorrowfully: "Ah me, poor children, poor fiends, they have rights, and she said true – I never thought of that. God forgive me, I am to blame."

Mark Twain, *Personal Recollections of Joan of Arc*

New Histories of American Law

Series Editors

Michael Grossberg, *Indiana University*
Christopher L. Tomlins, *University of California, Berkeley*

New Histories of American Law is a series of bold, synthetic, and path-breaking interpretive books that will address the key topics in the field of American legal history, written by the leaders of the field and designed for scholars and students throughout universities, colleges, and law schools.

Law and Religion in American History

Public Values and Private Conscience

MARK DOUGLAS MCGARVIE

College of William & Mary

CAMBRIDGE
UNIVERSITY PRESS

CAMBRIDGE
UNIVERSITY PRESS

One Liberty Plaza, 20th Floor, New York, NY 10006, USA

Cambridge University Press is part of the University of Cambridge.

It furthers the University's mission by disseminating knowledge in the pursuit of education, learning, and research at the highest international levels of excellence.

www.cambridge.org
Information on this title: www.cambridge.org/9781316605462

© Mark Douglas McGarvie 2016

First published 2016

Printed in the United States of America by Sheridan Books, Inc.

A catalogue record for this publication is available from the British Library.

ISBN 978-1-107-15093-5 Hardback
ISBN 978-1-316-60546-2 Paperback

Certain lines or paragraphs in Chapter One are reprinted from chapters 5 and 6 of *One Nation under Law: America's Early National Struggles to Separate Church and State* by Mark Douglas McGarvie, 2004, with permission of Northern Illinois University Press.

Contents

Illustrations

Preface

"The legitimate powers of government extend to such acts only as
are injurious to others," Thomas Jefferson wrote in his *Notes on the
State of Virginia*.[1] "But it does me no injury for my neighbor to say
there are twenty gods, or no God. It neither picks my pocket nor breaks
my leg." Jefferson's words express a legalistic conception of religion as
rooted in individual conscience. Religion expresses an understanding
of life beyond that reality evident in the material world. It answers
questions common to humanity throughout time: Where does life
come from? Is there a grand purpose for life on earth? Is there life after
death? Jefferson implicitly argues that the answers to these questions
are unknowable. Individuals can therefore form various answers to
them, each of which constitutes a personal truth to its holder, but is of
little consequence to anyone else. Conversely, many Americans before,
during, and after Jefferson's lifetime have conceived of the answers
to these questions as revealed by God in the Bible. For them, the text
of the Bible provides an unerring and public truth that can and must
serve as the basis for society.

However, Jefferson's words address far more than a form of religious belief; they also outline a conception of society in which government is confined to acting within a circumscribed public sphere. The
need to limit the scope and power of the public sphere derived from a

[1] Thomas Jefferson, *Notes on the State of Virginia*, "Query XVII: Religion," in Merrill
D. Peterson, ed., *The Portable Jefferson* (New York: Penguin Books, 1975), 210.

recognition of rights as essential aspects of human existence; to deny or limit humanity in its enjoyment of rights constituted a prevention of human progress and happiness. Therefore, the founders created a private sphere in which people remained free to pursue their rights and a separate public sphere with limited authority to address the needs of civil society, the most significant of which was the protection of rights from injury. Jefferson's words place religion in that private sphere and therefore beyond the scope of government.

The humanistic philosophy popular during the late 1700s celebrated humanity's autonomy, reason, rationality, and ultimate ability to improve itself and the world around it. In the aftermath of the Revolution, liberals used humanist values to redesign the laws and institutions of the new republic, values that recognized the novel – for the eighteenth century – distinction between public and private realms. Yet, enforcing that distinction has never been easy. Jefferson's words hint at the difficulties Americans, both then and ever since, have had in accepting all the ramifications of that distinction, especially the removal of religion from the public sector.

Generations of Christians who accept the Bible as true have struggled to understand why God's word, presumably superior to anything humanity creates, cannot be the basis of law and public policy. Both the Old and New Testaments of the Bible encourage readers to subordinate themselves to God; fight their human desires for sex, vanity, and selfish gain as sinful; and express their love for God in a loving brotherhood with other people. Accordingly, despite tremendous variations among American Christians, they have been more willing to endorse the empowerment of government to enforce God's moral teachings and, in so doing, to pursue a communitarian society. Their success, since ratification of the Constitution, has depended on either (1) reading Christianity, particularly its moral proscriptions and prescriptions, into the laws of the nation and the various states, or (2) changing the laws of the country and the various states so as to better embody Christian values. Yet, in reliance on the Jeffersonian conception of religion as a personal matter outside the scope of government, the Constitution has largely prohibited law from endorsing, depending on, or encouraging any religious doctrine or belief. As a result, law has really only been relevant to religion when refracted through particular political and social activities that have raised constitutional issues.

This book, therefore, addresses the relationship between law and religion almost exclusively from a public-law perspective, contextualized in significant intellectual and religious movements that have framed their interaction.

Accordingly, the chapters of this book are demarcated by political, social, and intellectual periods that identify changing cultural milieus that shaped the development of the nation's public law and the relationship between law and religion. Legal history is presented as the primary focus of a broader intellectual, cultural, and political history of the influence of Christianity on America's public institutions. This approach recognizes actors other than litigants, lawyers, and judges as voicing conceptions of law that both challenged and contributed to national understandings of the doctrine of separation of church and state. Ministers, social reformers, and religious activists have expressed visions of American society frequently formed from personal attempts to integrate their religious beliefs and their citizenship. In the process, they have worked for change in America's laws.

The "culture wars" that have been at the core of a major political division in the United States since the late 1970s are not new; in fact, they have their origins in the founding era and have been a periodic source of political tension throughout the nation's history. They result from popular dissatisfaction with the Jeffersonian ideal. This book addresses the tension between the Jeffersonian ideal and the practices and attitudes of generations of Americans.

This attempt to explain cultural understandings of and reactions to the Jeffersonian ideal of separating church and state develops two arguments. First, the founders created a private sector, largely immune from governmental intervention, to protect rights, one of which was the freedom of conscience. Religion was placed in this private sector, producing the separation of church and state. Throughout this text, the word "public" generally refers to the government sector. Second, ardent Christians, unhappy with the removal of religion from the public sector, have intermittently attempted to restructure the laws and institutions of the country to embody a greater commitment to Christian ideals. Politically unable to succeed in these goals by themselves, they have formed tentative alliances with a variety of others who shared their goals for a more communitarian society, even though these others may have espoused very different beliefs.

These two arguments form the thesis of this book, augmented by a third argument recognizing a perpetual cultural attempt to identify the United States of America as a "Christian nation." Religious activists have used the idea of a Christian nation to justify increases in public-sector recognition and support of Christianity and have used history in support of their argument. In particular, they have cited Federalist Party invocations of religion as a necessary prop for both a moral society and democracy in the founding era, the adoption of "In God We Trust" as a motto in the nineteenth century, and the inclusion of the phrase "one nation, under God," in the Pledge of Allegiance in the mid-twentieth century. Yet, each of these examples is more representative of a civil religion that puts religion in service to humanity than it is of a cultural submission to Christianity's prescriptive and proscriptive doctrines and that religion's teachings of providence, judgment, and redemption. In many ways, the use of religion in this way is less evidence of a devoutly Christian people than of a popular acceptance of a God created in Americans' image of themselves. The "civil religion" brings flags into churches and crosses into warfare, commingling loyalties and devotions while excusing self-interest, pride, and cultural arrogance. Just how many gods have Americans placed above the one they profess to worship?

Throughout the nation's history, Americans have used various versions and permutations of Christianity in support of exclusionary politics, defining themselves in reference to what they are not. A desire for cultural and racial homogeneity has manifested in reliance on predominantly Old Testament passages, opportune conceptions of Christian duties and morals, and an assertion of a "Christian nation" to suppress groups of people perceived to threaten community norms. Indians, Africans, Quakers, Catholics, Mormons, humanists, atheistic communists, and Moslems are just some of the people who have been persecuted, ostracized, and vilified by Americans who have used Christianity rather than the cosmopolitan constitutional ideal to define themselves. At times, supporters of the Christian nation myth have tried to read their religion into the nation's primary law and civil institutions. But, as this book indicates, the fits and starts of this attempt reflect the difficulty of integrating an idea system predicated on faith in a revealed truth with one rooted in a dependence on verification of asserted truths using human reason and rationality.

Moreover, Christianity has variously served both as a critique of prevailing cultural values and as a justification of those same values. The Christian nation myth, the rise of the civil religion in the nineteenth century, and the growth of the Religious Right in the late twentieth century all ignore the prophetic role of Christianity in preference for a conception of religion that reinforces American social life. Legal endorsements of a public religion have likewise rejected a prophetic Christianity for a noncontentious form of Christianity. Yet, Christianity has frequently been at odds with mainstream American social behaviors and values.

Throughout most of American history, Christianity has fought to restrain individual freedoms that produce immoral societal consequences. Ministers have decried free-enterprise capitalism as promoting poverty and suffering, democracy as too celebratory of humanity's abilities, and the absence of laws restricting alcohol use, censoring sexual behavior, and limiting teaching history or science in contravention of Biblical pronouncements. In support of Christian moralism and human deference to God, America's religious leaders have, more often than not, been willing to align with those who have advocated a greater public embrace of communitarian values and accepted the increase in state power that the pursuit of these values required.

The founders' very clear and quite radical intention to create a legal system independent of religious belief resulted in two parallel systems of rules, conceptions of morality, and understandings of justice that are almost entirely irreconcilable. Both the law and religion tend to espouse and promote absolutes. The absolutes that hold sway in the legal arena are more easily identified than those that prevail in the religious realm. People commonly assert that English common law served as the basis of American law. While there is some truth in this assertion, it minimizes the degree to which Americans rewrote their law after the Revolution to embody republican ideals and to protect rights. Most significantly, Americans perceived the need, amounting to what one historian considers a "compulsive mania,"[2] for constitutions – social contracts that set parameters on future laws and governmental actions by recognizing both individual rights and delegations of

---

[2] Robert M. Cover, *Justice Accused: Antislavery and the Judicial Process* (New Haven, CT: Yale University Press, 1975), 27.

limited authority to address public needs. Rights became the chief concern of law, the absolute upon which every legal expression depends.

Despite the prioritization of rights, the dominant ideas of any given time influence the course of law. In fact, American jurisprudence may best be understood as a subset of ideas – a legal expression of the beliefs, values, and societal goals of the American people applied to practical purpose in governing. Understood in this way, American law is never static. Change, especially radical change, may occur slowly and by incremental degrees because of a legal inertia rooted in the need to conform to constitutional principles, obey rules of precedent, and follow procedural dictates that limit the force of radical social arguments. Yet, it does occur, and when it does, it embodies a recognition of changing intellectual patterns in American society. The American law dealing with religion serves as an excellent example of ideological influences on the development of American jurisprudence.

One might think that religion has been just as absolutist as law, but religion in America has always been complex and pluralistic. Despite the fact that the founders encouraged immigration to the United States by people of all faiths or none at all, Christianity, since the earliest days, has formed the most popular religion within the country. Yet, this fact has never produced uniformity regarding the doctrines, morals, values, or goals of Christianity. If, as many religionists have asserted throughout the nation's history, society is to be subject to the values and morals commanded by the Christian faith, as many questions are posed as are answered. What are even the commonly held values and morals of Christianity? Who is to determine them?

America's Christians have fought among themselves for centuries regarding doctrinal issues such as humanity's role in salvation and whether the Bible constitutes the true word of God or a collection of allegorical stories written by men. Yet, just as many contests have arisen in the social realm as in the doctrinal. Is salvation or the social good the primary goal of the church? Can homosexuals marry or be ministers? To what degree does Christianity condone extreme inequalities in wealth within its own community or even its own congregations? There is no single Christian answer to any of these questions.

The rights orientation of the American legal system has produced a very strong individualistic character within the people and their society. The Revolution served as much, if not more, to liberate individuals from oppressive control in their lives in America as to overthrow the political structure of Britain's imperial governance. A rights-oriented individualism justified not only political revolution but social revolution as well. The embodiment of rights in the Constitution empowered people in their private actions. Consistent with this rights orientation, the common law of the early republic, in primary reliance on contract law, redesigned society by promoting individual freedom and autonomy at the expense of communitarian values and social cohesion. Yet, various forms of Christian expressions encourage adherents to adopt a communitarianism premised upon human brotherhood and to recognize social duties rooted in the need of humanity to follow the commandments of God. Individual rights cannot be used as justification or excuses to sin, to ignore the needy, or to deny the relevance of God and his law in all circumstances.

During and after the Revolution, law dictated that religion, as a matter of personal conscience, and the churches, as private voluntary corporations, be placed in the private realm. Yet, many Christians throughout the nation's history, believing that God's teachings must be manifested in society at large, have challenged religion's place in the private sphere and aligned with other communitarians to bring about change. In other words, they have turned to politics to change the law, at times trying even to change the Constitution. This book presents an analysis and interpretation of these alliances and their attempts to restructure society. It is a history of ideas, a story of the power of belief, and a record of the persistence of law to sustain the values of the founding era.

The interaction between popular ideas, law, and belief presents a complicated history made even more difficult because of the repetitive use of words that garner new meanings over time. The analysis presented herein depends on explicating the evolving conception of the role of the individual within American society, particularly in relation to the authority presented by government and churches. Three distinct terms are used in the text. "Law and religion" addresses the broad conceptions of systems of governing and belief. "Church and state" refers to the institutions derived from these conceptual systems. "Religion and politics" refers to the behaviors of people within the conceptual systems. One can think of the latter two interactions as subsets of the first.

American liberalism, shortly after the Revolution, prioritized freedom, autonomy, and legal equality and created a private sphere of action largely exempt from governmental intrusion to protect the individual in his or her exercise of these priorities. Disestablishment of the churches coincided with the privatization of morality as liberals recognized religion as a matter of personal conscience. Both political and moral authority over people's range of pursuits diminished in the early republic. Conservatives at the same time evinced a Burkean acceptance of the need to restrain individuals to sustain a functioning society and willingly enlisted religion and moral legislation as means of doing so.

American liberals have consistently sought to protect a broad range of options for individuals within their society. Yet, the focus of that protection has changed. A libertarian endorsement of democracy and free-enterprise capitalism promoted expanded personal freedoms in the early 1800s, but by the close of the nineteenth century, liberals came to see new sources of power or authority, found in corporations and prevailing human prejudices, to be even more dangerous to individual autonomy than powerful churches and government. Choosing the lesser of two evils, twentieth-century liberals willingly invested government with the power to limit the personal freedoms of some in society, primarily in the economic realm, to secure essential opportunities for a broader segment of the population.

Given the vicissitudes in Americans' thinking, the Supreme Court has fought to maintain a line separating public and private spheres as a legal constant since the early days of the republic. But, both the position of that line and its permeability have been incessantly challenged and reconceived over the last 225 years. As a result, the history of law and religion can best be understood as one of periodic fluctuations in attitudes toward the legal line, its location, and its true meaning. Each of these fluctuations forces a reconsideration of questions concerning the importance of Christian conceptions of the public good relative to individual rights and liberties. Americans' respect for their primary law and the law's own disinclination to change have produced political contests that have reenacted debates over the intentions and meanings of the founders in drawing the line and the degree to which societal judgments, at any point in time, can adjust it.

Political reconsiderations of the appropriate relationship between church and state have repeatedly raised challenges not only to what the founders intended to do but also to the relevance of their intentions. As this book goes to press, Americans once again debate the appropriateness of judicial review as a means of determining constitutional meanings and whether the original intent of the founders should be given priority in ascertaining those meanings. As will be established in the pages that follow, the founding era constituted arguably the most secular age in the history of the United States, and its primary laws and legal precepts embody that secularism. In light of this recognition, evangelical conservatives' calls for greater public reliance on religion while simultaneously endorsing judicial recourse to original intent present a baffling intellectual inconsistency that has produced both some distorted histories and some awkward and confusing law.

Acknowledgments

I owe a tremendous thank-you to series editors Mike Grossberg and Chris Tomlins for their confidence, support, and patience during this project. In addition, I received important advice and counsel on early drafts from Betty Mensch (SUNY at Buffalo Law School, emeritus), Martin Marty (University of Chicago, emeritus), Bill Nelson (New York University School of Law, emeritus), Richard Bernstein (New York Law School), Sally Gordon (University of Pennsylvania), Woody Holton (University of South Carolina), Larry Friedman (Harvard University), Mark Valeri (Washington University), Doug Winiarski (University of Richmond), Dave Parsons, colleague in the practice of law, and my wife, Blythe McGarvie, an author and educator as well. Bob Gross (University of Connecticut, emeritus) offered significant help in understanding transcendentalism, even sharing with me some works in progress. The University of Richmond, acting through its chair of the History Department, Hugh West, kindly provided me with a one-year sabbatical from teaching to help me in the research stage of this project. Since my move to the Marshall-Wythe School of Law at the College of William & Mary, Dean Dave Douglas and Vice Dean Laura Heymann have been wonderfully encouraging and supportive. My colleague in legal history, Tom McSweeney, has helped by being a friend with whom I can talk history, even during semesters devoted to teaching more pragmatic legal concerns. A former college professor of mine, Timothy Breen, similarly offered counsel in his more recent role as "friend." My beloved westie, Pooka, watched me write every word of the text from a window box in my office at home. After her passing, our newly rescued mix-breeds, Lakota and Archie, encouraged me from the same position through numerous revisions and edits. Last, but certainly not least, I owe a debt of gratitude to two wonderful women who helped me by typing the manuscript through its myriad changes. Cary Hemphill and Debbie Govoruhk showed dedication and patience with an "old school" professor who still writes everything in longhand on lined paper.

Prologue

Colonial America Perpetuates State Religion

The Reformation can be understood, in part, as the substitution of Biblical authority for that of the Pope and his priests. The Protestants formed in the spiritual revolution of the sixteenth century accepted that salvation depended on faith alone, reconceiving of good works as a by-product of faith rather than as a means of salvation. Within a societal context, therefore, morality, or the invocation to do good, became both a duty owed to God and an obligation to one's neighbors. Moreover, faith and the morality it engendered could be expected of everyone, even if God limited salvation to a few. Protestant doctrines asserted that Christian duties exist for all people and, as they express one's relationship to God, render all people equal in God's eyes. That equality, however, while undermining the privileged position of priests as mediators between God and humanity, caused no diminution in political authorities and social hierarchies. The Bible, in fact, seemed to endorse them in Romans 13: 1–7: "Let every person be subject to the governing authorities. For there is no authority except from God, and those that exist must have been instituted by God."

In Europe, the Lutheran conception of magistrates as fathers of their communities contributed to the shift in authority and wealth from the church to the state and led to the state establishing churches, schools, and social welfare institutions. Lutheranism accepted the Bible as a guide to building an earthly kingdom but tempered reliance on it by making both Christian morality and human reason equally important considerations in governing. Calvinism, which exerted tremendous influence in the English-American colonies in the 1600s, conversely considered it the duty of people to transform earth into an approximation of heaven, with the Bible serving as the expression of God's desires for human community. Therefore, throughout much of Europe, churches served in support of the secular authorities, while in America during the same time period, civil governments worked to support the churches. Calvinism distinguished, yet integrated, civil and religious lives. Throughout the colonies, public and private realms were indistinguishable, and in fact, the terms had little, if any, legal significance.

Legal establishments of religion in the colonies preferred a designated sect of the Protestant Christian religion over all others. Laws required residents to support the established church with tax dollars and to attend its worship services. The established church held sole authority to perform sacraments and exercised tremendous influence over the laws and morals of its community. Established churches also acted as quasi-public entities in providing nearly all the education in the colonies, raising taxes and contributing aid to the poor, and keeping most of the public records, including those for births, deaths, marriages, property transfers, and taxes.

Certainly the colonies along the Atlantic seaboard exhibited diversity in political structure, religious preference, and social composition, and the theocratic model of Calvin existed briefly only in New England. Yet, throughout the colonies, Christian precepts and morality influenced law, shaped communities, and directed people in their daily activities. Eleven of the thirteen colonies had some form of religious establishment, but even in Pennsylvania and Rhode Island religious doctrine and values exercised great influence. Every colony criminalized blasphemy, regulated economic activities consistent with Christian conceptions of ethics and the social good, and restricted sexual practices. Several colonies considered "hard dealing" or "oppression," which most often meant relying on market forces rather than morality and the communal good to determine prices, not only to be unlawful but also sinful. Virginia's laws regulated work hours, staffing, and prices. Colonies punished idleness for its deleterious effects on the community's productivity and for its disrespect of God. Idleness ignored God's gifts, properly expressed in one's "calling" as the fulfillment of one's duty to work for the good of the whole. And while the inhabitants of Massachusetts are frequently perceived as preoccupied with sex, or at least the control of it, they were hardly alone in regulating this activity. Pennsylvania flogged adulterers and sodomizers, and the Chesapeake colonies similarly punished fornicators. The punishment of sexual offenses ostensibly expressed the law's support of Biblical proscriptions of behavior, yet it originally arose in Europe in the 1500s as much from fears of syphilis as from fears of God's wrath. Perhaps more significantly, it implicitly asserted the legitimacy of societal restraints on basic human desires, ambitions, and longings and justified those restraints in reference to God's laws.

People in the 1600s could accept such restrictions in large part because they believed their place and role in society to be a result of God's intentions rather than of human abilities and actions. Society in Stuart England conformed to God's designs. All of creation could be expressed in a ceaseless hierarchical chain of being that structured the duties of people, animals, and even plants in relation to those above and below them. In this context the colonial integration of law and religion has been seen by some as a means of justifying the social power of the governing class. However, this reductionist argument minimizes both the sincerity of belief among the colonists and the role of religion in constructing both individual and community identities. Most people in the 1600s accepted God's revealed truth concerning the origins of humanity and the world, the power and efficacy of God, and the proper behavior of people as absolutes. To the colonists, Christian doctrine and the morals it prescribed were no less objectively true than the fact that the sun rose in the morning – a fact that only further confirmed both God's design and his active providence. Certainly colonists expressed awareness of doctrinal inconsistencies between Christian sects, using them as bases for persecution and ostracism. But, rather than raising doubts about the dogmatic interpretation of ancient texts translated multiple times from both dead and living languages and subjected to innumerable cultural and contextual meanings, those inconsistencies constituted evidence of the threat posed by religious error and the need for vigilant defense of the true creed.

Accepting the universal truth of a particular Christian doctrine, various colonies enforced religious conformity to reduce the threat of religious error. In 1624, John Cotton of Massachusetts expressed the reasoning behind the persecution of dissenters to the established

FIGURE P.1. Mary Dyer led to her execution on Boston Common, June 1, 1660. Religious dissenters, such as Quaker Mary Dyer, were whipped, imprisoned, banished, and even executed in colonial America. Artist unknown, nineteenth-century colored engraving, The Granger Collection, New York, Image #0061778.

religion in his sermon, "The Bloody Tenent, Washed and Made White in the Bloud of the Lambe":

If they [those holding false beliefs] be infectious, and leprous, and have plague sores running upon them, and think it their glory to infect others; it is no want of mercy and, charity, to set such at a distance: It is a merciless mercy, to pity such as are incurably contagious, and mischievous, and not to pity many scores or hundreds of the souls of such, as will be infected and destroyed by the toleration of the other.[1]

Colonists used the same reasoning not only to prosecute citizens for blasphemy, heresy (Figure P.1), and violations of the Sabbath, but also to sanction the slaughter of Indians unwilling to convert to Christianity

---

[1] John Cotton, "The Bloody Tenent, Washed and Made White in the Bloud of the Lambe" (1624).

and the enslavement of heathen Africans. Colonial communities strove for a pure homogeneity in belief, thought, and action and relied on religious precepts as the primary means of pursuing it.

Calvinism understands humanity to be inherently sinful and inclined to evil. People need strict rules to guide them, severe punishments to motivate them, and constant public reminders of their submission to God and his designated civil authorities. As already noted, the Bible provides considerable support for the respect and perpetuation of hierarchies and social order. The integration of law and religion reinforced colonial police powers with the authority of the faith. Throughout colonial America, police powers punished sin while simultaneously constructing a communitarian society by establishing social duties, promoting Christian morality, and preserving the social order. Laws rooted in faith subordinated individualism to the public good.

The integration of religion and law in colonial America results from two conditions that made the integration not only possible but also inevitable. The first is the understanding that Christianity expressed a universal and absolute truth. In this intellectual milieu, it only made sense for government to endorse that truth and the derivative duties of people in the promulgation and enforcement of its laws. The second is the absence of any modern recognition of individual rights or of a private sphere immune from public intervention. A social hierarchy, not dissimilar to old feudalistic social models, imposed duties on the rich and powerful to take care of those "beneath" them and for the poorer and less fortunate to willingly subordinate, show deference to, and obey their social "betters." Christianity reinforced this social model in its doctrinal expressions of the innate sinfulness and unworthiness of people, their duties to subordinate themselves to God, and its characterizing of lust, greed, and selfishness as evil. The law relied on these widely accepted understandings in promoting a social good by assigning duties and roles for the community's welfare. Private rights, and a private sphere necessary for their protection, were not relevant considerations in colonial America.

An example of the construction of a mill in a river town illustrates the absence of a distinctly private sphere. A colonial-era farming community on a river, but without a mill, becomes aware that it is losing money as its residents take their grains downriver to be ground. Furthermore, the absence of a mill inconveniences the local citizens. So

the magistrates decide to build a mill. They do so by seeking proposals from various bidders expressing their experience, a design of the
mill, and a plan of operations. The magistrates accept one proposal
and authorize its principal to construct a mill in the town. It will be
the only mill in town – a monopoly of sorts. The magistrates approve
the design, determine how many people will work there, the hours of
its operation, the days of the week on which various grains will be
ground, the hours of labor of the employees, the prices to be charged,
and the fair profit due the owner/operator. Is this a private or a public
mill? To colonial Americans, the question made no sense – it was more
meaningless than irrelevant. Similarly, the town church was neither
public nor private – it simply was a church.

Of course, the relative lack of any legal recognition of rights before
about 1700 imposed limitations on the freedoms of nearly all the colonists. Yet, perhaps no group of colonists suffered as much as women
did from the incorporation of Biblical ideas into law. Reformation
theology limited the rights and opportunities of women by considering God to have created husbands superior to their wives. Colonial
Americans perceived the household headed by a father/husband as the
primary political, economic, social, and religious unit. The male head
of the household made all the decisions regarding each of those cat-
egories of behavior for members of the household as a whole. Women
had no political voice, little opportunity to hold property, and generally lacked control over their own marriages. Laws in various colonies
furthered the extent of the authority of the head of the household
by permitting his use of corporal punishment over wives, children,
servants, and slaves alike. The perception of a household as a distinct
political entity also furthered communitarian sentiment, an ethical
perspective codified in laws imposing duties on the wealthy to assist,
even by taking into their homes, if necessary, orphans and indigents.
Christian duties and responsibilities underlay social status and reinforced hierarchies in colonial societies.

Religious establishment did not eliminate dissent from the preferred faith; it merely denied dissenters equal civil rights, subjected
them to punishment for practicing their faiths, and required them
to support the established church. Throughout the 1600s, colonists
exhibited little, if any, toleration of Jews, atheists, or Christians of
dissenting sects. England attempted to impose religious freedom, but

colonists largely ignored the attempt until Parliament passed the Act of Toleration in 1689. The recalcitrance of Massachusetts resulted in the revocation of its charter and the installation of a royal governor. Maryland, though created as a Catholic refuge necessitated by the persecution of Catholics along the entire Atlantic seaboard, quickly became dominated by Anglicans who exercised tyrannical control until Queen Anne secured limited religious freedom in that colony in 1702.

By the early 1700s, expanding business opportunities bringing diverse sailors and settlers to the colonies; the diffusion of people into less easily monitored western areas; new ideas spawned in the Enlightenment expressing human equality, natural rights, and a cosmopolitanism that scorned religious parochialism; and the growing professionalism, relative luxury, and sophistication of life in the colonies all contributed to an increase in religious toleration. Nascent capitalism fostered a growing individualism that threatened older Christian values and communitarian ethics while it encouraged modifications in religious doctrine and the laws prescribing it. Social and intellectual changes also spurred a reconsideration of religious belief and practice. The Great Awakening, beginning in the 1730s, can be seen either as a reformulation of religion to accommodate the ideas of the early Enlightenment, especially a growing individualism, or as a conservative reaction to those developments.

Awakening preaching reinvigorated a religion that had lost some of its significance to many Americans. It generated interest through emotional appeals to individuals to repent of sin, substituting a simple traditional message for the esoteric preaching of the previous thirty or forty years. Doctrinally, the Great Awakening combined a human-centered assertion of an ability to receive the grace of God through personal exertion with reassertions of human depravity and the need for a God-centered communal existence. In focusing on individual sensory receptivity to grace, the Awakening expressed an empowering message of personal responsibility that recognized each person as equal both before the Lord and in society. The Awakening therefore contributed a challenge to the authority of the churches and the social hierarchies they supported. The Awakening even broke down some barriers based on race, sex, class, and literacy. Yet, it also contributed to a new prestige among preachers as means of grace and reinforced communitarian ideas in calling for a new social order formed by a union of believers that would hasten the Biblical promise of a Second Coming.

Traditional, or "Old Light," ministers who expressed alarm at religious enthusiasm as a means of conversion minimized the Awakening's important theological contributions. "New Light" ministers such as Jonathan Edwards accommodated traditional Calvinist thought to ideas and attitudes of their time. Critics saw frenzied revival meetings as an indication that New Light preaching endorsed a dangerous individualism rooted in emotion more than reason. Yet, Calvinism had always denigrated human reason as a means of attaining salvation. The esoteric and sometimes tortured preaching and writing of the preceding generation, also prompted by desires to conform traditional belief to Enlightenment ideology and social change, had increasingly invoked reason to explain doctrinal changes as consistent with traditional understandings of Biblical meanings, if not with prior practices. The New Light preachers of the Awakening rejected these recent amendments to Calvinist thought and substituted those that, they argued, more accurately reflected the word of God and the traditions of their predecessors.

The division between Old and New Light preaching styles and doctrines fragmented nearly every sect within America. Established church leaders responded in fear, securing laws that prohibited itinerant preachers expressing New Light theologies. Yet, laws and punishments failed to restrain the religious enthusiasm of the 1730s and 1740s. Dissenters from the established religions flocked to the new Baptist and Methodist churches born in the Awakening, making them the fastest-growing denominations in the country. Three parties emerged within America's Calvinist churches: liberals who espoused a foundational Unitarianism, establishmentarians who used religion primarily as a means of preserving social order and morality, and pietistic evangelicals, born in the Awakening, who saw religion as more of a personal than a social concern. Though the liberals and the establishmentarians shared a greater doctrinal perspective, the liberals and the evangelicals combined to pose a social threat to established religion.

By motivating people to assume control over their religious beliefs, the Great Awakening encouraged a challenge to colonial authority. Some historians see in this a prelude to Revolution. However, the

Awakening as an ideological rather than a social movement sought to return both to an earlier version of Calvinist theology and to an older ideal of homogeneous Christian communities. The seeds of revolution took root in neither of these desires.

Yet, incontrovertibly, the Great Awakening realigned colonial America. As religious sects proliferated, established churches could make little claim to espousing the one true faith, even within a particular colony. Toleration became essential in nearly every business and social context. However, toleration is not the same as freedom. On the eve of the Revolution, one or another expression of Christianity served as the established religion in nearly every colony, and Christian ethics remained a vital aspect of the colonial legal culture. Atheists, Jews, and even Christian dissenters continued to be denied full civic participation. Still, Americans increasingly responded to religious diversity by ignoring what they saw as minor doctrinal differences. By 1749 in Boston's West Church, the Reverend Lemuel Briant could assert that "the perfect religion of Jesus was nothing other than a refined system of morality,"[2] foreshadowing future developments in Christian thought. Sectarian differences still mattered by the late 1700s, but more for social than for theological reasons. America, in the 1770s, was poised for a major reconsideration of the role of religion in society.

[2] Quoted in Harry S. Stout, *The New England Soul: Preaching and Religious Culture in Colonial New England* (New York: Oxford University Press, 1986), 223–4.

Revolution in Thought and Social Organization

The Legal Hegemony of Jeffersonian Liberalism, 1776–1828

Americans generally may think of their Revolution almost exclusively as a process of winning independence from Great Britain. In doing so, they vastly underestimate the transformative nature of the Revolution on American society. Americans expressed a widespread acceptance of natural rights, profoundly changing the nature of Americans' religious beliefs and restructuring the role of the individual in society, especially relative to the authority of the government and the churches.

The idea of natural rights derived from the Newtonian construct, an intellectual understanding of the world as governed by natural laws. Natural laws applied not only in the realms of physics and biology but also to all earthly activity. People, as inherently reasonable and rational and possessed of an innate benevolence permitting the formation of society, could discover and conform to the natural laws in shaping human laws and institutions. Natural law vested humanity with inherent rights. Creating a civil society that recognized and protected these rights required reconceptualizing the nature of the state and ultimately delineating public and private spheres, with the public or governmental sphere limited in its ability to interfere with the rights of individuals in the private sphere. Inevitably, the existence of the private sphere produced a more individualistic, even an atomistic society.

Thinkers during the intellectual age known as the Enlightenment (roughly the late 1600s to the early 1800s), though captivated by the exercise of their minds in scientific experimentation and discovery, also could accept dogmatic truths spawned entirely through intuitive reasoning and use those truths as bases for deducing governing principles consistent with them. Thomas Jefferson and the signatories to the Declaration of Independence could boldly assert that they held certain "truths to be self-evident," needing no further elucidation or substantiation. The Revolution accordingly could be fought for both equality and individual freedom, with only a slight awareness of the tension that may exist between these two goals. Ultimately, adoption of free-enterprise capitalism, initially perceived as a means of achieving both goals, focused attention on the tension between them and simultaneously resolved it in favor of personal freedom, endorsing a high degree of individualism. Law, through its protection of private rights rather than the public welfare, limited the idea of equality to legal considerations, deeming social equality inconsistent with American ideas of liberty.

The Revolutionary era lasted almost twenty years, from the Stamp Act crisis in 1765 to the Treaty of Paris in 1783. This era marked a change in American attitudes from a classical republicanism to liberalism. Classical republicanism prioritized the commonwealth and accepted Whig conceptions of rights rooted in the English constitution. Liberalism prioritized freedom and accepted natural rights common to all humans. To some degree, this transition corresponds to a broader intellectual movement within Western culture from the Moderate Enlightenment to the Radical Enlightenment. The Moderate Enlightenment of the late 1600s and early 1700s integrated Protestantism with new scientific and philosophical ideas. Moderate Enlightenment figures such as John Locke defended Christianity, but by the late 1700s, the writings of Rousseau expressed little patience with religion.

The rise in people's reliance on reason coincided with a sharp decline in religiosity. If "secularism" is used as a descriptor of observed behavior and not as a term defining a specific school of thought, the Revolutionary and Constitutional eras and the early republic constituted a secular age. In other words, relative to the time periods that preceded and followed it, Americans during this roughly sixty-year period of time relied less on religion as a means of understanding the world and the place of humanity in it and less on Biblical prescriptions and proscriptions as determinants of how people should live on earth. Estimates of church membership during and immediately after the Revolution range from 4 to 14 percent, with approximately 70 percent of those members being women. As late as the early 1800s in Virginia, only 40 of 107 Episcopal parishes had churches and ministers. Even in New England, religion declined. In Vermont and New Hampshire, 140 Congregational parishes were without a minister at the time the Constitution was drafted, and while the population increased by 150 percent between 1780 and 1820, the number of Congregational churches increased by only 40 percent during the same period. Ministers of the time complained of what they saw as a "republic of atheism" born in the humanist ideology of the Enlightenment. Roger Sherman of Connecticut said that in the late 1700s, Christianity "was fearfully threatened with extermination."[1]

The Revolutionary War constituted only the first stage of the transition from a hierarchical communitarian society governed by laws respecting Christian conceptions of truth and moral duty to an individualistic society in which laws respecting more liberal conceptions of rights reconceived of religion as a matter of personal conscience and considered truth limited to those matters provable by science and logically deducible from its principles. The war years encouraged Americans to think about the meaning of their Revolution and the ideals that supported it. This thinking process gained clarity through the constitutional era and produced a fulfillment of revolutionary ideals in the "second revolution" – the election of Thomas Jefferson to the presidency in 1800 – which marked popular rejection of an older republican model for a liberal mode of governance.

Republicanism and a Usable Religion

Republicanism's ultimate evolution into liberalism should minimize neither the importance nor the innovativeness of it as a political idea. However, the ability of republicanism, as a body of ideas

---

[1] Quoted in Sidney Earl Mead, *Nathaniel William Taylor, 1786–1858: A Connecticut Liberal* (Chicago: Archon Books, 1967, orig. 1942), 47.

that promotes a system of governance, to radically transform society was tempered by its assertion that democracy depended upon virtue. Virtue recognized both the need for a natural aristocracy of gifted men to selflessly devote themselves to governing and for the populace to respect the good of the whole as more instructive of voting behavior than self-interest. Most Americans at the time of the Revolution believed religion served a vital role in inculcating the virtue necessary for self-government. The reliance on virtue that underlay American republicanism during the Revolution mitigated efforts to separate church and state and even to recognize complete religious tolerance during the war years.

Revolutionary-era Americans struggled to reconcile relatively new understandings of individual rights and legal equality with lifelong understandings of religion, churches, and ministers as authorities. Ministers generally supported the war, giving hundreds, if not thousands, of sermons in support of Revolution and holding days of prayer and fasting to solicit God's help in their cause. In these efforts they encouraged a cultural integration of political and religious goals. Dissenting ministers defined liberty as both a Christian and a political imperative and openly hoped that the Revolution would bring religious freedom that would topple all sectarian establishments.

More conceptually, republicanism, at least in the 1770s, continued to accept governance or leadership by an elite, albeit one arguably determined by merit rather than title or class, that knew best what was good for everyone. In this context, religion, and its message of deference and submission, could be a useful political tool to restrain excessive liberty. It continued to endorse a moral ethic that restrained the individualistic aspects of republicanism that frightened some of its more socially conservative proponents. However, republicanism's endorsement of Christianity as a tool for promoting virtue implicitly reversed the traditional order of religious deference and placed God in service to humanity, indicating the changing role of religion in society.

Religion itself was anything but immune from the influences of Enlightenment thought. Christianity became increasingly Arminian, embracing human determinism, after 1750. American beliefs in providence and trinitarianism declined, while liberal forms of religion, such as Deism and Universalist-Unitarianism, grew so rapidly during the founding era that Jefferson believed they would form the religious beliefs of a majority of Americans within a generation. Deists believed in a "Creator" who, having once made the world, absented itself, leaving the world to be governed by natural laws. Universalists accepted God's love as ensuring universal salvation, and Unitarians denied the divinity of Jesus and the efficacy of the Holy Spirit. Together these forms of liberal religion repudiated the Christian ideas of providence, a judgment day, and the Holy Trinity. Many, if not most, of the men regarded as the Founding Fathers adopted a form of liberal religion, rejecting both the mysticism of Christianity and its imposition of moral duties.

Liberal religionists and more secular humanists shared a commitment to individual autonomy that fostered a relativistic approach to religion. People living in Europe and the American colonies during the 1600s had generally accepted one or another form of Christian doctrine as true, thereby justifying public-sector endorsement of Christianity and its moral teachings. By the late 1700s, growing numbers of people harbored substantial doubt as to the truth of the espoused tenets of Christianity. Many late-eighteenth-century Americans came to see religion as concerning matters unknowable and therefore beyond the powers of any just government to impose on its citizens. At the same time, a new conception of rights as derived from natural law recognized an inherent freedom of individuals to think and believe for themselves. Together the conception of religion as concerning matters unknowable and the understanding of a right of individual conscience contributed to a new and radical conception of society in which religion and morality were left to the consciences of individuals.

The cultural embrace of individualism challenged the idea of public truths and promoted freethinking. The creation of a realm of civic debate in the eighteenth century constituted a radical departure from the ideal of social order that pervaded the *ancien regime* in Europe and colonial governing patterns in America. Arguments, differing opinions, and even divisiveness between citizens or groups of people became not only commonplace but also desirable. A growing cultural respect for each person as an equal, rational, and reasonable thinker arose contemporaneously with society's appreciation of an open forum as a place for civic debate.

In no realm did an appreciation or respect for differences of opinion foster greater tolerance than that of religion. The works of John

Locke, written in the late seventeenth century, influenced American ideas on the nature of rights, government, and religion. In his *Essay Concerning Toleration*, Locke considered matters of doctrinal religious belief to be "purely speculative opinions" and the worship of any God to be a personal matter between each individual and his or her deity. Accordingly, he endorsed a tolerance of various religious beliefs and practices because "in religion men must in this necessarily follow what they themselves thought best."[2] The more liberal-minded of the founders, such as James Madison, adopted Locke's thinking in referring to religion as concerning "matters unknowable." Conceiving of religion in this way complemented the growing recognition of a right of conscience.

The Reverend John Cotton could argue in 1624 that the Puritans in Massachusetts Bay should remove nonbelievers from their community because the official interpretation of Christianity served as a public truth. The law considered dissenters from that truth to be wrong or "in error." Personal judgment or individual conscience, as Anne Hutchison, Roger Williams, and Mary Dyer learned, did not function as a basis for belief – ministers, speaking with the authority of the state, expressed the public truth of the scriptures that all within the community should believe. Conversely, once religious "truth" became a private matter of individual conscience, political leaders and laws could not prescribe beliefs or use them as bases for policy (see Figure 1.1).

Respect for religion as a private matter of personal conscience coincided with a growing understanding of good government serving a largely negative function. No better example of this thinking exists than the Declaration of Independence, in which Jefferson, writing "that in order to secure these rights, governments are instituted among men," predicated the creation of government on the need to protect rights. Conceiving of government as serving negative functions to protect individual rights and a realm for their free expression raised major questions about the legitimacy not only of any public establishment of a religion, but also of basing laws on moral imperatives rooted in religious belief.

---

[2] John Locke, *An Essay Concerning Toleration* in *An Essay Concerning Toleration and Other Writings on Law and Politics, 1667–1683*, ed. by J. R. Milton and Philip Milton (Oxford: Clarendon Press, 2006), 303–4.

FIGURE 1.1 John Waller shown preaching from the jail window in Virginia, where he was imprisoned for unlawful preaching in August 1771. The scene shows local Baptists bringing food to feed the imprisoned preacher. Waller, an effective evangelist, was imprisoned in five Virginia jails for a total of some 180 days for preaching. He also received twenty-one lashes with a horsewhip for preaching in Caroline County, Virginia. Persecutions of dissenters continued in colonial America until laws respecting the right of conscience, during and after the Revolution, established religious toleration. These persecutions encouraged evangelical dissenters to align with Jeffersonian liberals to separate church and state. Painting by Sidney E. King from the Virginia Baptist Historical Society, Richmond, VA. Used by permission.

The late or Radical Enlightenment imposed its own moral under-standings, eventually expressed in the new nation's laws that con-ceived of justice, addressing individual rights, as a public concern and morality as a personal concern. Adam Smith, in his *Theory of Moral Sentiments*, contrasted the use of the law to serve moral ends with its use to serve justice:

Beneficence is always free, it cannot be extorted by force, the mere want of it exposes to no punishment; because the mere want of beneficence tends to do no real positive evil. It may disappoint of the good which might reasonably have been expected, and upon that account it may justly excite dislike and disapprobation: it cannot, however, provoke any resentment which mankind will go along with....

There is, however, another virtue, of which the observance is not left to the freedom of our own wills, which may be extorted by force, and of which the violation exposes to resentment, and consequently to punish-ment. This virtue is justice: the violation of justice is injury: it does real and positive hurt to some particular persons, from motives which are naturally disapproved of....

[J]ustice is, upon most occasions, but a negative virtue, and only hinders us from hurting our neighbor.

Smith bases the argument that society cannot impose moral duties on people on the recognition of their equality, implicitly asserting the right of each person to adopt his or her own moral code as a matter of conscience: "Even the most ordinary degree of kindness or benef-icence, however, cannot, among equals, be extorted by force." Smith uses what has subsequently become a well-known allegory to clarify this Enlightenment-era conception of morality:

In the race for wealth, and honours, and preferments, he may run as hard as he can, and strain every nerve and every muscle, in order to outstrip all his competitors. But if he should justle, or throw down any of them, the indul-gence of the spectators is entirely at an end. It is a violation of fair play, which they cannot admit of. This man is to them, in every respect, as good as he.[3]

Even during the Revolution, Christian invocations to retain a commu-nitarian ethic exposed tensions between a rights-oriented humanism,

---

[3] Adam Smith, *The Theory of Moral Sentiments*, ed. by D. D. Raphael and A. L. Macfie (Indianapolis, IN: Liberty Classics, 1982), 78–89, 82, 85.

advanced by thinkers such as Adam Smith, and the Christian message. Many communities experienced severe economic distress as Atlantic trade suffered and Congress raised funds for the war effort. Working men in Philadelphia proposed a form of moral economy, common in the colonial era, in which communities would oversee market relations in order to ensure everyone's well-being. In August 1779, the city imposed price fixing by a newly created Committee of Trade. The action had widespread support of ministers, and even its secular endorsers used Biblical references and invocations of Christian moral duties to secure passage of the program. However, by this time it appeared to many people as an outdated and unappealing idea. Revolutionary ideals recognized a legal equality that precluded a restraint of one person's freedom to aid another. Differences in wealth and social position were seen to derive from ability, effort, and intelligence. The freedom to pursue one's own desires implied the freedom also to enjoy the profits one's pursuits generated. Philadelphia's merchants asserted that in "placing individual gain first, ... the community as a whole would benefit," and that "the limitation of prices is in the principle unjust because it invades the laws of property."[4]

By the late 1770s, a division within the country surfaced regarding just how much individual freedom the Revolution actually meant to create. This division would subsequently be expressed in the rise of two political parties: the Federalists, espousing some restrictions on personal freedom justified by Christian faith and morals to serve the social good, and the Jeffersonian Republicans, who, in the words of their leader, recognized that no such thing as the social good ever existed other than through "each individual seeking his own good in his own way."[5] The first major battles between these antagonists arose in constitutional efforts to disestablish religion.

---

[4] Quoted in A. Kristen Foster, *Moral Visions and Material Ambitions: Philadelphia Struggles to Define the Republic, 1776–1836* (Lanham, MD: Lexington Books, 2004), 34.

[5] Quoted in Gordon S. Wood, "Interests and Disinterestedness in the Making of the Constitution," in *Beyond Confederation: Origins of the Constitution and American National Identity*, ed. by Richard Beeman, Stephen Botein, and Edward C. Carter (Chapel Hill: University of North Carolina Press, 1987), 102.

Considerations of Religion in the Federal and State Constitutions

Religion as a Matter of Conscience

From 1776 until 1833, the various states and the nation created the first Western societies in well over a thousand years to separate religious beliefs, morals, and practices from law and public policy. By the end of that period, each state, with strong direction in some cases from federal law, had taken positive and decisive steps to disestablish religion, in the process not only endorsing religious freedom but also separating church and state. The law accomplished this task by defining two separate and distinct realms within society: (1) the public sector, which serves as the province of governmental action; and (2) the private sector, in which individual rights to think, act, and pursue dreams are protected from governmental interference as long as they do not impair another's equal rights. During this era, Americans placed religion in the private sector and protected each person's freedom of conscience from any governmental prescription or interference.

Locke's ideas had great currency during the founding era, and his language entered into debates regarding the role of religion in the new republic. During a debate on whether or not to require a Protestant test oath for state office holding in North Carolina, delegate Jacob Henry argued: "[T]he day, I trust, has long passed, when principles *merely speculative* were propagated by force."[6] James Madison expressed the same attitude in writing to his friend Thomas Jefferson concerning religious freedom: "I flatter myself [that] this country [has] extinguished forever the ambitious hope of making laws for the human mind."[7] As a product or concern of each individual's mind, religious belief, much like political opinion or taste in music, art, or beauty, had to be protected from the coercive authority of the state.

During the founding era, Americans generally recognized freedom of conscience as a broad right inclusive of religious judgment, defining it as "a freedom and exemption from human impositions, and

---

[6] Jacob Henry, "Speech in the North Carolina House of Democrats" (1809), reprinted in *Cornerstones of Religious Freedom in America*, ed. by Joseph L. Blau (Boston: Beacon Press, 1949), 93 (italics added).

[7] James Madison letter to Thomas Jefferson, January 22, 1786, in *The Writings of James Madison*, 9 vols., ed. by Gaillard Hunt (New York: G. P. Putnam's Sons, 1904), 2: 216.

legal restraints, in matters of religion and conscience" or immunity from "civil duties and restrictions that [one] ... could not in good conscience, accept or obey." James Madison, similarly, wrote: "The religion then of every man must be left to the conviction and conscience of every man; and it is the right of every man to exercise it as these may dictate."[8] Importantly, the founders protected an individual right to hold personal religious convictions and moral judgments not out of a special concern for religion but from an overwhelming need to protect individual autonomy in various contexts. As early as 1776, Richard Price's pamphlet, "Observations on the Nature of Civil Liberty," asserted that the protection of rights to physical safety, civil or political equality, freedom of conscience, and one's own moral judgment springs from "one general idea that runs through them all, the idea of self-direction or self-government."[9] Considering religious belief a matter of individual conscience made it possible, even essential, to treat it like any other private matter to be protected from state interference.

Americans used the freedom expressed in the idea of liberty of conscience to resist financial impositions to further any publicly sponsored religious message. In "A Bill for Establishing Religious Freedom," which condemns the use of tax money to support churches and religious teachings, Jefferson expresses both the essentially negative aspect of the founders' conceptions of law and its role in protecting rights to property and conscience.[10] The assertion of a right to conscience precludes government action interfering with that right. Jefferson's language conveys this message in its implicit acknowledgment of the division between private and public realms. Recognizing religious belief as a private matter protects the rights not only of dissenters, but also of all people regardless of their beliefs. Public authority cannot compel religious behaviors even from one who generally agrees with the public perspective being asserted. Americans' reconception

---

[8] Quoted in John Witte, Jr., and M. Christian Green, "The American Constitutional Experiment in Religious Human Rights: The Perennial Search for Principle" in *Religious Human Rights in Global Perspective*, ed. by Johan D. Van der Vyver and John Witte, Jr. (Cambridge, MA: Kluwer Law International, 1996), 517, 518.

[9] Quoted in Willi Paul Adams, *The First American Constitutions: Republican Ideology and the Making of the State Constitutions in the Revolutionary Era* (Chapel Hill: University of North Carolina Press, 1980), 156.

[10] "A Bill for Establishing Religious Freedom," in *The Portable Thomas Jefferson*, ed. by Merrill D. Peterson (New York: Penguin Books, 1975), 252.

of religion as a matter of individual conscience arose contemporaneously with acceptance of the primary role of government as protecting individuals in securing their individual rights. Together these understandings doomed laws that established churches as public institutions or that required pronouncements of religious faith or belief as conditions to securing any political, civil, or economic rights. Wartime constitutions of various states offered the first dramatic break from the old colonial system.

Revolutionary-Era Constitutions Struggle to Define Religious Freedom

Immediately following the Declaration of Independence, the Continental Congress urged the newly independent states to solidify their political legitimacy through the drafting of new constitutions. An additional purpose – that of redesigning society to more closely conform to republican ideals – would also be served in this process. The Revolutionary-era constitutions expressed the deep divisions then existing on the public treatment of religion and represent a mixed legacy on the issue of disestablishment. However, in no instance did early constitutional language determine the ultimate outcome of the disestablishment controversy within a state. Rather, the war-era constitutions served as the first attempt in what would be nearly a fifty-year struggle to reshape America into a secular nation in which civil institutions conformed to a new form of law that created its own morality. They expressed the wartime acceptance of a form of republicanism still dependent on a virtuous citizenry aided by religion. These early primary laws generally eliminated state support for religion and protected citizens from compelled religious behavior. Yet, during the war years, several states continued to condition full civil rights and political participation on expressed Christian belief. Americans were only just beginning to conceive of religion as a personal choice instead of a public truth and of a republic in which personal rights and liberties were always threatened by any government that gained power at their expense. Moreover, churches in colonial America had assumed primary responsibility for education and poor relief, expensive services that wartime state governments were woefully incapable of providing. Total disestablishment would require a complete restructuring of institutional life in America that could not happen overnight.

The disestablishment battles during and after the Revolution pro-vide evidence of the persistence of the communitarian worldviews of the colonial era existing in tension with the individualistic views prevalent in the founding era. Just as important, they show how dis-senters had to compromise in implementing their beliefs by aligning with others to pursue their social goals. Throughout much of the sec-ond half of the eighteenth century, dissenters, most prominently mem-bers of the evangelical and pietistic sects that grew rapidly after the Great Awakening, formed America's most spiritually and politically active group of Christians. These Baptists and Methodists constituted significant minorities in every state, but nonetheless were ostracized by laws that established the Anglican (Episcopal), Congregational, or Presbyterian Church as the authorized religious institution. Laws in several states prevented dissenters from conducting their own mar-riages and required children of dissenters to attend schools run by the established churches. Dissenters who ran afoul of the law or who upset local communities encountered beatings and jail sentences. They hoped that the Revolution would bring about religious equality. These dissenters joined with liberal religionists and secularists to pursue their shared political goal of disestablishment. Yet, their conceptions of American society after disestablishment differed considerably from those of the liberals.

The 1776 constitution of North Carolina disestablished the Anglican Church, banned the clergy from holding office, and prohib-ited state support of any religion. Yet, the same document prohib-ited any person who denied the "being of God or the truth of the Protestant religion, or the divine authority of either of the Old or New Testaments" from holding public office. North Carolinians hoped to disestablish Anglicanism while preserving a Christian community. Similarly, the 1776 constitution of Maryland provided that no per-son could be forced "to maintain any particular place of worship or any particular ministry," effectively ending Episcopalian supremacy but not religious establishment. The new Maryland constitution reads as follows: "Yet, the legislature may, in their [*sic*] discretion, lay a gen-eral and equal tax, for the support of the Christian religion." However, when the Maryland legislature attempted to act on this authority in 1780, the bill for a general Christian establishment encountered an early demise.

The mid-Atlantic states, though accustomed to greater religious diversity and toleration throughout the colonial period, acted only somewhat more aggressively in drafting their wartime constitutions. New Jersey in 1776 ensured that no person would "ever be obliged to pay tithes, taxes, or any other rates, for the purpose of building or repairing any other church or churches, place or places of worship, or for the minister or ministry, contrary to what he believes to be right, or has deliberately or voluntarily engaged himself to perform." Although Pennsylvania's 1776 constitution is frequently trumpeted as the most radically democratic of its age, even it did not secure complete religious freedom for its citizens. Pennsylvania allowed that "[n]o man ought or of right can be compelled to attend any religious worship, or erect or support any place of worship, or maintain any ministry, contrary to, or against, his own free will and consent."[11] However, the state also expressed the ideological conflict inherent in American values at that time by requiring an oath in the belief of God in order to vote. Pennsylvania eliminated public support for its sectarian churches and church schools but retained support for a Christian ethic among its citizenry.

New York went further, not only disestablishing the Anglican Church but also securing full religious liberty. Yet, certain Christians sought to impede secularization. A committee formed in August 1776 to prepare a new constitution heard a proposal for a general Christian establishment raised by Presbyterian Minister John Rodgers. Several clergymen supported the idea of religious freedom only so long as religion would remain a vital part of governance. Typical were the words of Pastor J. H. Livingston, who encouraged the state to "promote religion in general" as well as "defend it from all persecution."[12] Others demanded religious tests for voters and officeholders in order to secure Christian government. However, the committee not only disestablished the Anglican Church but also repudiated the establishment of the past

---

[11] Ben Perley Poore, ed., *The Federal and State Constitutions, Colonial Charters, and Other Organic Laws of the United States*, 2nd ed., 2 vols. (Union, NJ: Lawbook Exchange, 2001); Constitution of North Carolina, 1776, Art. XXXIV, 1413; Constitution of Maryland, 1776, Art. XXXIII, p. 819; Constitution of New Jersey, 1776, Art. XVIII, 1313; Constitution of Pennsylvania, 1776, Art. II, p. 1541.

[12] Quoted in John Webb Pratt, *Religion, Politics, and Diversity: The Church-State Theme in New York History* (Ithaca, NY: Cornell University Press, 1967), 114–15.

years, publishing a statement that any laws "as may be construed to establish or maintain any particular denomination of Christians or their ministers ... be and they hereby are, abrogated and rejected."[13] Having at once asserted that a state religion had never been established, the committee nonetheless rescinded all laws that could "inaccurately" be construed as establishing a religion. The constitution recognized a right of conscience free from public-sector interference and banned ministers of any religious faith from holding state office. The early legislature of the state proceeded to clarify and strengthen the constitutional provisions separating religion from governance by seizing the property of the church.

During the Revolution, the radicalism evident in New York in 1776 spread to other states. Churches, especially Anglican churches, came to be seen as unwanted authorities. Virginia followed the lead of New York in condemning church property. Yet, a mere aversion to authority does not explain the action taken in many states to prohibit ministers from voting or taking public office. As some Revolutionary-era Americans came to see religion as a threat to republican self-government, they moved toward a more complete separation of religion and government.

The 1777 constitution of Georgia expressed a popular embrace of secular humanism. Parishes once named St. Paul, St. George, Christ Church, and St. James were renamed Richmond, Burke, Chatham, and Liberty counties, respectively. The Georgia constitution, like those of Tennessee, Delaware, Kentucky, New York, and the Carolinas, prohibited clergymen of any denomination from holding public office and protected people in "the free exercise of their religion; provided it be not repugnant to the peace and safety of the state." The only limits on religious freedom concerned public order, not religious doctrine. While the Georgia constitution did allow for the possibility of a legislative enactment creating a multiple establishment, bills for this purpose introduced in 1782 and 1784 were quickly defeated.[14]

---

[13] Thorpe, Francis Newton, ed., *The Federal and State Constitutions, Colonial Charters and other Organic Laws of the State Territories and Colonies Now or Heretofore Forming the United States of America*, 7 vols. (Washington, DC: US Government Printing Office, 1909), 5: 2636.

[14] Poore, *Federal and State Constitutions*, 378, 383 (Georgia Constitution of 1777, Arts. IV, LVI, and LXII).

Dissenters became increasingly active politically during and after the Revolution in pursuit of disestablishment. However, they lacked the political power to realize their vision of the new nation: a country that embraced freedom of religion while still premising its policies on Christian beliefs, morals, and ethics. Establishing a broadly understood Christianity or multiple Christian churches would have satisfied them. Yet, to achieve the short-term goal of toleration, or equal status for churches expressing their dissenting beliefs, they formed a political alliance with liberal Americans who opposed all religious establishments as violations of human rights. Isaac Backus, perhaps the leading Baptist crusader for disestablishment, contrasted the views of these wary allies on religious freedom. He claimed that the liberals "despise government" and root their conceptions of liberty in that hatred, while "the true liberty of man is to know, obey, and enjoy his creator and to do all the good unto, and enjoy all the happiness with and in his fellow creatures that he is capable of."[15] Yet, generally, the allies used the same language, temporarily masking their underlying disagreements. Both espoused the need for the protection of liberty of conscience, free exercise of religion, and religious equality. Both also endorsed the disestablishment of religion and the separation of church and state but meant different things by their endorsements of these policies. The dissenters largely followed the traditional Protestant conception of liberty as the freedom to practice the true religion. Much like Roger Williams, they desired a separation of church and state to protect religion from unavoidable contamination from political processes, but they still recognized ways in which religion could influence public policies, laws, and morals. The Jeffersonian liberals sought to remove all spiritual influences from the governing process, while the evangelicals sought only a legal recognition of each church as an institution separate and protected from the government. The evangelicals desired a literal separation of church and state as institutions; the liberals, a separation of religion from law and governance. The liberals perceived religion as entirely the province of each individual, while the evangelicals perceived religion as a public concern, though each

---

[15] Isaac Backus "An Appeal to the Public for Religious Liberty," in *Isaac Backus on Church, State, and Calvinism: Pamphlets, 1754–1789,* ed. by William G. McLoughlin (Cambridge, MA: Belknap Press, 1968), 309.

individual might express it in his or her own way. Backus desired to keep test oaths for officeholders and laws prohibiting blasphemy, gambling, and violation of the Sabbath. Each of the allies had to rely on law to accomplish its purpose, and law, recognizing the primacy of protecting rights, tended to promote a more secular understanding of disestablishment and the separation of church and state. In the 1780s and 1790s, state laws increasingly recognized the idea of religion as a private matter protected from public interference, thereby circumscribing the extent to which the public sphere could even consider religion in its policy making.

The Federal Constitution Creates a Rights-Oriented Legal System

While disestablishment occurred over time on a state-by-state basis, the debates concerning law and religion at the Constitutional Convention focused national attention on the ideological bases for separating church and state. Liberals controlled the drafting process and tempered the influence of their evangelical allies in shaping the form of disestablishment. During ratification, the national debates confirmed an understanding of religion as a private matter to be protected from state action.

Virginia's statute on religious freedom served as a model for the nation's consideration of religion. Jefferson drafted his "Bill for Religious Freedom" as a means of securing rights for Virginians not yet protected in the state constitution. Jefferson expressed his view of a social contract as limiting the powers of all future legislators. He argued that the government only had authority over those considerations that the people delegated to it – and that "the rights of conscience we never submitted, we could not submit."[16] In the draft of his bill, Jefferson noted that its protections are only the acts of a legislature and therefore inferior to both natural law and constitutional law. In the absence of a constitutional provision, Jefferson thought that the bill would have to do. During the Revolution, his state recognized religious belief as a private matter of individual conscience, banned all clergymen from holding office, and suspended the Act for the Support of the Clergy, yet it refused to pass his bill. While serving his country

---

[16] Thomas Jefferson, *Notes on the State of Virginia*, "Query XVII: Religion," in Peterson, ed., *Portable Jefferson*, 210.

in Paris in the early 1780s, Jefferson expressed regret that Virginia had not yet protected its citizens from tyrannical laws. Jefferson recognized the tolerant attitudes that existed in Virginia and the country, but knew enough about human nature to doubt they would last forever.

In 1784, while Jefferson was in Paris, Patrick Henry proposed "A Bill for Establishing a Provision for Teachers of the Christian Religion" that would have taxed all Virginians "to restore and propagate the holy Christian religion." In response, Madison drafted his "Memorial and Remonstrance Against Religious Assessments." In this document, he outlines the liberal perspective on the role of religion in society. Madison asserts that "the religion ... of every man must be left to the conviction and conscience of every man" and that this "inalienable right" of conscience is rooted in the indisputable fact that "the opinions of every man, depending only on the evidence contemplated by their own minds, cannot follow the dictates of other men." He makes it clear that all matters of religion are "wholly exempt" from the "cognizance" of "Civil Society" or any "Legislative Body." Madison claims that in infringing on the right of conscience, Henry's proposal "violates the equality which ought to be the basis of every law" by assuming one person's or one group of people's spiritual beliefs to be superior to those of any other equal human being. Law cannot render such a judgment. He asserts that "government will be best supported by protecting every citizen in the enjoyment of his religion with the same equal hand which protects his person and property." In closing his document, he reasserts that "the equal right of every citizen to the free exercise of his religion according to dictates of conscience is held by the same tenure with all our other rights."[17]

The legislature never even put Henry's proposal to a vote. The strong support of freedom of conscience convinced Madison to write to Jefferson asking his permission to reintroduce his bill. Jefferson agreed. Madison credited the sentiments of the majority of Virginians for the passage of the law in 1786, support that surprised and frustrated the pro-establishment forces. Dissenters played a huge role in passage of the bill, but so too did devotees of liberalism.

[17] James Madison, "Memorial and Remonstrance."

Jefferson later said that he drafted the language of the bill very broadly so as "to comprehend within the mantle of its protection the Jew and Gentile, the Christian and Mahomedan, the Hindoo and infidel." Significantly, Jefferson distinguished various religious believers from infidels or nonbelievers, recognized them all as equals, and protected the freedom of conscience of everyone.

Madison prepared the working draft of the United States Constitution shortly thereafter. Following the Jeffersonian model, law was reconceived in the Constitutional Convention from supporting the social good through communitarian ideals consistent with Christian morality to serving ideals of individual liberty through a new understanding of rights as private concerns beyond government authority. To accomplish this end, the founders conceived of a private sphere of human activity protected from public interference and placed religion and the churches in that realm.

The draft prepared at the Constitutional Convention recognized a right of individuals to pursue their own desires through private contracts immune from public-sector interference. The contract clause of the Constitution provides that "No state shall ... pass any ... law impairing the obligations owing to contracts"; in other words, no perceived public interest, assertion of moral duty, or communitarian ethic shall be deemed superior to the rights of private individuals to contract for their own betterment. Nowhere is the protection of individual rights more evident than in Article 1, Section 10 of the Constitution. And nowhere is it more evident than in this section that contract law, embodying liberal ideas of individual autonomy, was to be the chief means of protecting individual liberty. During the ratification process, more Americans supported this provision than any other – and most considered it a necessity.

The clear intent of the founders to create a private realm of action protected from public interference also finds expression in the takings clause in the Fifth Amendment. Each of the Amendments restricts government action in respect of individual rights. Following the protection of due process, the Fifth Amendment provides "[N]or shall private property be taken for public use, without just compensation." This clause protects private-property rights from majoritarian exploitation, a protection absolutely dependent on a recognition of distinct private and public spheres. While colonial America paid little attention to this distinction in harnessing all available resources to address societal needs, the Constitution provided for the independence of noncriminal private actions from governmental interference and of private institutions from public control. The Constitution effectively prohibited a governmental reliance on private means to serve public ends.

The debates in Philadelphia in 1787 focused on the protection of individual rights to believe or not believe; they did not focus on protecting religion per se. Convention discussions of religion never mentioned the Ten Commandments or the Bible and did not refer to Christianity as a true religion, the need to form the government in accordance with God's teachings, or the desirability or inevitability of subordinating human will to God's plan or providence. The delegates did consider referencing religion as a guide to moral behavior, noting that morality depended as much on human reason as on God's dictates. Yet, even this minimal endorsement was left out of the draft of the Constitution. Religion, understood as a matter of individual conscience, became, by the 1780s, if not before, a strictly private matter placed in the private realm. President George Washington recognized this distinction in responding to a letter from New Hampshire and Massachusetts Presbyterians. Its drafters feared a moral collapse resulting from the Constitution's rejection of providence. Washington responded by writing that "true piety" could not be the province of "public councils." He encouraged the Presbyterians to look not to government but to "the guidance of the Ministers of the Gospel [to whom] this important object is ... more properly committed."[18]

Many Americans expressed discontent that their fellow citizens rejected any recognition of God's role in winning independence or of a commitment to religious truth in the new government. As Americans of this perspective reviewed the proposed Constitution, creating the first Western society in several hundred years not to establish a Christian church, they wondered whether the republic could survive without a publicly recognized faith. A New Hampshire man wrote in 1788 that "civil governments can't well be supported without the assistance of religion."[19] Certainly the drafters were aware that

---

[18] Letter from President George Washington to the Presbytery of the Eastward, convened in Newberry-Port (New England) (Nov. 2, 1789), as cited in Carl H. Esbeck, "Uses and Abuses of Textualism and Originalism in Establishment Clause Interpretation," *Utah L. Rev.* 2 (2011), 489–623, at 505.

[19] New Hampshire polemicist quoted in Herbert Storing, ed., *The Complete Anti-Federalist*, 7 vols. (Chicago: University of Chicago Press, 1981), 4: 242.

many ardent Christians believed that their work diminished the roles of religion and the church in the new republic. Most of the men in Philadelphia for the drafting simply did not care. Social conservative and future leader of the Federalist Party, Alexander Hamilton, "when asked why the Constitution mentioned neither God nor religion ... is reported to have smiled and answered, 'we forgot.'"[20] The cavalier rejection of piety, deference, and religious duty was not confined to the Jeffersonians.

While the question of republican virtue raised a conceptual issue regarding the place of religion in the new republic, specific Constitutional provisions fostered debates more threatening to ratification. Religion arose during the ratification process as a significant concern in three contexts: the use of religious tests for federal office holding, the absence of any national religion or commitment to God, and the protection of religious liberty. Each issue was resolved in favor of individual liberty instead of perpetuating a community premised on Christian belief.

The draft submitted to the people of the United States for ratification banned any and all religious test oaths. Neither voters nor candidates for office could be required to acknowledge a belief in God, Christian doctrine, or an afterlife as a condition of exercising their inherent civil rights. The draft also contained no reference to God for having aided in the crusade for independence or protecting the American people in the early years of nationhood, provisions that had figured prominently in earlier state constitutions and had been proposed by delegates at the convention in Philadelphia. During the ratification process, Americans further clarified the absence of any role for religion in governing by demanding a bill of rights securing freedom of conscience.

In ratifying conventions held in the various states, citizens expressed concern over the failure of the Constitution to protect the essential rights of individual citizens from the power of the government. Though in Paris, Jefferson found the absence of a bill of rights a significant omission. From across the country, citizens called for a bill of rights as a means of protecting individuals from government power, specifically designating rights that could not be relinquished and must

---

[20] Quoted in Paul E. Johnson, *The Early American Republic, 1789–1829* (New York: Oxford University Press, 2007), 112.

be safeguarded from future legislative action. They overwhelmingly cited freedom of conscience as the right most in need of protection. The language they used indicates the nature of the right they sought to protect. "Centinel" (Samuel Bryan), a Philadelphia merchant, wrote to his city's *Freeman's Journal* "that all men have a natural and unalienable right ... to the dictates of their own consciences."[21] Richard Henry Lee's letter to Governor Randolph on December 6, 1787, published in the *Virginia Gazette*, encouraged Virginia not to ratify the Constitution without a bill of rights that provided in some form "that the right of conscience in matters of religion shall be secured."[22] The American people did not seek to protect religion or their churches, but rather their freedom to think and believe without governmental interference or prescription.

Several states published their ratifications of the Constitution with resolutions seeking protection for essential rights, including specific suggestions to guarantee the individual right to freedom of conscience. Virginia asserted that "all men have an equal, natural, and unalienable right to the free exercise of religion, according to the dictates of conscience." New Hampshire offered: "Congress shall make no laws touching religion or to infringe on the rights of conscience." North Carolina insisted on a guarantee of religious freedom without offering specific wording. New York asserted "that the people have an equal, natural, and inalienable right freely and peaceably to exercise their religion according to the dictates of conscience." Maryland suggested "[t]hat there be no national religion established by law, but that all persons be equally entitled to protection in their religious liberty." South Carolina declined to make a specific suggestion as to the need for an amendment establishing religious freedom, but Charles Pinckney, speaking on May 14, 1788, at his state's ratifying convention voiced sentiments consistent with the invocations of the other states. He asserted that the people's rights must be superior to governmental authority: "We have been taught here to believe that all power of right belongs to THE PEOPLE – that it flows immediately from them, and is delegated to their officers for the public good – that

---

[21] "Centinel" [Samuel Bryan] to the *Freeman's Journal (Philadelphia)*, October 24, 1787, in ibid., 77–91.

[22] "Richard Henry Lee to Governor Edmund Randolph, October 16, 1787," published by the *Virginia Gazette*, December 6, 1787, in ibid., 465–72.

our rulers are the servants of the people, amenable to their will, and created for their use." He specifically sought protection for religious belief to make Americans "the first perfectly free people the world had ever seen." While Pennsylvania, by a very slim majority, approved the Constitution without calling for amendments, the minority, led by Robert Whitehall, published a separate dissent expressing a need for a bill of rights "establishing these unalienable and personal rights of men, without the full, free, and secure enjoyment of which there can be no liberty, and over which it is not necessary for a good government to have control." The first of those listed provided: "The right of conscience shall be held inviolate and neither the legislative, executive, nor judicial powers of the United States shall have authority to alter, abrogate, or infringe any part of the Constitutions of the several states which provide for the preservation of liberty in matters of religion."[23]

Throughout the debates in the various states, in the written proposals for amendments offered by the states, and in the promulgation of the amendments themselves, the right to absolute liberty of conscience regarding religious belief is recognized as beyond the reach of a legitimate government. This right derived from human nature and was accorded respect in the implementation of a political theory conceiving of a limited government in service to its citizens. References to freedom of religion refer to it as "full," "natural," "perfect," and "inviolable" and define it further as a matter of "conscience," "reason," or "conviction." The breadth of the limitation placed on government was referred to as prohibiting any laws from even "touching" or "infringing" on matters of individual conscience. One searches in vain for any indication of an intent to protect religion or churches. The First Amendment protected human rights, not religion or the religious institutions designed for its dissemination.

---

[23] Historians differ on whether the states offered "amendments" as such or rather, in the words of Anson Phelps Stokes and Leo Pfeffer, merely "urged or suggested" the need for further rights protection. In either case, the perceived need for protecting freedom of conscience was expressed. For New Hampshire, see Anson Phelps Stokes and Leo Pfeffer, *Church and State in the United States* (New York: Harper & Row, 1964), 151; for Virginia, North Carolina, and New York, see Stokes and Pfeffer, *Church and State*, 152; see also Bailyn, *Debate*, 2: 537; for Maryland, see Bailyn, *Debate*, 2: 554; for South Carolina, see Bailyn, *Debate*, 2: 578; for Pennsylvania, see Bailyn, *Debate*, 2: 541, 532.

The final language of the First Amendment prohibiting a "law respecting an establishment of religion, or prohibiting the free exercise thereof" is often read as separate clauses, which can even appear contradictory. Yet, when placed in the intellectual context of the debates that produced it, the language can be seen as protecting a right of conscience from various forms of laws that would interfere with it. The focus must be on each individual's right of conscience being protected, not on the nature of government action being prohibited. Only when the clauses are read together in the context of the ideas they sought to clarify does Madison's assertion that "'the separation between Religion and Government in the Constitution' was the surest guarantee of 'the sacred principle of religious liberty'" make any sense.[24] The founders placed freedom of conscience, like other natural rights, in the private realm to protect it from public action.

The debate in 1787 through 1789 centered on a legalistic conception of belief as a private matter of conscience beyond the scope of governmental authority. This history challenges those supporters of public recognition of a "Christian nation" who maintain that the First Amendment only precludes the government favoring one sect at the expense of all others. It also contradicts extremists who argue that the First Amendment protects churches or even religion instead of or in addition to protecting individual rights of citizens. Neither the convention nor the ratifying process provides any support for the "Christian nation" argument. Numerous early state constitutions prohibited governments from establishing one sect or religious society in preference to others, and language consistent with that intent was proposed and rejected during the debates on the Amendments to the federal Constitution. Such a provision clearly would have permitted nonpreferential support for the Christian religion, and the founders regarded that as an establishment of religion.

There is in fact no evidence either of a final intent to limit the protection of liberty of conscience to Christians or to consider that protection apart from a separation of religion and governance. The country's first two presidents, Washington and Adams, relied on the First Amendment to encourage Jews and Moslems to come to

---

[24] Quoted in Frank Lambert, *The Founding Fathers and the Place of Religion in America* (Princeton, NJ: Princeton University Press, 2003), 4.

America, assuring them that "the government of the United States is not, in any sense, founded on the Christian religion."[25] Delegates to the Constitutional Convention had expressed admiration for the Virginia state constitution's declaration of rights well before the ratification controversy over a bill of rights. Attention had focused on the provision of religious freedom, which Madison rewrote for George Mason to clarify that the intent was not toleration, but rather a recognition of belief as a matter of individual conscience beyond the scope of government. Calls for a bill of rights securing religious freedom made clear that the right derived from the nature of humanity. No matter how pervasive the Christian religion might be, it could not be allowed to limit one's right to freedom of conscience. That popular opinion supported an amendment to secure absolute freedom of belief, not just to limit any citizen's options to a selection among one of various competing Christian sects, is evident in the language used in calling for a bill of rights.

Confirmation of this conclusion also comes from the writings of many Christians at that time, who recognized the secular nature of the primary law and expressed concern over the spread of secularism. Expressing growing fears that a secular Constitution would diminish the influence of God and religion in the new nation, sermons and pamphlets during this era criticized the irreligiosity of the Constitution, the separation of religion from morality, and the preoccupation of the people with money and personal gratification. Such protestations were of little consequence in the republican afterglow of revolution, and those protesting found themselves to be political outliers.

Ratification clarified the popular support for the creation of a private sphere as the means of protecting rights and for the understanding of religion as a matter of conscience placed within that private sphere. Ultimately, the Constitutional separation of church and state derived less from the provisions addressing religion than from the broad liberal interpretation given the primary law by the Marshall Court in its exposition of the contract clause. The Marshall Court required all

---

[25] US Congress, *American State Papers: Documents, Legislative and Executive at the Congress of the United States* (Washington, DC: Gales and Seaton, 1832–62), 2: 18. See also Washington, *Letter to the Hebrew Congregation in Newport, Aug., 1790,* in *George Washington: A Collection,* ed. by W. B. Allen (Indianapolis, IN: Liberty Classics, 1988), 521.

private organizations to incorporate in order to take advantage of the protections of the contract clause.[26] Each church or private voluntary religious association, after disestablishment, so long as it adopted the private corporate form, had an equal legal right to hold property and to recruit members, proselytize, and even criticize public policy from its own unique spiritual perspective. But, in assuming a private corporate form, churches separated themselves and their messages from the public sector. Rather than create a separate category for religion, the founders considered it a private matter and dealt with it like other private concerns – in the marketplace.

Marshall's liberal understanding of the role of contracts in protecting individual liberty surprises some who see the Federalist judge as a defender of government power. His opinions indicate the breadth of Americans' acceptance of contract law principles as the primary means of transforming a hierarchical and communitarian society into one respecting equality and individual freedoms. Contract law, in its embodiment of Enlightenment precepts, expressed the means of redefining the role of the individual within society. It recognized the parties to a contract as equals, bound by law to perform their respective obligations. It assumed that any potential party to a contract was reasonable, rational, and capable of making his or her own bargain. Community status, Christian brotherhood, and social deference, once relevant factors in colonial jurisprudence, became irrelevant in the enforcement of a wide range of social activities ranging from the sale of goods and labor to marriage and care for one's elderly parents. Moreover, contract law asserted its own system of morality. Performing one's contractual obligations, nothing more nor less, established one as trustworthy. Frequently this morality was at odds with both Christian teachings and America's communitarian heritage.

State courts served as the primary vehicles by which contract law transformed American society. Predominately members of Jefferson's Republican Party, state court judges relied on contract law principles to redesign a myriad of personal relationships and institutions. At the same time, state legislators used these same principles to reshape the role of the churches in American society. Quasi-public institutions

---

[26] *Trustees of Philadelphia Baptist Assoc. v. Hart's Executors*, 17 US (Wheat) 1 (1819).

during colonial times, churches, after the Revolution, had to adopt a corporate form and learn to behave as private institutions.

States Follow the Federal Model

Following the Revolution, the states had the luxury of rewriting their constitutions to better conform to the theoretical model of the social contract. The new constitutions would be drafted not by sitting legislatures but in conventions specifically called for that purpose and then ratified through popular consent expressed in voting. These constitutions evince a rise in secular attitudes and in limitations on the conceptions of state power in recognition of the rights of individuals to maintain their own religious beliefs and practices. Distinguishing public and private realms provided the means of protecting individual rights.

Pennsylvania, in its 1790 constitution, eliminated its religious test for voting, providing that "every [resident] freeman of the age of twenty-one years ... shall enjoy the rights of an election." In its 1792 constitution, Delaware eliminated an oath for state officeholders that acknowledged belief in God, Jesus as his son, and the Bible as divine inspiration, and in reasserting a right to religious freedom referred not to "God" but to a "Creator." Maryland, in 1795, exempted Quakers and others unable to take oaths, agnostics and atheists among them, from having to do so to hold office.[27]

South Carolina provides perhaps the best example of postwar disestablishment in which the tentative political alliance between evangelical Christian activists and Jeffersonian liberals fragmented over time. During the Revolution, liberals and dissenters worked together to disestablish the state's Anglican Church, which held considerable social and political prestige. The breakdown of the alliance after the war forced voters to choose between a nonsectarian Christian establishment and a liberal rights-oriented secular republic.

Evangelical minister Oliver Hart wrote to Henry Laurens of his hopes for religious reform days before the drafting of the state's wartime constitution. His hopes were dashed when he saw the new plan of government perpetuating an Anglican establishment. In the spring

---

[27] Poore, *Federal and State Constitutions*, Pennsylvania Constitution of 1790, Art. III, Sect. 1, pp. 1551–2; Amendment to the Maryland Constitution, Art. III, 1795, p. 829.

of 1776, the dissenting clergy, including Oliver Hart, gathered under the direction of Reverend William Tennant to plan for "securing an equality in religious privileges."[28] The group chose Tennant to present its work, a petition for disestablishment, before the general assembly, a task he performed on September 11, 1776. His comments before the assembly reflected the priorities of dissenting ministers. The petition specifically objected to the establishment of one "particular denomination of Protestants in distinction from and preference to all other denominations." The ministers referred to the prejudicial treatment of one sect fomenting discord and a dangerous discontent within society. In closing, the petition called for a guarantee "[t]hat there never shall be any establishment of any one religious denomination or sect of Protestant Christians in this state by way of preference to another." If these provisions of the dissenters' petition were not adequately clear, Tennant's own comments left no room for confusion. He cited the inability of dissenting clergy "to marry their own people" and the unfair competition between the Anglicans, for whom "the law builds superb churches," and those denominations who must "build their own." Perhaps the most significant problem, he felt, was that the law allowed only one church to incorporate; it alone could hold property, sue in the court system, and collect alms and bequests. Tennant made certain the assembly understood that the dissenters did not wish the state's legislators to abstain from addressing religion, but only to stop favoring one sect over another: "The state may do anything for the support of religion without partiality to particular societies or imposition upon the rights of private judgment." Tennant championed the authority of the assembly to punish vice and encourage virtue.[29]

The wartime constitution of South Carolina, adopted in 1778, declared that "[t]he Christian Protestant religion [is] the established religion of this State." Further, "no person shall, by law, be obliged to pay towards the maintenance and support of a religious worship that he does not freely join in, or has not voluntarily engaged to support." Yet, all voters and officeholders were required to swear to their belief in "God, heaven, and hell" as understood in Protestant Christian

---

[28] Hart to Henry Laurens, March 19, 1776, Hart Papers.
[29] Tennant, "Writings," *South Carolina Historical Magazine* 61 (4) (1960): 194–7 (all quotations).

doctrine; while the new document recognized due process protection and liberty of the press, religious freedom was limited to Protestant Christians.[30] Individual Episcopal congregations needed to reform themselves by incorporating as private independent bodies, but though law made all churches equals, the wealth and status of Episcopalian church members rendered their denomination socially superior.

By the 1780s, liberal exponents of Jeffersonian democracy in South Carolina began to question the restrictive nature of their own state constitution. Proposals for a constitutional convention started to appear in the press by the mid-1780s. In an editorial on September 7, 1786, the *Gazette of the State of South Carolina* argued that, though the war was won, "the American Revolution is just begun [as] the whole government must be made to conform to democratic principles."[31] Calls for a new state constitution focused primarily on the need to protect civil rights. Liberal concepts of political equality and freedom of conscience required a reconceptualization of South Carolina's social institutions.

By 1787, complete religious freedom, requiring abolition of the Protestant Christian establishment of 1778, had become a rallying point for the liberals. Unlike the earlier disestablishment campaign, this crusade was carried by those who premised their position on both the need of the government to recognize natural rights and the perception of religion as a matter of personal conscience. In this debate, the liberals expressed significant distaste for all organized religion. At the climax of the debate, the *City Gazette* of Charleston published a letter from an American living in Paris: "France is indeed upon the eve of complete freedom; a new era is evidently approaching; political liberty in Europe must copy the example of America and will certainly be followed by a great and general change in many religious tenets of the present day, as soon as the empire of reason shall have established itself a little further over the minds of men." This writer found political freedom best expressed by those philosophers who sought to challenge religious beliefs that kept people subordinate not only to a god but inevitably also to other people. These philosophers, "by

---

[30] Poore, *Federal and State Constitutions*, South Carolina Constitution 1778, Art. 28, Art. XXXIIII, pp. 1626–7.

[31] Untitled editorial dated September 7, 1787, *Gazette of the State of South Carolina*.

drawing a distinct line of separation between spiritual and temporal concerns, have paved the way for universal peace, harmony, and good will among men."[32]

Ministers of what had once been dissenting denominations and who had earlier united with liberals to fight the Episcopalian establishment now recognized a need to clarify for their parishioners on which side of the battle line they were to stand. They chose to bind themselves to other Christians in opposing liberal reform. Methodist Bishop George Foster Pierce scorned those who rejected God's truth for one devised by humanity: "This specious, insinuating infidelity is distilling its poison under the patronage of science, education, and knowledge." Reverend Thomas Reese wrote that God has "favored us," but "if we abuse the gifts of Providence, turn our liberty into licentiousness, and provoke the vengeance of Heaven by our daring impiety, and shocking immoralities, what can we expect, but that a righteous God will give us up to the fatal consequences of our own vices, and inflict upon us a punishment which we justly deserve." More liberal pastors found it more difficult to openly support a Christian establishment. Reverend Richard Furman, Oliver Hart's successor at the Charleston Baptist Church, remained silent on the disestablishment issue but advocated defeat of a companion provision that would prevent ministers from serving in a state office.[33]

The 1790 constitution rejected the more conservative views of the dissenters in preference for the liberal views protecting a liberty of conscience; it abolished parishes (substituting counties) and denied all clergymen the opportunity to hold state office.[34] The new constitution further signaled an intention to remove the churches from their roles in public governance. In this change can be seen the importance of ideological debate to the disestablishment issue and the radical nature of the legal prescriptions. Liberal republican values came to replace

[32] "Extract of a letter from an American gentleman in France," dated October 14, 1789, *City Gazette (Charleston, South Carolina),* January 5, 1790.

[33] Pierce quoted in Mark D. McGarvie, "Disestablishing Religion and Protecting Religious Liberty in State Laws and Constitutions (1776–1833)" in *No Establishment of Religion: America's Original Contribution to Religious Liberty,* ed. by T. Jeremy Gunn and John Witte, Jr. (New York: Oxford University Press, 2012), 87; Reverend Thomas Reese, "An Essay on the Influence of Religion" (Charleston, 1788; microfiche in the Presbyterian Historical Society Library).

[34] Poore, *Constitutions,* 1628–34.

Christian ethics in people's value systems, and public institutions came to express those new values. Prior to 1790, churches in South Carolina had served as the public instruments of poor relief, record keeping, and, to a lesser degree, education. After adoption of the new constitution, either government or private charities would have to assume these responsibilities. Wasting no time in implementing social change, the legislature of the state first addressed the issue of assisting the poor in 1791, passing a statute that provided for the election of county commissioners of the poor, as public employees, to assume the duties previously held by parish church wardens. In 1794, the state created an Orphan House to shelter unemployable children, and in 1795, it created its first penitentiary. Appointees to public boards administered both facilities and relied exclusively on state funding. Public control ensured that secular rather than religious values, priorities, and goals would inform the programs. As elsewhere, the need for secular public action arose in South Carolina primarily over the provision of education. Although the Jeffersonians generally abhorred the growth of government to address social needs, they recognized education as an exception. Perpetuation of the republic depended on an educated citizenry, and the state was required to recognize and perform its duties to secure its future.

Though the public school movement experienced minimal growth in South Carolina, it produced a response from the churches. Their response shows how churches had to adapt to their new roles as private institutions. Threatened by the idea of public schools teaching liberal and practical knowledge, they responded by starting private schools of their own. Nearly all denominations attempted to combat the threat of secular education and, in the words of the Charter of the Columbia, South Carolina, Theological Seminary, to finally extinguish "the twilight of unenlightened reason."[35] In adoption of the corporate form to protect their funds and their message in a sometimes hostile environment, the churches recognized and conformed to their new role as private institutions outside the realm of governance but free to dissent from and criticize public action.

---

[35] Charter quoted in Erskine Clarke, *Our Southern Zion: A History of Calvinism in the South Carolina Low Country, 1890–1900* (Tuscaloosa: University of Alabama Press, 1996), 116.

During the same decade, New York's legislature took measures to attach church property and secure total freedom of conscience. The wartime constitution of New York had disestablished the Anglican Church and protected freedom of conscience. By the 1780s, liberals demanded more. In late 1784, the New York State legislature passed four laws asserting a new legal status for churches in the state. Each was enacted with near-unanimous support and excited almost no attention in newspapers, sermons, or other forums of civic debate. The laws created a system of general incorporation for all religious bodies to follow, recreating churches as private institutions protected by rights of incorporation. Accordingly, New York, unable to interfere with private contract rights, would have to find new means of addressing public needs. By separating public and private institutions, the legislature implicitly separated state and church as well. Legal doctrine determined the form of church-state separation in New York, but legislative liberals committed to removing religion from government showed how use of the form could serve liberal principles.

In both the substance and tone of the legislative enactments of the 1780s, the New York legislature evinced a hostility toward both the Episcopalian Church and the use of state authority in furtherance of religious goals. However, New Yorkers found it difficult to remove the churches from past roles without accepting a significant diminution in public services. In 1784, legislative action abolished the parish as a civic designation and repealed all laws calling for churches to use tax money in performance of public functions. The colonial model of church-provided education proved untenable in a secular republic that recognized societal dependence on an educated citizenry. Governor Clinton's first address to the New York legislature in 1783 encouraged creating public schools for young students. In the 1790s, new government agencies formed to construct highways, keep public records, provide aid to the poor, and collect taxes.

While southern and mid-Atlantic states completed the separation of church and state in the constitutional era, disestablishment did not come to New England until the second decade of the nineteenth century, and then it was largely imposed by national law. In 1815, the Jeffersonian Republicans in control of the governor's office and legislature in New Hampshire tried to take over Dartmouth College, a Congregational Church seminary, to transform it into a liberal university to teach the skills necessary for success in a free-enterprise republic. Similar actions had been taken previously in many states without prompting litigation. However, in New Hampshire, the church-affiliated school challenged the legislature's action in court. In 1819, the Supreme Court issued its decision in *Trustees of Dartmouth College v. Woodward*.[36] In a pyrrhic victory for the church, the Court prevented the takeover on the basis of the contract clause of the Constitution, holding the school's charter to be a contract. In the process, the court reminded all Americans of the heavy black line dividing public and private spheres and of the place of churches on the private side of that line. The college stood apart from the state as a private religious institution; it served the private interests of its trustees and not the public interests of the state. Subsequently, states stopped contributing to the support of church-affiliated schools and began instead to build secular state universities. The decision had the further effect of hastening the disestablishment of religion in New England.

Early constitutions in New England attempted to perpetuate the old colonial model of a corporate society. Article III of the Massachusetts Declaration of Rights, part of the state's 1780 constitution, continued state support for religion, asserting that religion was necessary for "the good order and preservation of civil government" that depend on people's "piety, religion, and morality." In 1785, the Massachusetts Supreme Court recognized only incorporated churches as deserving of the support provided in Article III and upheld the policy that only established churches could incorporate. Dissenters' churches "had no legal existence." But, the incorporated churches retained a public quality as they were supported by tax dollars and legally bound to serve the state's articulated needs. The Federalist Party, dominant in state politics throughout the early republic, continued to use the churches as part of its vision of a commonwealth in which people worked together, through government and chartered corporations, to benefit the public and promote the social good.

In 1807, religious dissenters contributed to a temporary interruption of the Federalist Party's control of Massachusetts by electing a Republican governor and a Republican majority in each house. In June of that year, a proposed bill would have excused dissenters from

[36] *Trustees of Dartmouth College v. Woodward*, 17 US (4 Wheat) 518, 634 (1819).

taxes supporting the established church if they belonged to any other church, whether or not it was incorporated. Despite Republican control of the government, the bill failed when Federalists raised public antagonism to the bill by referring to it as the "infidel bill."[37] More serious challenges to the state's establishment arose in court cases.

By the second decade of the nineteenth century, the state's position that unincorporated churches were private voluntary associations while incorporated established churches were quasi-public entities serving the public good stood at odds with the developing corporate law rooted in contract law theory. While traditional Congregational Church doctrine understood a church as controlled by its members, state law recognized a parish church as a public institution serving the needs of its local residents, all of whom paid for its support. As residents in several parishes voted to bring in Unitarian ministers, traditionalists opted to leave those parishes to found new churches, taking the accumulated wealth of the parish church with them. The parish residents sued for the return of their property. In 1812, Judge Theophilus Parsons, in a decision clearly at odds with Constitutional law and prevailing liberal ideas, had held that parishes were public entities. All residents, whether members or not, controlled the election of parish ministers and officers, who were civil servants.[38] Obviously, this decision could not be the last word on the matter. Yet, before the courts could resolve the property law cases, the voters expressed continued support for some form of religious establishment.

Just months after the *Dartmouth College* decision, Massachusetts held a constitutional convention to consider eliminating its religious test oath for officeholders and public support for religion. The convention also considered, in light of the *Dartmouth College* decision, the advisability of starting a state school in contrast to continuing support for Harvard, a school owned by the Congregational Church. Despite the Supreme Court's clear legal precedent curtailing a state's power to control a private religious school, Massachusetts voters rejected the chance to fund a state school and retained the test oath and an established church. The issues were framed in terms of preserving the

---

[37] Johann N. Neem, *Creating a Nation of Joiners: Democracy and Civil Society in Early National Massachusetts* (Cambridge, MA: Harvard University Press, 2008), 20–1, quoting 1780 Massachusetts Constitution, 51, citing *Cutler v. Frost*, 53.

[38] *Burr vs. First Parish in Sandwich*, 9 Tyng 277 (1812).

traditional community of the state. Religion was depicted as the glue that held society together and formed its values. An editorial asked "whether Infidels and Nothingarians shall enjoy the blessings of a government that derives its stability and equity from Christianity?"[39] This position stood in abject contradiction to liberal republican concepts of political equality. Yet, in 1820, it held sway in Massachusetts.

While the voters in 1820 could reject prevailing ideology and law, the courts could not. Churches were either public or private entities – they could not be both. Between 1812 and 1821, traditional Congregationalists lost four cases in which they tried to retain church property while losing control of the church ministry to Unitarians. In the last of these, concerning the town of Dedham, Judge Isaac Parker held that each established church served as a public body and that the property of that church belonged to the parish as a political entity. Moreover, the dissenters could not incorporate a separate church and therefore could not take or hold property. The decision attempted to harmonize the Supreme Court's decisions on the rights of incorporated churches, culminating in the *Dartmouth College* decision, with state law and policy that provided public support and special legal protection for established churches.[40] However, the decision angered a large number of Congregationalists who had long supported establishment. Their loss of property prompted a reconsideration of the state's system of public churches, which seemed archaic in the context of liberal corporate law doctrine. Only in response to these court decisions did the citizens support disestablishment, reforming the churches as private corporations and putting them on equal footing in 1833. Contract law succeeded where politics would not in overcoming public support of religion.

Cultural Division in the Afterglow of Nation Building

In the years following the Revolutionary and Constitutional periods, American society experienced tremendous religious diversity. The cosmopolitan attitudes expressed in the separation of church and state indicated the growing power of liberalism as a social philosophy. An

---

[39] *Boston Recorder*, September 16, 1820, 151.
[40] *Baker v. Fales*, 16 Mass. 487 (1821).

almost atomistic individualism came to dominate American values
and laws and reached its full expression in the acceptance of a free
market not only as a means of economic organization but also as a
system of social or political organization in which every idea or possibility competed for support from among masses of potential voters,
purchasers, contributors, or adherents. Religion, too, competed in this
free market of ideas.

Liberalism endorsed a strict legal equality that forbade government
from favoring one individual or group at the expense of another. The
societal acceptance of legal equality found expression in the world's
first attempt to implement the moral values described by Adam Smith.
Free-enterprise capitalism and democracy constituted two sides of the
same coin. Contract law, endorsed in the Constitution as an expression of human liberty and legal equality, became the means of radical changes in social relations, elevating individuals' goals and desires
above concerns for the common good. This assertion of individual
autonomy constituted a social revolution following the political one,
involving a transition from classical republicanism to liberalism. In
this change, the individual became the primary political, economic,
and social actor – invested with the legal authority and autonomy to
vote, purchase, work, marry, relocate, and make a myriad other decisions as a private individual. Jefferson conceived of a free republic
as predicated on open commerce – and the absence of archaic duties
based on family relations, social class, or religion – existing between
all Americans and ultimately between all the people of the world. Law,
after the Revolution, embodied these ideas of individuality and freedom. Law replaced the multiple sources of authority that had existed
in colonial America: family, religion, and community. The rule of law
expressed a new ideology in which individual rights and freedoms
dominated.

Religion and even morality became matters of individual choice.
Government endorsement of any religion or the morality derived from
it would favor the beliefs of one person over another. Inevitably, liberalism's defense of individualism led not only to a rejection of government support for religion but also to a type of moral relativism.
Asserting the privacy of individual rights, liberalism expressed discom-
fort with imposing prescriptions of what another person should do
out of moral duty. If each individual is possessed of an internal moral

compass that enables him or her to distinguish good from evil, right from wrong, and if people are equal, no one person can impose his or her understanding of moral duties on another. Every state severely limited the extent to which law interfered in people's behaviors.

Of course, moral relativism existed largely as a philosophical fiction, for liberal humanism imposed its own moralism. Yet, the Jeffersonian liberals argued that this moralism derived from truths deducible from natural law: people's natural equality and their right to freedom of action in pursuit of personal goals. Christian morality, conversely, derived from a faith in spiritual matters unknowable.[41] As religious truth is ultimately unverifiable and therefore solely a matter of individual judgment, it forms an imperfect source of broadly conceived societal values. Respect of an individual's freedom of choice, action, and belief necessarily requires a tentative rejection of any religiously based moral absolutism and therefore of any public prescription of moral duty.

In 1784, Ethan Allen, a self-taught rural farmer who gained fame for his heroics in the Revolution, published *Reason the Only Oracle of Man* describing his understanding of a morality derived from natural laws rather than from religion. Allen contended that morality derives solely from an understanding of the nature and environment of humanity. Reason can be used to understand what is good, for what is good produces happiness. This human-centered belief disputes what Allen describes as the Christian message that humans are "born in a state of enmity to God and moral good."[42] The new conception of morality that prevailed after the Revolution shaped how people behaved and grew up. It considered virtue to be the appreciation of each person's right to his or her own ideas and behaviors. Law endorsed these new moral attitudes by protecting individual rights to conscience and respecting relations formed by will, not social duty. Law substituted liberalism's commitment to individual autonomy for republicanism's commitment to virtue.

The relative importance of religion to governing in the early republic is perhaps best seen in Jefferson's election to the presidency in 1800.

---

[41] When natural law, in the twentieth century, also was perceived as speculative, it too lost its authority to serve as the basis of morality. See Chapter 3.

[42] Ethan Allen, *Reason the Only Oracle of Man* (New York: Scholar's Facsimiles and Reprints, 1940), 467.

By that time, the differences between the Federalist and Republican Parties had become well defined, with the Federalists supporting a classical republican vision for America in which established religion encouraged virtuous behaviors, and the Republicans endorsing a liberal worldview of individual freedom and the disestablishment of religion. During the campaign, scores of ministers favoring the Federalist Party attempted to besmirch Jefferson's reputation by referring to him as an atheist. Reverend Thomas Robbins said to his congregation in Connecticut that he could "not believe that the Most High will permit a howling atheist to sit at the head of the nation."[43] Reverend Aaron Bancroft said that without a Christian president to lead it, the United States would devolve into the social chaos confronting France.[44] Federalist supporters used the same arguments in the press. The *Newark Gazette* claimed that the main issue before voters was "God – and a Religious President; or ... Jefferson – and no God!!!"[45] Politics encouraged some prominent figures to reconsider their positions on the role of religion in society. In less contentious times, Alexander Hamilton, when discussing the rejection of opening each morning of the Constitutional Convention in Philadelphia with a prayer, remarked that the delegates had no need for recourse to "foreign aid."[46] In 1800, he was not a practicing Christian, and his favorite for the presidency, Charles Cotesworth Pinckney, espoused religious views similar to Jefferson's. Yet, he spoke of the need to prevent "an atheist in Religion" from becoming president.[47]

Jefferson's election promised greater adoption of the liberals' agenda. The new president asserted that the First Amendment had built "a wall of separation between church and state."[48] Yet, the most significant changes in America's moral culture resulted not from federal policy but

---

[43] Quoted in Edwin S. Gaustad, "The Emergence of Religious Freedom in the Early Republic," in *Religion and the State: Essays in Honor of Lew Pfeffer*, ed. by James E. Wood, Jr. (Waco, TX: Baylor University Press, 1985), 42.

[44] Quoted in Neem, *Creating a Nation of Joiners*, 23.

[45] *Newark Gazette*, September 20, 1800, n.p.

[46] Thomas Fleming, *Duel: Alexander Hamilton, Aaron Burr, and the Future of America* (New York: Basic Books, 1999), 4–5.

[47] Quoted in Gregg L. Frazer, "Alexander Hamilton: Theistic Rationalist," in *The Forgotten Founders on Religion and Public Life*, ed. by Daniel Dreisbach, Mark David Hall, and Jeffrey H. Morrison (Notre Dame, IN: University of Notre Dame Press, 2009), 111.

[48] Letter of Thomas Jefferson to Danbury Association, January 1, 1802.

from Republican state court judges using liberal ideology to resolve private law cases. Legal historian James Willard Hurst has shown that the developing contract law of the early republic, protecting private rights and individual initiative, resulted in a tremendous "release of energy" that redesigned American society.[49] In the process, it also substituted a liberal moral code, rooted in the preeminence of individual rights and freedoms, for the more communitarian morality derived from Christianity that governed for most of the eighteenth century.

In the early 1800s, law transformed business disputes from public to private concerns. In colonial America, law supported a Christian communitarian view of the public good and frequently limited an individual's use of property when a community deemed that use to be contrary to its public interest. By 1805, in the case of *Palmer v. Mulligan*, the New York Supreme Court asserted the right of a property owner to develop property as inherent in the concept of ownership. Law protected private rights even when doing so frustrated old colonial common law precedents of restricting individual actions to protect the values, ethics, or conceptions of social good within a community.[50]

Liberalism recognized not only people's inherent reason, rationality, and moral compass but also their equality. This way of thinking necessitated a restructuring of a myriad of interpersonal relationships. Authority within the society, beginning with the government and the church but also including husbands, fathers, and community sentiment, diminished. Contract law served as the means of changing society to conform to liberal ideals. Law, in the early republic, recognized each person's private individual right to sell his or her labor on the open market – a concept known as free labor. In asserting the doctrine of free labor, law rejected community restrictions on wages and various forms of labor combinations, now seen as conspiracies or restraints on trade, that had been popular in the colonial era. Courts in six different states considered twenty-three cases of labor combinations in the early 1800s as criminal prosecutions. These cases involved attempts by workers to force individuals to join with them in demanding certain wages or employment terms rather than to accept work on their own terms. In

[49] James Willard Hurst, *Law and the Conditions of Freedom in the Nineteenth-Century United States* (Madison: University of Wisconsin Press, 1956), 3–32.

[50] *Palmer v. Mulligan*, 3 NY (Caines) 307 (1805).

every instance, the court protected private individual rights by finding labor combinations injurious to the free-labor ideal. In a case concerning journeyman tailors in Philadelphia, the defense counsel used old moralistic and communitarian arguments in attempting to sway the jury. He argued from an old colonial perspective that law could restrict individual freedoms and even impose greater duties on owners and prominent people in order to serve the public good. But the jury did not see the case as involving class issues, only the rights of tailors who did not want to affiliate, but rather to contract to sell their labor freely as individuals. In these decisions, American law expressed primary concern for individual rights and freedoms, including all rights to property. Law protected individual spheres of action, not community values or Christian morals.

Liberalization of the law shaped personal or family relationships as much as it did business relationships. In particular, law expressed changing cultural attitudes regarding female autonomy. After the Revolution, a few outspoken people argued that the denial of the vote to women and the perpetuation of coverture, through which a woman lost control of her property in marriage, were inconsistent with Enlightenment assertions of human equality and Revolutionary ideals. New Jersey even extended the right to vote to women in its wartime constitution, a right extended by legislation in 1797, though property thresholds restricted the franchise. The development of separate spheres on the basis of gender in the early republic inarguably limited married women to the home, but nonetheless provided a distinct means for women to pursue a valued political and social function. Ironically, perhaps, in daily life, men and women grew to see themselves as largely equal, especially as partners in marriage.

In fact, perhaps no personal legal matter better illustrates the change in values in late eighteenth-century America than does marriage. First, the decision to marry became less a concern of family economics and more a consideration of personal desire. The new concept of "companionate marriage" referred to a mutual love, affection, and respect between spouses. William Ellery Channing, speaking in 1816, referred to a new "tenderness and dignity which have rarely distinguished it [marriage]" in the past.[51] Second, new laws allowed for marriages in

---

[51] Quoted in Timothy Kenslea, *The Sedgwicks in Love, Courtship, Engagement, and Marriage in the Early Republic* (Boston: Northeastern University Press, 2006), 169.

civil ceremonies before justices of the peace and greater acceptance of common law marriages. Third, during the Revolutionary era and the early republic, laws recognized a greater liberality to granting divorces. Marriage had to protect, in the words of a 1775 magazine article, the "reasonable liberty" of the two parties to the marriage "contract."[52] Divorce laws after the Revolution repudiated the old colonial idea that husband and wife, or even the entire colonial household, constitute a single political economic and social entity. In some divorce cases, the courts gave custody of the children to ex-wives in consideration of the individual interests of each person. A marriage contract, like all others, had to be a voluntary agreement between two equal parties.

Americans during the early republic abandoned primogeniture, allowing daughters to inherit real and personal property, and instituted reforms to intestacy laws recognizing the right of widows and widowers as nearly equal. Certainly these changes recognize that Revolutionary-era Americans defined people as individuals rather than by their roles in a family. Yet, they also indicate the attempt by Americans of this era to break down social hierarchies and eliminate artificial preferences, such as aristocracy, monopolies, and established churches. Each individual became a free actor, able to make decisions based on her or his own self-interest. In according greater respect for the rights of daughters and widows, legal reform limited the impositions on sons to care for their sisters, mothers, or stepmothers.

Outside of marriage, women exercised greater autonomy in pursuing educational and business opportunities. Public awareness of women as autonomous sexual actors also increased. Popular songs, poems, and stories depicted women as having sexual desires equal to those of men. A simultaneous decline in adherence to traditional Christian admonitions against extramarital sex resulted from recognition of a new respect for privacy and diminished parental and church authority. Between one-third and one-half of all first births between 1776 and 1828 resulted from premarital or extramarital affairs, and the era witnessed the highest rate of illegitimate children in the nation's history.

The endorsement of an unprecedented degree of individual self-interest combined with democratic forms of governing to frighten

---

[52] "An Essay on Marriage or the Lawfulness of Divorce," *Pennsylvania Magazine*, December 1775, Supplement, 602.

many social conservatives, especially traditional Christians. Some clergy condemned economic freedom and society's embrace of capitalism as vehemently as they attacked social freedoms. In 1793, during the yellow fever outbreak in Philadelphia, a Lutheran minister blamed the city's preoccupation with theatergoing, sexual freedom, and "the luxury and dissipation among all classes of people" for the epidemic.[53] Many evangelicals openly criticized the growth of capitalism since the Revolution and looked back to the Puritan communities of New England as establishing a more virtuous way of life.

Dissenting ministers, who had once championed the cause of disestablishment, now felt betrayed by their liberal allies and bemoaned the reduced status of Christianity and its ministers in the early republic. Reverend Lyman Beecher believed in 1817, as Connecticut effectuated disestablishment, that Christians and their ministers "shall become slaves ... and slaves to the worst of masters."[54] Several prominent Christian leaders, among them Yale President Timothy Dwight, criticized the post-Revolutionary culture, even condemning the Revolution itself as a victory for infidelity. Dwight saw the erosion of the religious significance of marriage as just one indication of the need to fight back against liberalism: "You must take your side.... [W]ill you make marriage the mockery of the registrar's office? Will you enthrone a Goddess of Reason before the table of Christ?"[55] Certainly different conceptions of human nature formed the essence of the philosophical disagreement. Reverend Beecher, bemoaning the protection of rights in post-Revolutionary America, called for "laws against immorality [to] be restored to their ancient vigor."[56] Yet, ministers such as Dwight and Beecher were far from alone in questioning what that effort had produced. Samuel Adams, a hero of the Revolution, expressed dismay that old laws that once suppressed "idleness[,] Dissipation[,] and Extravagancy" had been repealed and replaced by a legal culture that

---

[53] J. Henry C. Helmuth, *A Short Account of the Yellow Fever in Philadelphia, for the Reflecting Christian* (Philadelphia: Jones, Hoff, & Derrick, 1794), 21.

[54] Lyman Beecher, *Autobiography of Lyman Beecher*, 2 vols., ed. by Barbara H. Cross (Cambridge, MA: Belknap Press/Harvard University Press, 1961), 1: 192.

[55] Timothy Dwight, "A Discourse on Some Events of the Last Century," in *American Christianity: An Historical Interpretation with Representative Documents*, ed. by H. Shelton Smith, Robert J. Handy, and Lefferts A. Loetscher (New York: Scribner's, 1963), 1: 530–9, 538.

[56] Lyman Beecher, "A Reformation of Morals," 14, 15, 16.

tolerated all degrees of freedom.[57] At the root of their concerns was the disestablishment not only of the churches as public institutions endorsing Biblical truth and the community's morals but of religion as a force in governing public morals and educating the young. They believed that a public endorsement of religion was necessary for the health of "true religion and good morals."[58] They desired a return to the Christian communitarianism of the late colonial era, albeit without the political control of Britain.

The election of Thomas Jefferson to the presidency in 1800 crystallized the conservative Christians' fears and prompted action to save their country from atheism. They had two means for doing so at their disposal. The Federalist Party provided a political option. Though it had lost the 1800 election, the Party remained a vibrant expositor of classical republican ideals, including the need for public acceptance and recognition of religion. The other option involved using private voluntary associations to express the evangelical message and fight the growth of liberalism.

The "Second Awakening" arose in part as a reaction to liberalism's endorsement of individual freedoms, moral relativism, and market capitalism. Its leaders revived their evangelical predecessors' commitments to a truly Christian society, but did so by employing the same legal and entrepreneurial strategies that had replaced a Christian communitarian society with a secular and individualistic one. Yet, the real growth in evangelical use of these corporations came after the War of 1812. Until then, the Federalist Party served as the primary means of combating liberalism.

Significant Federalist Party leaders appealed to Christian voters through calls for a greater role for religion in the public realm. Federalist Party doctrine endorsed Christianity as necessary to promote public order and the virtue required for democratic governance, expressing an alternative vision of America to that of the Jeffersonians. Alexander Hamilton saw popular acceptance of Adam Smith's theory of a self-regulating market economy as a dangerous and "speculative paradox" of rights-based law and hoped that religion could serve as

[57] Quoted in Gary Scott Smith, "Samuel Adams," in *The Forgotten Founders*, 49.
[58] Quoted in Mead, *Nathaniel William Taylor*, 41. Beecher, at p. 81, is quoted as stating: "[T]he time has come when it becomes every friend of the state [CT] to wake up and exert his whole influence to save it from innovation and democracy."

a means of rebuilding a communitarian ethic.[59] Similarly, John Jay believed that Americans had lost their sense of duty to God with disastrous consequences for public morality. Perhaps conflating his religious and his political goals, Reverend Beecher sought to convert the "Sabbath-breakers, rum selling tippling folk, infidels, and ruff-scruff" so as to cease the Republican threat to New England's standing order.[60]

Federalist judges also fought to stem the tide of liberalism washing over the nation. New York Supreme Court Justice James Kent launched a personal crusade from the bench to return Christian morality to American society. In 1811, he considered the case of Mr. Ruggles, who publicly stated, "Jesus Christ was a bastard and his mother must be a whore." Despite the fact that New York had repealed its law making blasphemy a crime, Judge Kent convicted him of that offense on the grounds that no statutory law prohibiting blasphemy was needed as Christianity formed a part of the society's common law. Kent added that Christianity provided a necessary basis for "moral discipline [and] those principles of virtue which help to bind society together," especially to combat the individualistic forces of capitalism.[61]

The *Ruggles* decision stood out as anomalous in 1811, provoking only scattered reaction – liberals were more inclined to be dismissive of Kent and his radically conservative jurisprudence than overly alarmed by it. The *Ruggles* case nonetheless served as a voice of Christian activism, if not of significant legal precedent. Kent's decision was never cited in New York and received judicial support only in one other state, Pennsylvania, in three cases brought over the following thirteen years: one for "behavior destructive of morality in general,"[62] one for working on the Sabbath,[63] and another for blasphemy.[64] Kent's legal theories actually found greater acceptance later in the nineteenth century than in the early republic; by the 1840s, they would have widespread public acceptance. During the early 1800s, they appear as an

---

[59] Quoted in Joyce Appleby, *Thomas Jefferson* (New York: Henry Holt & Co., 2003), 68.

[60] Quoted in Mead, *Nathaniel William Taylor*, 48, 80.

[61] *People v. Ruggles*, 8 Johns. 290 (NY, 1811), 290, 294.

[62] *Commonwealth v. Sharpless*, 2 Serg. & Rawle 91, 103 (Pa., 1815).

[63] *Commonwealth v. Wolf*, 3 Serg. & Rawle 48 (Pa., 1817).

[64] *Updegraph v. Commonwealth*, 11 Serg. & Rawle 394 (Pa., 1824).

isolated example of Federalist attempts to impose the old Christian communitarianism of the colonial era on post-Revolutionary society.

Pennsylvania's prosecution of a man who worked on Sunday contradicted a national trend to embrace productive labor on all days of the week. The United States Post Office not only delivered and received mail on Sundays but also presented an opportunity for men in small towns to gather for drinks with friends. The disregard of the Sabbath so alienated some evangelicals that by 1810 Lyman Beecher and Senator Theodore Frelinghuysen of New Jersey started the first nationwide campaign to close the post office on Sundays. The brief effort produced enthusiasm among evangelical activists but mostly resentment among other Americans. It did, however, alert evangelicals to the opportunities voluntary organizations created to influence public policy. In 1812, Timothy Dwight organized "a general society for the suppression of vice and the promotion of good morals." Beecher described it as a political response in "anticipation of the impending revolution" in morals.[65] These early Christian political societies failed largely because they could not attract less fervent and nonbelievers to their causes. In the early 1800s, Christian activists lacked the numbers to win political battles on their own. To succeed in future campaigns, they would have to find new allies who supported their social or political cause, if not the Christian justification for the positions taken in these movements.

Jefferson's election in 1800 proved to be only the beginning of an extended period of Republican Party dominance – not ended at the national level until Andrew Jackson's election in 1828. The overwhelming political support for Jeffersonian liberalism solidified the Constitutional delineation between public and private spheres. The Republican successors to Jefferson each endorsed the idea of the private sphere promoting economic and social progress. They defined justice as the securement of private rights. Law during their administrations recognized happiness as a personal concern and therefore a matter of private, not public, consideration. Monroe's election in 1816 was heralded by the *Columbian Centinel*, a Boston newspaper published in the heart of Federalist strength, as the dawning of an "era

---

[65] Quoted in Mead, *Nathaniel William Taylor*, 81.

of good feelings." After 1816, the Federalist Party became largely irrelevant in national politics.

The Republican presidents from Jefferson through John Quincy Adams recognized that public and private spheres must be separated to protect individual rights. While colonial governments had licensed private initiatives, often protected as monopolies, to address public needs, the Republicans committed themselves to enforcing the new public-private distinction. They inquired whether government had the right to act in a certain realm – if it did, then public action was taken; if it did not, then the action was left to private enterprise to handle. But, when private enterprise acted, it did so in pursuit of private goals and values, free from government concern and direction.

Jefferson delayed acting on the Louisiana Purchase, despite strong personal desires for western growth and an equally strong conviction that the purchase was in the best interests of the nation, until he secured a legal opinion on its constitutionality. Following Jefferson's example in pursuing the Louisiana Purchase, both Madison and Monroe requested advisory opinions from the Supreme Court on whether the federal government had constitutional authority to undertake improvements to the national infrastructure. Only on the Court's advice that it did, did they build the National Road and propose further roads and canals. New York, under Republican leadership, funded the construction of the Erie Canal and collected its own tolls rather than licensing a private firm to dig and profit from the project. President John Quincy Adams did not need the authorization his predecessors did, for they had already determined the constitutionality of federal action to improve the infrastructure, but in his First Annual Message to Congress he cited Adam Smith for recognizing government's ability to provide roads, canals, and education and encouraged the legislature to undertake these ventures and a stagecoach line west. The Republicans' willingness to use public means to address societal needs for education, road and canal construction, and the defense of free commerce on the high seas stands in sharp contrast to their refusal to treat religion and morality as anything but private concerns.

They accepted that the Jeffersonian assertion of "life, liberty, and the pursuit of happiness" as inherent individual rights meant that no government could ever deliver them; all it could do is not interfere with them. Colonial governments had exercised tremendous police powers to create a civil society through communitarian prescriptions of social order. The Republicans refused to do likewise in the early republic. In the process, they created a society in which private individuals pursued their own goals in the private sphere while protected by law from most public-sector interference. Impositions of religion and morality would have constituted two forms of public interference. The Federalist Party continued to represent communitarian and religious interests that challenged the Republican vision, but after 1816 did so almost exclusively in New England.

2

A Christian Counter-revolution and a
New Vision of American Society, 1828–1865

The alliance between the Jeffersonian liberals and the evangelical pietists that produced the disestablishment of religion in most of the country during the Revolutionary and Constitutional eras fragmented shortly afterward in the election of Jefferson and the ascendancy of liberalism. By the 1820s, these one-time allies engaged in open political warfare over the values of the new nation. In the decades prior to the Civil War, Christian reformers undertook several measures to restructure the United States as a Christian nation. In furtherance of this goal, activist Christians asserted that separation of church and state concerned only those institutions, banning laws requiring membership or monetary contributions to churches, and did not require the divorce of religious beliefs or principles from governing. Yet, to pursue this goal, they aligned with social reformers who sought only a more equitable and communitarian society than that created at the founding. Together these new allies hoped to change the law to express new visions of society.

By the 1830s, religion assumed more forms and embraced a greater range of beliefs than at any earlier period in the history of English America. This variation of religious expression resulted, in part, from the fact that law had made religion a matter of personal choice. Each church or religious organization had equal status as a private voluntary association using the corporate form. As religion conformed to the democratic structure of the society, people defined their own beliefs and formed their own churches, sects, or communities for expressing them. Christianity, while the largest religious expression in Jacksonian America, constituted anything but a united front in its challenge to the secular republic. Yet, as Americans came to battle one another over slavery by the era's end, they also began to come together in an attempt to integrate their religious values with their secular interests, forming a civil religion that would last well into the twentieth century.

As the United States celebrated its fiftieth anniversary in 1826, it reveled not only in the winning of its independence and the establishment of its constitutional government, but also in its burgeoning economy, the doubling of its geographic size, the growth of its transportation and communication infrastructure, and its growing military and diplomatic power. Certainly some Christian Americans saw in this national success evidence of God's grace and of Americans as his chosen people. Others, however, harbored misgivings over America's progress, seeing it as the product of a liberal ideology that ignored or refuted God's directions for how people were to live. Preachers walked a fine line when they credited God with earthly progress while condemning the freedoms that produced it. As early as 1812, Reverend Lyman Beecher, in a sermon delivered in New Haven, Connecticut, asked his listeners, "Did the late war [the Revolution] produce in our own land no change for the worse?" He answered that it had – the Revolution and the rise of Jeffersonian liberalism had contributed to a diminished stature of religion and its ministers, an increase in selfish business pursuits, a decline in morality and respect for parents and authority, a diminished reliance on the Bible as the true word of God, and an insensitivity to the less fortunate. Beecher and other evangelicals bemoaned the excesses of individual freedom and the coincident loss of community that had occurred after the Revolution. Recognizing that the churches, and even religion itself, were removed from the province of government, he called on all Christians to form "a sort of disciplined moral militia ... to devise ways and means of suppressing vice and guarding public morals."[1] Specifically, he encouraged his followers to put their religious beliefs into social action by forming private voluntary

---

[1] Lyman Beecher, "*A Reformation of Morals Practicable and Indispensable*" (sermon delivered at New Haven, Connecticut, October 27, 1812) (Utica, NY: Merrill and Camp, 1813), 8, 17.

associations that would work to reform American society by rendering it more attentive to moral duties and the needs of people for spiritual as well as economic sustenance.

Christian reform would address every aspect of society in the new nation, from family and personal relations to the way business was conducted. Christian reformers sought to remake the United States into a less individualistic, competitive, and insensitive society by infusing the people and their institutions with a new appreciation of Christian duties and communal interdependence. Private charity and political involvement formed a two-pronged approach to social change. In both, ardent Christians had to align with non-Christian communitarians to achieve their goals.

Despite profound spiritual and doctrinal divisions, antebellum reformers found common cause in their alienation from prevailing social values and their awareness of social problems. Contemporary historians may well underappreciate Romanticism as an intellectual movement, studying it largely as a literary and artistic phase in Western cultural history. Romanticism arose in reaction to the Enlightenment's emphasis on reason. The founders largely accepted that humanity could use its reason to discover the laws of nature, absolutes that governed a rationally ordered world. Romanticists, who believed that people were as much spirit as intellect, found that this assertion deprecated humanity's emotional needs. The Romantic movement fostered a wide assortment of spiritual expressions from Transcendentalism to experiments in phrenology, diet, and sexual abstinence. Several spiritualities encouraged the creation of utopian communes of believers set apart from mainstream society. Each contained a significant reformist impulse.

By the 1830s, growing numbers of Americans desired not only their own economic prosperity, but also improvements in the quality of life of the less fortunate. Recognizing the desire of many Americans for a stronger community and greater attention to moral responsibilities, Christian denominations during the antebellum era made social reform a major focus of their religious messages and worked with people of various beliefs toward that goal. In so doing they championed a reintegration of Christian morality, and even Christian beliefs, into the laws and institutions of the country. They experienced some successes at the state level, but no real change in the nation's laws.

Two weaknesses, each a product of tentative intellectual commitment, prevented the reformers from reaching greater successes. First, reformers in Jacksonian America exhibited a tacit acceptance of the liberal institutions created during the nation's founding. Most of the Christian reformers deferred to, even if not endorsing, the primacy of rights, the bifurcation of private and public spheres, and the need for churches to adopt the corporate form. Still, their criticism of contemporary evils exposed the tension they felt between their acceptance of national laws and institutions and their desire for a more moral and Christian society. In this they embodied a lack of ideological clarity that undoubtedly hindered them in pursuing radical changes. Second, the multiplicity of actors seeking a more communitarian society shared little but their communitarian sympathies. They divided over religion, women's rights, and the role of the market in society.

President Andrew Jackson himself epitomized the lack of ideological clarity of his age while also expressing a new spirit of American culture and politics less cosmopolitan and ecumenical than that of the founders. He was the first national candidate to appeal to voters using race and religion, to openly support slavery, and to advocate clearing lands of Indians for settlement by white men. Ironically, he fashioned himself as the heir to Jefferson's political mantle, despite the fact that Jefferson could not tolerate the man. By the 1820s, if not before, Jefferson had become widely recognized as having initiated a revolution in American political, legal, and cultural thought. Subsequent disciples, assuming the authority to speak for Jefferson, subjected his views and policies to sometimes grotesque caricature to justify their own positions. Jackson was perhaps the most self-aggrandizing of these political opportunists. Never a sophisticated thinker, his own positions, attitudes, and perspectives resemble different threads of the man's thought that are not easily woven into a whole cloth. Eschewing intellectual consistency, he made no pretense to being a thought leader. His inconsistency expressed itself in his endorsement of "rugged individualism" while comfortably making moral judgments and imposing duties on others; he was not alone in this inconsistency.

Spiritual Rebirth Energizes Americans

The Second Awakening

The reform initiatives of the Jacksonian era depended on a reassertion of Christian faith commonly called the Second Awakening. Two integrated yet distinct phases composed the Second Awakening. In the first phase, lasting from the late 1790s into the second decade of the nineteenth century, New England preachers reacted to perceptions of cultural irreligion, the diminished stature of the clergy, and the growth of liberal religion by developing a new Christian doctrine that asserted the importance of Christian behavior and social duty as at least equal to concern for salvation. In the second phase, ministers and Christian laypeople organized themselves into private voluntary associations to spread the Christian message at home and abroad and to produce social change consistent with that message.

The preachers of the Second Awakening led what one historian describes as a Christian "*reconquista*" of American society to combat the rationalism and individualism of the Revolutionary and Constitutional eras.[2] Doctrinal changes, such as a reconception of humanity as capable of moral action, an acceptance of postmillennialism (which predicted that the Second Coming would follow construction of a peaceful and moral earthly society), and the prioritization of communal brotherhood as a sign of godliness all encouraged an outward religious expression. Reformist Christians hoped to reintegrate religion into the social fabric of the country, establishing social controls through new laws that would reshape cultural values and temper what they perceived to be an excess of freedom.

The Second Awakening succeeded in reenergizing Americans to religion. By 1850, approximately 35 percent of Americans had joined churches. From 1820 to 1860, the American population tripled; during those same forty years, the number of congregations in the United States grew by a factor of five. The Great Awakening gave birth to the evangelical sects, but the Second Awakening empowered them; Methodists and Baptists became large and influential denominations.

Second Awakening preachers spoke with great attention to popular religious needs, appealing to people who felt adrift in an individualistic society that seemed to offer little, if any, compassion, emotional support, or spiritual comfort. In so doing, evangelical clergymen both regained some of the social status lost after the Revolution and redefined the purpose and function of religion in post-Revolutionary America. To create a moral society and prepare for Christ's return, Christian reformers fought to help the poor and unfortunate, eliminate

[2] Howe, *What Hath God Wrought*, 168 (quote).

prostitution, encourage temperance, and ban slavery. In asserting a religion focused on social reform, evangelicals created a basis for working with liberal Christians and nonbelievers.

The Transcendentalist Alternative

Despite the growth of evangelical Christianity in antebellum America, Transcendentalism perhaps better captured the spirit of the Romantic Age, and it, too, promoted societal reform. Transcendentalism had its birth in the Transcendental Club, a group of Bostonians that included public intellectuals such as Ralph Waldo Emerson, Henry David Thoreau, Margaret Fuller, Bronson Alcott, and William Ellery Channing. The club formed to share ideas concerning the sterility of Enlightenment thought and its religious expressions of Deism and Unitarianism. While many of the members were Congregational ministers with Unitarian leanings, they criticized the church for its devaluation of mysticism and its rejection of the literary romanticism of the Bible. Transcendentalists believed that human reason must be supported by transcendent human capacities for knowing – a spiritualism that rejected miracles while accepting the mystical aspects of human love, compassion, and understanding. The more doctrinally inclined Transcendentalists accepted Jesus as an exemplary moral man who had realized his transcendent potential. Religion expressed humanity's quest for that very same transcendent potential that constitutes the divine. However, as the quest must be an individual one, religious traditions, doctrines, and institutions may hamper as much as aid its success. Increasingly at odds with even liberal Congregationalists, Emerson resigned his ministerial appointment at the Second Church of Boston in 1832 because he could no longer accept the myth that underlay his administration of the Lord's Supper. Fellow Transcendentalists Orestes Brownson, George Ripley, and Theodore Parker soon reached the same decision.

The Transcendentalists advocated wide-ranging social change that would temper some of the effects of liberalism and build a more communitarian society. Men like Bronson Alcott feared that commercial interests and the capitalists who created them might take permanent control of the country. Reverend William Ellery Channing argued that free enterprise contravened God's designs for humanity and endangered its soul. Transcendentalists led many Americans in asking,

"Given the proper degree of freedom necessary for human fulfillment, what should people do?" In particular, did Americans have any duties in exercising their freedoms? They answered that people were not only to live in harmony with nature, but also to free themselves from convention, competition, and conformity, to exercise freedom of thought, and to work for the social good by addressing social problems such as slavery, poverty, and the subordination of women.

Transcendentalists came to very similar conclusions as their more traditional Christian counterparts regarding both the need for reform and the basis for it. These groups used the same values – human compassion, sympathy, and a desire for social harmony – as bases for judging American society. Competitive individualism, the social by-product of the recent Revolution, came under attack from Transcendentalist and Christian reformers alike. To contain the rabid individualism they perceived, nearly all the Transcendentalists endorsed some increase in communitarianism. In so doing, they largely ignored or refuted the Jeffersonian delineation between public and private spheres and conceived of moral duty as a shared concern.

Margaret Fuller argued for an expansion of the idea of equality to include social considerations and suggested recognition of a moral law. In 1845, she encouraged the government, at any level, to assume greater responsibility for caring for the poor, the insane, and the imprisoned, writing that "[t]here is wealth enough" for the society to assume greater responsibilities: "[L]et not economy but utility be the rule of expenditure, for, here, parsimony is the worst prodigality."[3] Similarly, *The Dial*, a Transcendentalist journal, criticized employers for their selfishness but asserted that their "sin" belonged to the entire society that applauded their priorities. Several Transcendentalists argued that laws, and even the Constitution, were not final authorities. Thoreau questioned any citizen's duty to obey unjust laws, even advocating civil disobedience.

Public Attitudes Encourage Legal Change
Free-enterprise capitalism contributed to the growth of a new middle class, first distinguishable by the 1820s. Yet, by the 1840s, economic

---

[3] Margaret Fuller, "Our City Charities: Visit to Bellevue Alms House, to the Farm School, the Asylum for the Insane, and Penitentiary on Blackwell's' Island," in *The Portable Margaret Fuller*, ed. by Mary Kelley (New York: Penguin Books, 1994), 375–6.

change had produced greater wealth disparities than ever before known in America. In cities, the richest 5 percent of free males owned 70 percent of all the real estate and personal wealth. Cities suffered from poor housing, poor air quality, poor water quality, and poor sanitation. Rats infested every major city. A newborn baby in Philadelphia or New York in the 1830s or 1840s had a life expectancy of twenty-four years, six years less than a baby born into slavery.

Concerned Americans addressed poverty entirely through philanthropy, implicitly endorsing the liberal ideas expressed in the Constitution protecting private property and legal equality. The law could neither prefer a group of people to advance its interests, even to balance the social scales, nor take property from those who earned it to benefit those who did not. In this environment, prevailing Christian morals created private, not public, responsibilities. Private charities remained the only significant means of helping the less fortunate. As most of the public-aid charities in the antebellum era had religious affiliations, these private voluntary benevolent associations reinforced the idea of religion as a private matter expressed and taught through private institutions. However, reformers quickly learned to combine charity with political calls for social change, and much of that social change involved rewriting the laws.

For many Christians, reform of society began with reform of the family. A reassertion of traditional Christian attitudes regarding gender difference strongly influenced antebellum conceptions of family structure, eroding gains made toward sexual equality in the founding era. Three assumptions supported societal recognition of that difference: (1) biological distinctions that not only made women more appropriate caregivers to children but also rendered them physically weaker; (2) emotional and intellectual distinctions that rendered women both more moral and more sensitive and less reasonable, rational, and thoughtful; and (3) Biblical passages that required women to submit to men and warned that women, if not restrained, can be temptresses and seducers. Christian activists soon recognized that changes in the common law came very slowly and were unlikely to overturn the precedents established in the first sixty years of nationhood. Accordingly, they lobbied their legislatures for statutory reforms that would reverse the liberal policies of the preceding decades. Statutory reforms in family law expressed the reformers' desires to limit individual freedoms to achieve their moralistic and communitarian goals. Reformers referenced the Bible in asserting family roles prescribed by God. Judges James Kent and Joseph Story even gave judicial sanction to these views in their individual commentaries. Legislation placed new restrictions on marriage, created new protections for women from breaches of promises to marry that might sully their reputations, made abortion and other forms of family planning illegal, limited expansions of the rights of illegitimate children, and empowered state governments, especially courts, with authority to intercede in family matters to serve societal interests in child welfare and family stability. Through this legislation, reformers reasserted an image of the family as a social unit rather than as a group of individuals; in this unit, women and children needed protection as weak and dependent entities, and the law imposed duties on husbands and fathers first and the state second to provide that protection.

As women pursued activities such as writing novels for profit during the print revolution, factory work in New England's textile mills in the early industrial revolution, and social reform in the "Benevolent Empire," they acted on the freedoms created in the founding era and challenged Christian conceptions of morality and patriarchal authority. The common law of the early republic had recognized, at least to some degree, a woman as an individual legal actor with authority to enter into contracts, including marriage. This legal ideal proved inconsistent with the growing cultural image of a woman as a vulnerable and powerless female in need of protection. Victorian society imposed new responsibilities on women to conform the legal ideal to the cultural one as the law increasingly assumed the role of defender of womanhood. New cultural norms reduced a woman's individual and sexual freedoms by creating new duties for her to act morally superior and control herself so as not to harm those she loved. Law reinforced growing Victorian-era cultural attitudes regarding proper behaviors for women.

The Romantic era's respect for emotional and sympathetic impulses proved to be a double-edged sword. Many saw female participation in social reform as an outgrowth of women's natural role as caregivers and moral leaders. Yet, the prevailing Christian stereotype excoriated single women living on their own and working in factories or writing or reading popular novels celebrating freedom and sensual experiences.

A conservative Christian reaction to women's expanded role outside of the home sought to narrow even further the acceptable realm of female activities and used the Bible to do so. Ministers molded the new role of women, as republican mothers, into a Christian responsibility. In so doing, they reinforced the old message of female limitations with a duty to keep the family moral by staying at home. An evangelical minister in Utica, New York, stated: "Man profits from connection with the world, but women never; their constituents [*sic*] of mind are different. The one is raised and exalted by mingled association. The purity of the other is sustained in silence and seclusion."[4] In other words, both to retain their own morality and to inculcate it in their children, women must be restricted to their homes.

As a girl reading books in her father's law office, Elizabeth Cady Stanton came to resent the influence of Christianity on American law. Noting the misogynistic aspects of the Bible, beginning in Genesis as woman is made the temptress of man and punished for her sin by God through an increase in her pain during childbirth and the designation of a man, as husband, to rule over her, she found the text an unsuitable basis for the laws of reasonable people. Yet, ministers continued to cite those very passages in support of laws and customs restricting women's societal options and sexual inclinations. In 1838, petitions to various state legislatures submitted by a Christian group known as the Female Moral Reform Society noted the absence of laws criminalizing "Seduction and Adultery" and called for prison terms for female seducers. Religious influences on sexual identities contributed to changes in sexual behaviors. By the 1820s, some of the liberal attitudes of the late 1700s had succumbed to a new sense of propriety. Growing numbers of young couples reacted both to the high rate of premarital pregnancies in the 1790s and early 1800s and to new invocations of Christian morality by restraining themselves from intercourse until married.

Among the social changes affecting women in the early republic, perhaps the increase in female education promised the greatest long-term significance. However, by 1830, education also became a battleground between the old liberalism of the founding era and the early republic and the new Christian conservatism of the antebellum

---

[4] Quoted in Johnson, *Early American Republic*, 115.

years. Americans had taken much of the responsibility for educating young people away from the churches, but had done little, prior to the 1830s, to provide public education. Between 1790 and 1830, numerous plans for public education received popular support, and a few even gained legislative endorsement. However, the voters' aversion to taxes left the plans unfunded. In the 1830s, Horace Mann, Secretary of the Massachusetts State Board of Education, asserted the need for "common schools" that would provide tuition-free education to the whole population. Echoing Jefferson, he contended that democracy depended on an educated citizenry that could only be produced by schools with common standards for teaching, textbooks, and curricula provided at public expense. Mann hoped to build on the liberal educational theories of Locke and Rousseau that recognized children as essentially moral beings with great intellectual potential. Education, from this perspective, should provide the freedom and incentive to develop thinking people capable of moral, social, political, and intellectual autonomy. Yet, Mann encountered a backlash from evangelicals, who believed that liberal education had already gone too far in eroding respect for morality and deference to authority in young people. In 1812, Lyman Beecher had ridiculed the liberalism that had "exiled from the school ... not only the rod, but government and catechetical instruction, and a regard to the moral conduct of children." Claiming that "man is desperately wicked, and cannot be qualified for good membership in society without moral restraint," he called for greater discipline and teaching of Christian doctrine and morals in the schools.[5] By the 1830s, many preachers had taken up the battle for returning strict authority and moral direction to the classrooms while also arguing that girls needed little, if any, higher education to become wives and mothers.

The same Christian attitudes that compelled a reconsideration of family structure in Jacksonian America prompted a reappraisal of the principles and goals of American law. By the mid-1830s, Americans desirous of greater brotherhood in their society had begun to waver in their commitment to separating religion and government. Pastoral calls for a greater acceptance of legal or public recognition of morality

[5] Lyman Beecher, "A Reformation of Morals," 14, 15.

expressed a growing recognition that religious beliefs, as much as any other, could be a legitimate basis for social and political actions.

American law risks its effectiveness if it strays too far from popular understandings of right and wrong. Jacksonian America experienced an unprecedented disrespect for law, a cultural phenomenon that may well have influenced the direction that law took beginning in the 1830s. Christian communitarians, resenting law's refusal to invade the private realm of morality, began to take action into their own hands. An increase in vigilante justice imposed moral standards on behaviors when law failed to do so. In 1834, a mob attacked prostitutes in the city of New York, and in 1835, another mob in Vicksburg, Mississippi, hung several men to purge the town of gamblers. Across America, citizens turned to extralegal means to establish community morals. In 1838, a young Abraham Lincoln noted "the increasing disregard for law which pervades the country; the growing disposition to substitute the wild and furious passions, in lieu of the sober judgment of Courts; and the worse than savage mobs, for the executive ministers of justice."[6] President Andrew Jackson himself seemed to condone extralegal practices when he told the Supreme Court that while it might pronounce law, it would be unable to enforce it under his administration.[7]

In order to create a Christian society, reformers had to destroy, or at least severely limit, the law's protection of individual rights and liberties. By the 1830s, popular support for tempering law's devotion to rights was growing throughout the country. Some scholars at the time, such as Congregational Pastor Mark Hopkins at Williams College, asserted a rather utilitarian conception of rights to replace the founders' absolutist conception: "A man has rights in order that he may do right."[8] In 1833, Nathaniel Chipman published *Principles of Government*, in which he

---

[6] Abraham Lincoln, "The Perpetuation of Our Political Institutions: Address Before the Young Men's Lyceum of Springfield, Illinois, January 27, 1838," in *Abraham Lincoln: His Speeches and Writings*, ed. by Roy P. Basler (New York: Da Capo Press, 1946), 77.

[7] The statement, given in reaction to the Court's decision in *Worcester v. Georgia*, 31 US 515 (1832), is understood to be "John Marshall has made his decision; now let him enforce it."

[8] Hopkins quoted in William M. Novak, *The People's Welfare: Law and Regulation in Nineteenth-Century America* (Chapel Hill: University of North Carolina Press, 1996), 33.

attacked Locke and Rousseau for their excessive prioritization of individual rights. Christian activists, and the laws they supported all across America, expressed a desire for greater attention to the social good – a social good that embodied Christian conceptions of moral duty and benevolence.

The police powers of a state constitute a legally recognized authority to limit certain individual liberties to secure a greater public good. Created by legislative action, they depend on the electorate's prioritization of communal goals and values over the protection of rights. Tremendously disfavored in the early republic, police powers found increased support from reformers as a means of legislating morality in Jacksonian America.

Legislation proved much more effective than common law in addressing the reformers' agenda. Antebellum legislation addressed myriad activities that implicated the social good. Building codes and public nuisance laws promoted safety, fire prevention, and cleanliness; licenses were required for a wide range of economic pursuits, from operating a theater or bowling alley to selling horses or firearms; market regulations were designed to prevent fraud and cheating; and numerous laws pertaining to railroads imposed duties for fences, crossing signs, and other protections for people and livestock. Yet, the greatest amount of new legislation focused on public morals. Laws of various states criminalized adultery, fornication, prostitution, incest, sodomy, Sabbath breaking, profane swearing, the use of corpses in medical education, obscenity and lewdness (including such behaviors as publishing obscene prints and writings, obscene speech, or public exposure), and any activity "which outrages decency, shocks humanity, or is contrary to good morals."[9] In 1830, Connecticut passed laws encouraging female chastity by prohibiting "lascivious carriage and behavior."[10] In 1860, Pennsylvania revived a law against blasphemy. State legislatures between 1830 and 1865 seemed to accede to Lyman Beecher's assertion that the purpose of society's laws is to restrain human wickedness. Moreover, state courts recognized police powers exercised to support morality as legitimate. In eighty-seven cases brought by businessmen objecting to Sabbath-day protection laws before 1920, not one succeeded.

[9] Joel Prentiss Bishop, *Commentaries on the Criminal Law*, 4th ed., 2 vols. (Boston: Little, Brown, 1865), I: 545–50.
[10] Public Statute Laws of Connecticut (1830), chap. I, 268–76.

An 1838 legal publication asserted that while church and state remained separate institutions and the law recognized no doctrinal beliefs, "ethical Christianity [and] the moral aspect of the gospel" infused the actions of "statesmen and politicians."[11] Some courts seized on the cultural change of the era to promulgate a moral Christian jurisprudence. Supreme Court Justice Joseph Story, committed to undoing the Jeffersonian influence on American law, in 1833 asserted that Christianity formed a part of America's common law. His decisions show a corresponding tendency to impose moral values. In 1823, he overturned what he perceived to be inequitable labor contracts, and he supported the Taney Court's expansion of state police powers. Ironically, President Jackson, who evinced little respect for law or the Supreme Court, was able to appoint five justices, in part because in 1837 Congress expanded the size of the Court from seven to nine justices. Jackson selected each of his appointees from southern slaveholding states. His Chief Justice, Roger Taney, became infamous for his opinion in the *Dred Scott* case, but was equally important in strengthening the police power of the states at the expense of both federal authority and individual rights.[12]

Justice Story was not alone in eschewing a strict application of contract law to avoid what some judges perceived to be unjust hardships. An increase in the acceptability of Christian humanitarianism as a basis for law led judges to ameliorate the sometimes harsh effects of contract law either through restricting application of that law or by blatantly refusing to enforce harsh contract language. Some judges even cited the Bible in justifying their decisions, while others asserted spiritual influences more obliquely as the need for law to recognize the common feelings of humanity.

Those judges who resented the changes brought by the post-Revolutionary law began to read Christian conceptions of morality and communitarian ethics into American law as a means of upholding state police powers infringing on protected rights. Judge Lemuel Shaw in Massachusetts, much like Chancellor Kent in New York, became notorious for this practice. In a blasphemy case brought

[11] *An Inquiry into the Moral and Religious Character of the American Government* (New York: Wiley and Putnam, 1833), 185.
[12] See *Brown v. Maryland*, 12 Wheat 419 (1827), in which Taney represented Maryland, and *License Cases*, 5 Howard 504 (1847).

against a man who asserted a right to be free from religion and fight superstition, Judge Shaw, on the Massachusetts Supreme Court, wrote in 1838 that law could not tolerate "an intended design to calumniate and disparage the Supreme Being, and to destroy the veneration due to him."[13] During this same time period, some southern judges began citing the Bible in legal decisions in order to support threatened conceptions of a social hierarchy protecting slaveholding and a master's dominion over his slaves. In North Carolina, a judge wrote: "[T]here is no appeal from his master; that his power is in no instance usurped; but it is conferred by the laws of man at least, if not by the law of God."[14] In Georgia, a court justified slaveholding on the basis that white paternalism toward black slaves was a Christian duty.[15]

Christian victories in combating secular individualism came about as a result of the ambitious reform program started by Lyman Beecher. Like his mentor, Timothy Dwight, Beecher felt anger and dismay toward liberal society. He identified a selfish and sinful lust for drink and luxurious living as being at the heart of America's problems – a lust seemingly encouraged by liberal laws promoting individual freedoms and economic competition. He defined sin as indifference to society or a selfish individualism that denied one's moral duties to his community. Beecher displayed a Manichaen worldview typical of evangelical preachers during the Second Awakening. They saw the world as sharply divided between Christian adherents to prescribed morality and heathens who ignored God's prescriptions. Yet, to establish a godly order, Beecher and his fellow reformers had to wade into the devil's den and use liberal law for their own purposes.

The Benevolent Empire Attempts to Rebuild a Christian Community

When Lyman Beecher, in 1812, called for "a disciplined moral militia" to transform the United States into a Christian nation, he proposed an idea born in frustration. The country had not only neglected to mention

---

[13] Accounts of the *Kneeland* trials can be found in Octavius Pickering, ed., *Reports of Cases Argued and Determined in the Supreme Judicial Court of Massachusetts*, 24 vols. (Boston: Little, Brown, 1954), 20: 220; John D. Larson, ed., *American State Trials*, 17 vols. (St. Louis: Thomas Law, 1921), 13: 450–575.

[14] *State v. Mann*, 13 N.C. 263, 267 (1829).

[15] *Neal v. Farmer*, 9 Ga. 555, 582 (1851).

God and to secure a public role for Christianity in its Constitution, but it was well on its way toward complete disestablishment. Secular humanism seemed to have controlled the nation's course since its founding. In the years immediately following the Supreme Court's 1819 decision in the *Dartmouth College* case, private incorporation clearly put churches and religious organizations in the private sector, reinforcing perceptions of the separation of church and state and of religion as a matter of private conscience. The Whig Party, in some key ways a worthier successor to liberal democratic traditions than the Jacksonians, endorsed the legal distinction between public and private realms as a means of protecting the autonomy of each citizen to make his or her own moral choices, and encouraged the creation of private voluntary associations in furtherance of personal values and beliefs.

Beecher acknowledged the need to play by a new set of rules. Christians would form private voluntary associations, incorporate them so as to raise money and be protected from government interference, and use them to proselytize, petition, lobby, and protest. They would use new political means to shape public attitudes and ultimately to shape laws. They would beat the liberals at their own game. Doing so indicates the extent to which corporations, and the contract law that spawned them, had already become an integral part of the American culture. Alexis de Tocqueville, writing in 1831, noted Americans' preference for private-sector initiatives over public ones: "The citizen of the United States is taught from infancy to rely on his own exertions ... he looks upon the social authority with an eye of mistrust and anxiety, and claims its assistance only when he is unable to do without it."[16]

Private voluntary corporations expressed a new democratic impulse as they pursued Christian goals. While private societies, they nonetheless constituted powerful political vehicles to further particular visions of American society. The "Benevolent Empire" describes loosely affiliated private corporations composed almost entirely of volunteers that shared commitment to communitarian goals shaped by Christian moral duty. One society noted that the governing boards of these corporations worked "harmoniously ... [to realize] that last command of

---

[16] Alexis de Tocqueville, *Democracy in America*, ed. by Richard D. Heffner (New York: Penguin Press, 1956, 1984), 95.

our ascended Lord, to Go and spread the influence of the gospel over every creature."[17]

Historians must ask to what degree the liberal rules of the contest dictated the outcome of the crusade. Christian reformers sought nothing less than radical change in American values, attitudes, institutions, and laws. As Reverend James G. Birney said, reform was the means of "purifying governments, and bringing them to a perfect conformity with the principles of Divine government." He added that government could only hope to restrain "human wickedness" by conforming civil law to divine law.[18] This vision of government and law was completely irreconcilable with that created by the United States Constitution. Did acceptance of the Constitution requiring compliance with liberal legal ideals and institutional forms doom the Christian counter-revolution from the start? Short-term successes before the Civil War indicated that it did not, but the Christians' failure to make any real changes in constitutional law, the form of governing institutions, and the nation's broad-based cultural endorsement of individual rights and free-enterprise capitalism signify that perhaps it did. Christian reformers hoped to appeal to people who themselves enjoyed the benefits of political and economic freedoms and could not garner sufficient political power to take those freedoms away.

The Benevolent Empire required compromise from its leadership from its beginnings. The growth of private voluntary associations advocating social reform coincided with the granting of universal male suffrage. Yet, these philanthropic organizations attracted large numbers of people who had no other political voice: women, clergymen in some states, and free African Americans in most states. Women spearheaded most of what Lyman Beecher conceived of as "a gigantic religious power" organized to do God's work.[19] Though women composed approximately 75 percent of church members, their involvement in reform associations initially provoked criticism from some clergymen. The General Association of Massachusetts Congregational Churches condemned female activists as shameful and scandalous. Still, tens of

---

[17] Quoted in John Corrigan and Winthrop S. Hudson, *Religion in America*, 7th ed. (Upper Saddle River, NJ: Prentice-Hall, 2004), 165.

[18] Quoted in Donald B. Meyer, *The Protestant Search for Political Realism, 1919–1941* (Berkeley: University of California Press, 1960), 93, 92.

[19] Quoted in Corrigan and Hudson, *Religion in America*, 164.

thousands of mostly middle-class women flocked to staff private voluntary Christian associations from the 1820s through the 1840s.

Just as important, Christians recognized the need to work with non-Christians even if those non-Christians did not see their goals as steps toward the millennium, nor their dedication to them as expressions of Christian faith. In 1846, Reverend Charles Grandison Finney wrote that "the only way in which Christians in the churches who would do anything towards reforming mankind can make their influence is by forming societies, composed often partly of Christians and partly of those who profess no religion."[20] Similarly, Emerson expressed the Transcendentalists' willingness to work with evangelicals, with whom they shared little in thought and belief, if "[w]e are to revise the whole of our social structure" at a time he saw as crucial in American history.[21]

A renewed clerical emphasis on political activity to produce legal change contributed vitally to the antebellum reform movement. Following disestablishment and the election of Jefferson, the clergy had largely refrained from political activity. Their reticence receded in the 1820s as they gave voice to a commitment to taming the individualistic impulses and desires to which liberals had given free reign for decades. The means of doing so, in the absence of public recognition of the church's authority, would have to be coercive laws.

In 1833, the American Temperance Union asserted that as "the traffic in ardent spirits [is] morally wrong," laws should be passed to prohibit it.[22] Christian duty, in other words, should be reflected in public laws. The Christian crusade for temperance began decades earlier; as early as 1812, the General Assembly of the Presbyterian Church condemned drunkenness, and early temperance societies took shape in Massachusetts and Connecticut in 1813. In February 1826, the American Society for the Promotion of Temperance advocated total abstinence; by 1834, it had more than 1 million members. The Temperance Society, as it was known, contended that Christians had

---

[20] Charles Grandison Finney, "The Pernicious Attitude of the Church on the Reforms of the Age" (1846), in *Reforming America, 1915–1960*, ed. by Joshua D. Rothman (New York: W.W. Norton, 2010), 8–9.

[21] Ralph Waldo Emerson, "Man the Reformer" (1846), quoted in Rothman, ed., *Reforming America*, 13.

[22] Walters, *American Reformers*, 13 (quote).

FIGURE 2.1. "Neglected by Their Parents ... They Are Led to the Gin Shop."
Christian reformers in Jacksonian America linked alcohol use to female immorality and other social ills. Etching, 1848, by George Cruikshank from his
series, *The Drunkard's Children*. The Granger Collection, New York, Image
#0032788.

a duty to care for the souls of their fellow citizens and that drinking led to damnation. Non-Christian activists emphasized the societal
effects of alcoholism: poverty, violence, and broken homes. Together
Christian and non-Christian reformers undertook to change the country through moralistic legislation.

Temperance became a political and legal issue in Massachusetts
during the 1830s. A new law requiring vendors to have a license to
sell alcoholic beverages angered thousands who saw it as a moralistic
attack on the free market. Marcus Morton, governor of the state, said
that reform laws could not interfere with "individual rights, personal
habits, or private business."[23] The issue of whether the legislature,
influenced by Christian morals, had the power to promote the public good in contravention of free-market principles came before the
Massachusetts Supreme Court in 1837. Old Federalist Chief Justice
Lemuel Shaw, son of a Congregational minister, upheld the licensing

[23] Neem, *Creating a Nation of Joiners*, 158 (quote).

laws as an appropriate use of state police powers, contending that the legislature could preserve, encourage, and protect morality as much as peace, safety, and health.

While the temperance movement made little headway at the national level, the victory in Massachusetts rallied the reformers and showed them a new direction: state-by-state campaigns. In the same year as Shaw's decisions in the licensing cases, Reverend Charles Grandison Finney gave his famous "Oration in Temperance," encouraging greater efforts to the cause.[24] The state-by-state strategy, later to be employed by the right-to-life movement in the early twenty-first century, had some successes in requiring alcohol to be sold in very large containers, thereby making sales to private individuals unlikely, and in requiring liquor licenses. Yet, the greatest success came in 1851 in Maine with the prohibition of the manufacture or sale of alcoholic beverages in the state. Thirteen states subsequently enacted "Maine laws," but within a few years, all those laws had been repealed.

Proselytizing complemented Christian lobbying efforts for statutory reform. Bible reading provided the key component to transforming the United States into a Christian nation by instilling humility and morality. The American Tract Society and the American Bible Society, organizations largely funded by various churches, printed and distributed bibles as well as Christian magazines and pamphlets attacking vice, atheism, and liberalism in all its various forms. The founders of these societies referred to secularists as the enemy and enlisted followers for help in a holy war. In a complementary endeavor, the American Board of Commissioners of Foreign Ministers, associated with the Theological Seminary of Andover, sponsored missionaries, translated and distributed bibles, and founded Christian schools across the globe. In 1828, a group of activist Christians formed a Union for Sabbath-Day Protection. It found that secularism had eliminated respect for the Sabbath and altered the national conscience. The Union called for a boycott of businesses open on Sunday and lobbied for laws prohibiting commerce on that day.

Reverend Finney had come to New York in 1829 to see the extent and degree of urban poverty. At that time, he argued that converting

---

[24] Charles Grandison Finney, "Oration in Temperance," in *Lectures to Professing Christians* (London: Milner Press, 1837).

the poor to Christianity would build their self-sufficiency, an important counterpart to charitable aid. However, the panic of 1837 increased the poverty in American cities while simultaneously impairing the abilities of charities to raise relief funds. Expressing an increasing frustration with and alienation from mainstream society, Christian reformers saw the setback as yet another indication of the failings of the free market or as punishment from God for the societal embrace of individualist values.

No issue garnered more support from reformers than abolition, and no other cause brought together more people of various persuasions: liberal Christians, evangelicals, Quakers, Transcendentalists, and secular humanists. Christian abolitionists conceived of the cause as part of a broad evangelical crusade to use religion as a means of eradicating social evils. In 1829, a free African American who owned a clothing store in Boston published a condemnation of slavery as contrary to Biblical expressions of humanity's duties to God. The pamphlet gained distribution up and down the eastern seaboard. In 1831, William Lloyd Garrison, an evangelical reformer, published the first issue of the *Liberator*, an abolitionist journal, and soon thereafter founded what was to become the American Anti-Slavery Society (AASS); but, control of the Society soon passed to Arthur and Lewis Tappan in New York, significant figures in the Benevolent Empire, who had experience in other Protestant charities. At first, Garrison and the Tappan brothers agreed on the religious nature of the abolitionist crusade. The "Declaration of Sentiments" written by Garrison and adopted by the Society referred to slavery as "an audacious usurpation of the Divine prerogative, a daring infringement on the law of nature ... and a presumptuous transgression of all the holy commandments."[25] To many Christians, slavery hastened humanity's embrace of sin – violence, laziness, sexual predation, and family deterioration – and Americans had a moral duty to end it. The cause of abolition fit nicely into a Christian worldview that accepted perfectionism and postmillennialism.

Yet, Garrison soon split with the Tappans, evincing the tensions always present in varying forms of American Christianity. The Tappans endorsed the idea of a Christian nation and asserted that all of the

[25] *Liberator*, December 14, 1833.

society's laws must conform to God's laws. The sinful law of slavery was but one example of the need for complete legal change that would also again subordinate women to their male masters. Conversely, Garrison believed the state incapable of creating a Godly society and considered each human the appropriate vehicle for reform. He believed that no nation could enforce morality without succumbing to immorality itself by using force, violence, and coercion against its own citizens. The religious tensions simmered within the AASS until Sarah and Angelina Grimké undertook a speaking tour to rally support to the cause of abolition. The Tappans and some of their supporters, proclaiming reliance on St. Paul, saw women speaking in public as at least as great a moral threat as slavery. Reverend James G. Birney argued that the success of abolition must come only as a part of a broader restructuring of American laws and values to eliminate rampant individual freedoms and inclinations to sin, including women in public roles.

The election of Abigail Kelley to the governing committee of the AASS prompted the Tappans and their supporters to leave and found the American Missionary Association (AMA) to work for abolition within the "Christianization of the United States." Only people "of evangelical sentiments who profess faith in the Lord Jesus Christ" could become members of the AMA, and only men could become officers within the group.[26] Neither Garrison's nor the Tappans' societies persisted into the 1850s. Abolition, like the crusade for temperance, lost momentum on the national level and had to operate on state and local levels. The conflict between Garrison and the Tappans, however, split the movement at all levels. Some evangelicals worked closely with mainline Christians, Transcendentalists, and even secular liberals to oppose slavery, while others remained ensconced in "islands of holiness."[27]

Women's Rights Assertions Confirm the Need for Separation

Many of the women active in the abolitionist cause became leaders of the women's rights movement and continued their battles with religious

[26] Lewis Tappan, *History of the American Missionary Association: Its Constitution and Principles, Etc.* (New York, 1855), 21, 23.

[27] The term "islands of holiness" is most recently the title of a new book referencing the Biblical passage: Curtis D. Johnson, *Islands of Holiness: Rural Religion in Upstate New York, 1790–1860* (Ithaca, NY: Cornell University Press, 2012).

conservatives. The Grimké sisters, Elizabeth Cady Stanton, Lucretia Mott, Susan B. Anthony, and Lucy Stone all had their first experiences in reform in working to abolish slavery. The Benevolent Empire gave women a chance to use those qualities so valued at home – compassion and moral awareness among them – to benefit society at large. Yet, when women assumed leadership roles in the reform movement, they seemed to be acting outside of, not within, their prescribed roles. Doing so angered many Christians, who believed unequal sex roles to have been established by God. Conservative and moralistic laws being developed in some areas of the country reinforced these notions.

Christianity acted to limit some social change while it encouraged other forms of change; the women's rights movement found itself fighting Christian values as much as legal limitations. Susan B. Anthony wrote: "By law, public sentiment, and religion, from the time of Moses down to the present day, woman has never been thought of as other than a piece of property."[28] Though married herself, Anthony saw marriage as an expression of Christian ideals of female subordination and as a legal means of perpetuating women's submission to men. She objected to laws that asserted the family to be a social unit with divinely prescribed roles and duties for its components. She argued that women are by nature no more moral than men and that each individual is responsible for his or her own moral decisions. The Christian influences on law, she contended, had long taught that the individual must be "sacrificed to the highest good of society."[29] Turning to Jefferson, she saw just laws as celebrating and protecting individual freedoms. Lucy Stone concurred with Stanton: "My heart aches to have somebody, [but] what a mere thing the law makes a married woman."[30]

[28] *Proceedings of the Tenth National Woman's Rights Convention*, May 10 and 11, 1860 (Boston: Yerrington and Garrison, 1860), in Elizabeth Cady Stanton and Susan B. Anthony, *The Papers of Elizabeth Cady Stanton and Susan B. Anthony*, ed. by Patricia G. Holland and Ann D. Gordon (Wilmington, DE: Scholarly Resources, 1991), reel 9, frame 658.

[29] "Tenth National Woman's Rights Convention," in Elizabeth Cady Stanton and Susan B. Anthony, *The Selected Papers of Elizabeth Cady Stanton and Susan B. Anthony*, ed. by Ann D. Gordon (New Brunswick, NJ: Rutgers University Press, 1997) 1: 420.

[30] Lucy Stone to Antoinette Blackwell Brown, August 1849, in Lucy Stone and Antoinette Blackwell Brown, *Friends and Sisters: Letters Between Lucy Stone and Antoinette Blackwell Brown, 1846–1893*, ed. by Carol Lasser and Marlene Deahl Merrill (Urbana: University of Illinois Press, 1987), 56.

Resenting the Christian influences in law used to subordinate women, Stone committed herself to a total separation of church and state.

The 1848 Seneca Falls Conference on women's rights produced a document modeled on the Declaration of Independence that demanded that women be granted all the rights available to male citizens. As many Americans attempted to roll back what they perceived to be excessive freedoms gained in the founding era, the women in Seneca Falls looked to extend them by making the Revolution and its aftermath relevant to all people regardless of gender. Freedom of conscience formed a significant aspect of the women's rights movement as women sought respect for the right to hold opinions and to express them in public. Stanton and Mott specifically drew the dichotomy between rights that derived from liberal conceptions of human nature and those that were recognized only within religious parameters of what people were expected to do. Christianity limited women by defining them as needing male protection, counsel, and authority. Law's acceptance of these absurd notions transgressed the Constitutional commitment to freedom of conscience.

At the Women's Rights Convention in Syracuse four years later, the inconsistency between Christian laws and women's rights came to the fore. Antoinette Blackwell Brown, the first woman ordained as a minister in the United States, introduced a resolution recognizing the validity of law's reliance on Biblical truth while asserting that people had misused the Bible in claiming that it subordinated women. Brown said that the Bible recognized equality but that its readers had not. In a counterargument, Susan B. Anthony read a letter from Stanton in which she wrote that Christianity itself degrades and subjugates. Reverend Brown's resolution failed as attendees agreed that the Bible was subject to various interpretations and should not be the basis of asserting female equality.

Legal Challenges to the Separation of Church and State Arise

The Benevolent Empire, the women's rights movement, and the expansion of moral legislation in the 1830s and 1840s each asserted conceptions of the separation of church and state that expressed tensions within the doctrine. Courts, too, struggled to understand and apply the doctrine, repeatedly citing it in case law only to approve statutes promoting Christianity as legitimate uses of police powers. By 1850, most states had reinstituted laws protecting the Sabbath and punishing blasphemy, atheism, polygamy, and crimes against morality. Courts tolerated these state and local laws. It is difficult, if not impossible, to determine whether these laws embodied a change in cultural attitudes or worked to bring about that change by censoring behavior. Certainly Victorian America lacked the cosmopolitanism of the "Era of Good Feelings."

Americans generally accepted the idea of separation as fundamental to their society, but differed as to what it meant. In 1849, President John Tyler rejected a solicitation from the Methodists for a new church in Georgetown, prompting *The Baltimore Sun* to write: "The office of the President is exclusively secular, and for his religious sentiments he is responsible to no earthly being." However, a Washington newspaper, *National Era*, rebutted the *Sun*: "The *Sun* ... justifies him, on the ground that his office is 'exclusively secular!' Ridiculous! Do virtue, knowledge, and religion cease to have claims upon a man because he happens to hold a civil office?" The *Era* concluded that though it "believed in the separation of church and state," the concept did not prevent leaders from relying on or supporting religious precepts while in office. A few years later, Presbyterian Minister Erasmus Darwin MacMaster denied that the law mandated any separation of church and state and endorsed a Christian Amendment to the Constitution to clarify the issue. This proposal, like many similar ones, failed to gain popular support.

Numerous ministers attempted to minimize, in one way or another, the doctrine of strict separation that arose in the early republic. Lyman Beecher argued that human governance must be rooted in God's law to produce a moral society. Presbyterian Pastor Ezra Stiles Ely more aggressively urged all Christians to form a "union of church and state ... by adopting, avowing, and determining to act upon, truly religious principles in all civil matters." He advocated reliance on the Bible rather than on a mere Constitution: "We are a Christian nation: we have a right to demand that all our rulers in their conduct shall conform to Christian morality; and if they do not, it is the duty and privilege of Christian freemen to make a new and better election." Responding to those who endorsed a strict separation, he argued, "are Christians the only men in the community who may not be guided by their judgment, conscience, and choice in electing their rulers?"[31] Ely's plan for an evangelical alliance backfired as it so alienated liberals who feared disruption to the Constitutional norms that it resulted in defeats for Christian-sponsored legislation in his state.

Despite the greater legal and cultural attention to morality, many activists desired a more specific national recognition of the Christian faith. To these folks, no issue seemed so great a rejection of Christian prescriptions as Sunday postal deliveries. In 1810, Congress created the national mail system with a seven-day week of operations. By 1828, the changing cultural mood prompted Christians to initiate the first significant national discussion of the degree to which government should be influenced by religious doctrine. They demanded a cessation of Sunday mail deliveries in respect of the Sabbath, sending petitions to Washington, holding rallies in locales across the country, and raising their objections in sermons. Yet, the campaign soon fell apart. Americans generally appreciated the daily mail and saw little disrespect to religion in maintaining it. Liberals saw in the defeat of the proposal a demonstration of the viability of the Madisonian argument that the national government, led by the most intelligent and public-spirited politicians and focused on major issues, would be less susceptible to populist and parochial movements than state and local governments world.

The populism expressed in the Sabbatarian movement upset businessmen, liberal pastors, merchants, and secular intellectuals. William Ellery Channing accused evangelical ministers of building support for a political cause not on reasoned argument but rather on an abuse of the followers' faith in them as ministers, referring to their leadership as a form of despotism and to their followers as willing to "substitute the consciences of others for ... [their] own." He found the Sabbath-protection perspective "at war with the spirit of our institutions," rooted in a defense of individual freedoms.[32] Kentucky Senator Richard M. Johnson feared that the movement promised "religious combinations" that might overturn the legal and political foundations of the country. He asserted that "once the government

---

[31] Quoted in Hamburger, *Separation*, 198–9, 258, 269. See also Robert S. Handy, *A Christian America: Protestant Hopes and Historical Realities* (New York: Oxford University Press, 1991), 50.

[32] Quoted in Neem, *Creating a Nation of Joiners*, 115.

began to 'determine what are the laws of God,' ... there would be no stopping the rise of religious oppression."[33] The Sabbath-protection movement generated, by 1831, 900 petitions sent to Congress. Yet, rather than convincing the national leaders of the need for reform, they succeeded only in calling attention to the antagonism of many Christians to the liberal laws and institutions of the country, thereby alerting people to the political threat posed by the organized Christian activists.

While populist movements in support of building a Christian America faltered, movements that defined an American Christianity by ostracizing religious nonconformists experienced some degree of success. Large numbers of Americans embraced a broadly based non-sectarian Protestantism as a means to protect their values, cultural attitudes, and ethical moralities from perceived threats from Catholics, Mormons, and other newcomers. Ironically, to overcome the religious influences of non-Protestants on American laws and institutions, including the separation of church and state, Protestants encouraged a greater legal recognition of their own religious beliefs.

The first large wave of Catholic immigrants, arriving in the 1830s, found their beliefs incompatible with liberal ideas that considered religion a matter of individual conscience. In 1832, Pope Gregory XVI called the United States' defense of liberty "profane."[34] Closer to home, Father J.W. Cummings referred to the assertion that people have natural rights as "utter nonsense."[35] When Bishop Hughes of New York said, "Everybody should know that we have for our mission to convert the world, including the inhabitants of the United States," he spoke for many Catholics who saw their new environs filled not with fellow Christians but with heathens.[36]

These pronouncements fueled Protestant fears and distrust. Americans generally objected to hierarchies, though the increasingly racist justification for white master-class paternalism in the South constituted an exception to this inclination. Conversely, the Catholic

[33] Quoted in Noah Feldman, *Divided by God: America's Church-State Problem and What We Should Do about It* (New York: Farrar, Straus, & Giroux, 2005), 54–5.

[34] Quoted in Hamburger, *Separation*, 230–1.

[35] Quoted in John T. McGreevy, *Catholicism and American Freedom: A History* (New York: W.W. Norton, 2003), 37.

[36] Quoted in Hamburger, *Separation*, 210–11.

Church endorsed and depended on hierarchy: the Pope expressed the one true religion and God's true desires for man; only priests read the Bible and did so exclusively in Latin; and priests assumed almost divine authority in granting absolution of sins and paving one's way into heaven. To many non-Catholics, the Catholic Church appeared to threaten intellectual and spiritual independence and to require a docility in its followers that repudiated individual judgment and authority. The increase in Catholic immigration in the 1830s revived John Jay's argument that Catholics be denied the vote, lest the country be subject to a widespread expression of papal desires by his dutiful servants.

Bible reading returned to the classrooms in the 1830s as a result of both an increase in Christian sentiments and a fear of Catholic immigrants. Catholic laypeople, of course, were not permitted to read the Bible, which priests read to them in Latin during Sunday masses. Catholic protests against Bible reading in the schools far outnumbered those of atheists and humanists. The protests prompted violence from nativist groups, but more significantly politicized the issue and brought it before the courts. In every case the courts upheld Bible reading in the schools. In a case from Maine in 1854, the court held that use of the Bible was "merely as a reading book," and it was "consonant to the soundest principles of morality."[37] A court in Massachusetts upheld the school's authority to discipline a ten-year-old boy, who, on orders from his priest, refused to recite Protestant prayers, Bible verses, or the Ten Commandments. The decision set out a principle that many Americans then and subsequently would use to integrate their nationalistic pride with their religion, asserting that republican government rested on an acceptance of Christianity. Increasingly, Americans came to see themselves as "God's chosen people" and their national successes as evidence of his support for democracy and free-enterprise capitalism. Popular attitudes accepted the Jewish history in the Old Testament as relevant to America's destiny and saw Puritan leader John Winthrop as a new Moses. A revisionist history even reconceived of the Puritans as advocates for religious freedom, further confusing not only history but the meaning of that term. In this intellectual milieu, political actions reinforced judicial acceptance of school prayer

[37] *Donahoe v. Richards*, 38 Me. 379, 398, 400 (1854).

and Bible reading. Ohio, in 1851, amended its constitution to allow schools to teach religion and morality as essential to good government. Catholic leadership, sensing the powerlessness of the doctrine of separation of church and state when wielded in Catholic hands, encouraged Catholic parents to send their children to private Catholic schools.

Catholics were not alone in suffering from governmental endorsements of religion in the antebellum decades. In 1830, arguing that the world was in its "latter days" and the Second Coming was near, Joseph Smith published the *Book of Mormon* and founded the Church of Jesus Christ of Latter-day Saints. The Mormons, as Smith's adherents came to be called, adopted a patriarchal communalism at odds with the "profane" individualistic value system of the country. Most strikingly, they practiced plural marriage, in which men could have multiple wives. They were the first, but certainly not the last, group of Americans to learn that despite the liberalization of marriage laws, traditional Christian practices still underlay the institution of marriage. Viciously attacked in Ohio, Illinois, and Missouri, the Mormons ultimately found a temporary refuge in the Utah Territory. Popular acceptance of the idea of separation of church and state coexisted with laws that marginalized dissenters and perpetuated a value system rooted in contemporary Christian doctrine.

From 1830 through the 1850s, Protestant Christian activists used politics as a means of introducing their religious values into the law. They gained support from various groups – Transcendentalists, populists fearing new ideas, and communitarians disdainful of individualism and capitalism. Their successes came with the increase of state police powers to prescribe morality and encourage conformity to loosely conceived Christian ideals. Yet, most of their efforts fizzled before 1860. While the political allies shared a commitment to social reform, ultimately they differed as to the importance of religious doctrine to the reform process and the society it would produce. Differences among Christian and between Christian and non-Christian reformers divided activists in the abolition and temperance movements. Moreover, Christians themselves differed in their willingness to limit property rights and individual freedoms to reach Christian communitarian goals. Only in populist movements to ostracize nonconformists did Christian reform find lasting success. Not only had the founders created legal, social, and economic institutions that embodied and perpetuated their secular and individualistic values, but those values had taken root in the majority of Americans. Americans, on the brink of Civil War, were a largely Christian people who wanted to see no tension in being governed by largely secular laws.

Abraham Lincoln and Civil Religion

The popular assertion of Christianity as a means of defining American cultural values during the antebellum years produced few long-term changes in the law, but may well have provided a basis for the cultural embrace of Christianity later in the nineteenth century. A popular expression of nonsectarian Protestantism placed religion in service to humanity and democratic institutions. It fostered acceptance of Christian morality for the good of the whole. Yet, it expressed a weak religious doctrine – a lowest-common-denominator form of Christian belief. During the Civil War, President Lincoln saw this form of religion as a basis for unity and used it to sustain the nation during that tremendous upheaval.

Abraham Lincoln is an odd character to have elevated the role of Christianity in American laws and institutions. An ardent defender of liberal conceptions of rights and prosperity, he joined the Republican Party as much for its pro-capitalist platform as for its attack on slavery; in fact, he justified his opposition to slavery in large part on its inconsistency with capitalism and free-labor ideals. Early political opponents attempted to slander him by calling him a Deist in 1843 and an infidel in 1846, charges he barely refuted. In response to a handbill used in an 1846 campaign, Lincoln stated that though he was "not a member of any Christian Church ... [he had] never denied the truth of the Scriptures [nor] spoken with intentional disrespect of religion in general or any denomination of Christians in particular."[38] He not only never joined a church but also was never baptized, nor took communion. Lincoln never publicly referred to Jesus by name or by the term "Christ."

---

[38] Quoted in Mark E. Neely, *The Last Best Hope of Earth: Abraham Lincoln and the Promise of America* (Cambridge, MA: Harvard University Press, 1993), 23 (quotes).

His law partner, William Herndon, cites Lincoln's good friend, Jesse Fell, in describing the President's religion as most like that of Transcendentalist Theodore Parker, a position supported by Lincoln's relationships with Emerson and George Bancroft, both Transcendentalists.

Yet, as president, Lincoln probably did more to integrate Christianity into American culture, governance, and law than any other elected official in the country's history. In the process, he helped redefine American Christianity. He endorsed a liberal, broad-based, nonsectarian, nonorthodox Christianity – a form of faith defined as a civil religion. Lincoln may well have been the first person to use this term, doing so in his Young Men's Lyceum Address in 1838. In numerous subsequent public statements, Lincoln quoted Scripture, invoked God's aid, or credited providence for history's course. He asserted that God brought the Civil War as a way of purging the nation of its sin of slavery. In creating Thanksgiving as a national holiday in 1863, he implicitly acknowledged God's providence – an acknowledgment he made explicit in the enacting proclamation by calling for the "interposition of the almighty Hand" and referring to "the ever watchful providence of almighty God."[39] Perhaps most important, though, Lincoln seemed to embody an almost Christ-like morality, made only more real by his anguish over the War and the sufferings it caused and by his own death as a martyr for abolition and the survival of the country. He seemed to take on the nation's sins and, through his death, deliver the American people to a new world of promise and glory. Lincoln himself came to embody Christianity for the American people. One Methodist minister after the War said, "If Lincoln was not a Christian, it would make me feel like tearing myself away from the bonds of orthodox Christianity."[40] But, as Lincoln became the model for Christian behavior, in America, Christian belief became more secular, republican, and nationalistic – a blending of religious, political, and patriotic faiths. America's Christianity after the war became more concerned with establishing a shared value system and preserving the social order than with saving souls or doing God's will.

[39] Proclamation of Abraham Lincoln, October 3, 1863.
[40] Quoted in Merrill D. Peterson, *Lincoln in American Memory* (New York: Oxford University Press, 1994), 218.

The power of Lincoln's words not only defined the War's purpose for Americans, but it also defined their nation and themselves. The civil religion that took shape during the Civil War expressed three principles: (1) an American sense of mission supported by providence that persisted from Puritan settlements forward; (2) a commitment to democratic free enterprise as expressing God's plan for humanity in a moral society; and (3) a belief that God will protect and preserve the American people as long as they live up to the principles found in their institutions. Civil War–era Americans, with Lincoln's guidance, came to see their nation's founding in Biblical terms. The Puritan migration was the American exodus; the Revolution and Constitution, the establishment of the new Israel; and the Civil War, a punishment for slavery tantamount to the great flood.

The civil religion adopted by Americans integrated nationalism with loose conceptions of providence and Christian duty. It contained some aspects of Christianity, specifically its morality and acceptance of a higher authority, but was not necessarily Christian. Its celebration of earthly forms and human creations, especially democracy and capitalism; its invocation of God's name to serve human ends; and its nationalistic pride and militarism can all be seen as blasphemous devotions to false gods, violating the first commandment's invocation to "put no other gods before me." Still, Americans accepting the civil religion expressed their beliefs in increased devotion to Protestant churches. Ten percent of the soldiers in both armies who had not been Christians before the War converted to the faith and joined a church. Noncombatants converted in almost equal numbers.

The civil religion expressed in the Civil War may have had its roots in an earlier era, but Lincoln's use of it during the War did more to raise the importance of Christianity in America than all the preceding revivals, awakenings, and reform movements. Earlier crusades to build a Christian community encountered an inability of many Americans to square Christian values with American legal ideals promoting individual freedoms. Even Transcendentalist reformers expressed impatience with their evangelical brethren. William Ellery Channing wrote in 1839 that evangelical activists threatened American democracy by their disrespect of "independence of thought and action" and their desires for "designing men" to control others' lives. The reform movements they generated produced similar discontents. Orestes Brownson said:

Matters have come to such a pass, that a peaceable man can hardly venture to eat or drink, to go to bed or get up, to correct his children or kiss his wife, without obtaining the permission of some moral or other reform society.[41]

Conversely, the civil religion involved few moral limitations and threatened only cultural outliers such as Catholics and Mormons, whom populists could cast as un-American and non-Christian.

By the mid-1850s, the Benevolent Empire and the zeal of Christian activists that created it had largely dissipated. Despite forming alliances with lukewarm Christians and non-Christian moral reformers, the evangelicals could never create a critical mass necessary for reorienting the country. They remained a vocal minority. American individualism remained firmly entrenched in laws despite temporary victories in isolated areas by the reformers. National culture retained the institutions and laws constructed in the founding era embracing individualism, freedom, and legal equality – not Christian communitarianism. Despite the pooled efforts of Transcendentalists, utopians, and the leaders of the Second Awakening, the United States retained its individualistic character because Americans valued individual autonomy and private pursuits above all else. But, the civil religion promised change in that it wedded Christian ideals to American values and institutions. In so doing, it distorted both, but it would lead to a greater integration of church and state than at any time since before the Revolution.

---

[41] Quoted in Neem, *Creating a Nation of Joiners*, 159.

3

Regulating Behavior and Teaching Morals

The Uses of Religion, 1865–1937

The Second Awakening, the communitarian social initiatives of the Benevolent Empire, and the invocation of a civil religion by President Lincoln helped erode the nation's secular orientation and the clarity of disestablishment by the end of the Civil War. Yet, the laws in 1865 continued to assert the separation of church and state, even if many court decisions, public policies, and attitudes seemed to reject the doctrine. Separation continued largely because of the early republic's legal delineation of public and private spheres. While challenged from the 1830s onward, this legal delineation did not confront serious reconsideration until the late 1800s and early 1900s. Then the politicization of morality by both non-Christian Pragmatists and Christian reformers in pursuit of new conceptions of social justice demanded a form of legal positivism that rendered the classical liberal demarcation of government authority to a circumscribed public sphere an archaic impediment to social progress. These reformers not only reintroduced religion as a basis for moral action into political discourse, but also minimized the legal basis for the separation of church and state.

Postwar society created a fertile ground for reconsideration of the nation's purpose and values. The Civil War produced tremendous doubt among Americans that they were either God's chosen people or capable of democracy. Simultaneously, America experienced a transformation from a local to a national culture. Initially, this national culture expressed longings for a new sense of community rooted in discipline and traditional values. The anguish of the War defeated ideas of anti-institutional individualism, such as Thoreau's embrace of civil disobedience. However, by the 1880s, Americans were open to revising their values and looked to a new educated class of professionals and experts in pursuing efficiency, predictability, and conformity. The rigorous social code imposed in Victorian America can be seen as rooted in this culturally derived value system combined with Christian ethical prescriptions. It offered predictability and an appreciation of conformity in an era of tremendous social change and the anxiety it produced. Americans expected their institutional authorities to protect and encourage the new social code.

As law and religion form the two greatest institutional authorities in the United States, they were asked, singularly and together, to lead Americans' adaptation to a new society – at once protecting the values and lifestyles of the past while enabling people to prosper in a new social context. Amid the doubt about Americans' character and mission following the Civil War, the National Teachers' Association adopted a resolution declaring that "[t]he Bible should not only be studied, venerated, and honored as a classic for all ages ... but devotionally read, and its precepts inculcated in all the common schools of the land."[1] Other actions taken to address the national character focused more directly on purging society of recognized threats. Throughout the Old South, Jim Crow laws returned political and economic power to white people while restricting the liberties of black people. In the second half of the nineteenth century, Native Americans were increasingly restricted to and regulated on reservations. The United States government also established quotas for immigrants, limiting the entry of Asians and people from Southern and Eastern Europe in particular, especially Catholics and Jews. Religion influenced each of these actions, as well as the legislative enactments concerning Mormons and Catholics taken to protect Protestant Christian America from the threats these people were considered to pose. These laws focused less on belief than on behaviors, yet relied on Protestant values and morals to determine the boundaries of appropriate behavior. The court

---

[1] Quoted in Bruce J. Dierenfield, *The Battle over School Prayer: How Engel v. Vitale Changed America* (Landmark Law Cases in American Society Series), ed. by Peter Charles Hoffer and N. E. H. Hull (Lawrence: University of Kansas Press, 2007), 26.

system, up to and including the Supreme Court, accepted this moralistic regulation of behavior.

Most of the rewriting of the secular laws of the founding era continued to occur at the state level. The Supreme Court did not apply the First Amendment religion clauses to the states until the 1940s, facilitating the promulgation of new state laws. Before that time, the free exercise and establishment clauses were not understood to identify two distinct and independent protections, but rather to explain a conceptual limitation of government power necessary to protect freedom of conscience. States promised similar protection, as all but six state constitutions contained protection for liberty of conscience. Yet, increasingly they repudiated that protection. Twenty states came to permit test oaths for officeholding, and six states required political officers to believe in God. Nineteen state constitutions recognized a public authority able to sanction "licentious" or "immoral" conduct. The inconsistency in states' treatment of religion is never more apparent than in regard to education. Thirty-five state constitutions prohibited the use of public funds for religious schools, but most tolerated Bible reading and the teaching of explicitly Christian morality in public schools. State and local governments flew flags at half-mast on Good Friday, Easter, and other Christian holidays, mounted the Ten Commandments on public buildings, and erected crosses in public parks. Far from protecting a separation of church and state, state law generally, as expressed in constitutions, statutes, and hundreds of cases, endorsed a public religion rooted in vague Protestant beliefs and morality. Yet, as a national culture overcame local cultures during this time, so too did national attitudes on religion and law challenge this parochial system.

Historians have read different and contradictory meanings into the legal developments of the late nineteenth and early twentieth centuries, including an endorsement of Protestant values over Catholic and other minority perspectives, an endorsement of community homogeneity, or a growing acceptance of secularism. Certainly secularism, as a school of thought expressing agnostic or atheistic beliefs, experienced a tremendous increase in influence from the 1880s to the 1920s. Yet, the persistence of religious endorsements at the state and local levels, as well as federal legislative enactments and the court decisions they spawned, seem a greater endorsement of Protestant values and pervasive American fears than a recognition of the intentions of Jeffersonians to separate church and state by moving religion to the private sphere. Indeed, during this time period, the social and legal distinctions between public and private spheres blur.

Perhaps the era is best seen as transitional. In the late 1800s and early 1900s, American Christianity again fragmented and then changed. A new cultural value system and a revitalized Social Gospel produced little change in the national laws prior to 1937, but they served as the basis for tremendous legal and social change thereafter. The religious and political ideas that percolated in this period provoked considerable debate and challenged long-standing legal, economic, and social assumptions. By 1937, religious ideas had combined with new views of law and society to form a significant force for change.

Diversity, the Civil Religion, and Challenges to Separation

During the period from 1865 to 1937, American Christianity divided between two polarized expressions of faith, fundamentalism and a revitalized social gospel, each of which encouraged its adherents to work for dramatic change in the nation's values and laws. Despite the importance of these religious forms to legal change, a plurality of Americans accepted a third form of Christianity: a liberal religion that espoused a Christian morality quite compatible with prevailing secular values. This variant of liberal religion, referred to as a "civil religion" or as the "religion of the republic," combined a belief in the essential truth of Protestantism with patriotism rooted in secular and religious mythology. Many mainline Protestant denominations endorsed this doctrinally tepid religion, national expansion, and free-enterprise capitalism as fulfillments of God's promises for his new chosen people. The civil religion infused nationalistic and patriotic behaviors with religious significance. Significantly, it expressed an understanding of law's protection of rights as rooted in an acceptance of Christian religion: the First Amendment protected people's rights to give thanks to a Christian God who had chosen Americans as his people and secured their destiny for greatness through his gift of free-enterprise democracy. In the late 1800s and early 1900s, Americans placed the motto "In God We Trust" on coins and paper money and established Christian Holy Days, such as Christmas and Good Friday, as national holidays (along with Thanksgiving). The conflation of religion and nationalism is evident in the remarks of Supreme Court Justice David Brewer in an address at Yale in 1902. He referred to the voting booth as "the temple of American institutions" in which "each of us is a priest" entrusted with "the care of the ark of the covenant."[2] Even critics of the civil religion recognized its prominence. H. Richard Niebuhr, of Yale Divinity School, wrote: "[T]o be reconciled to God now meant to be reconciled to the established customs of a more or less Christianized society ... [with] [t]he life now lived in the land of promise ... regarded as the promised life."[3] The popularity of the civil religion eventually found expression in the nation's laws, rendering church and state less separate in 1937 than they were in 1865.

The legal recognition of the civil religion relied on intellectual inconsistencies ignored by both the general public and the legal elite. Both groups understood the First Amendment to prohibit direct aid to sectarian causes, but not to require removal of all religion from the public sphere. Yet, Americans still understood that religious freedom depended on a clear delineation between public and private realms. In 1868, Reverend Jesse Peck lauded the consignment of all matters of conscience to the private sphere. Similarly, the law continued to recite the maxims of the founders, only to betray them in nearly every court challenge. In 1872, the Supreme Court asserted the Madisonian ideal that the Constitution protected people from religious influences within their government: "The structure of our government has, for the preservation of civil liberty, rescued the temporal institutions from religious interference." In the same decision, the Court restated the law that in America, the practice and dissemination of religion rested with private voluntary associations.[4] Still, prevailing American values of the late 1800s rested on basic Christian understandings of morality that Americans were unwilling to leave to the care of private corporations. Accordingly, they expanded the public sphere to allow governmental involvement in the spread of Protestant Christian morality through the establishment of a civil religion. This "extra constitutional

---

[2] Quoted in Michael Walzer, *Exodus and Revolution* (New York: Basic Books, 1985), 113.
[3] Niebuhr quoted in Martin E. Marty, *Modern American Religion, Vol. 2: The Noise of Conflict, 1919–1941* (Chicago: University of Chicago Press, 1986), 317, 319.
[4] *Watson v. Jones*, 80 US 679 (1872), at 728–9.

arrangement," in the words of one scholar, constituted an unofficial establishment of religion inconsistent with the nation's cultural embrace of religious pluralism.[5]

While the civil religion itself diminished the separation of church and state, challenges to it from various minority sects further eroded the doctrine. To a degree far greater than Protestants, Catholic and Jewish immigrants from Europe had been taught values scornful of the individuality they found in America. The Catholic Church in Rome criticized American cultural attitudes that it perceived threatened the Church in the United States. In 1864, in the Papal Encyclical *Quanta Cura*, the Catholic Church called the idea that liberty of conscience existed as a universal right "insanity."[6] Pope Pius IX gave credence to a belief shared by many Catholics in America that their religion was "fundamentally at odds" with the American way of life.[7] The 1870 declaration by the First Vatican Council that the Pope is "infallible" on all that concerns human faith and morality only deepened divisions between rights-loving Americans and the Catholic Church. Yet, the most divisive pronouncements came in 1891 and 1899, when Pope Leo XIII condemned "Americanism" as destructive of the essential components of Catholic theology and the "modern capitalist system" as dependent on the "misery and wretchedness pressing so unjustly on the majority of the working class." In *Rerum Novarum*, issued in the latter year, the Pope blessed trade unions and government control of the economy as means of creating social justice.[8] The Catholic press in America picked up on Rome's themes. The *Catholic World* in February 1878 pilloried Adam Smith for making "the individual the [primary] unit of society. The true unit of society is the family."[9]

Catholic immigrants desired their own schools, and even their own charities, as protections from America's cultural influences. Not only did the public schools endorse individualism, but many had come to use

---

[5] William R. Hutchison, *Religious Pluralism in America: The Contentious History of a Founding Idea* (New Haven, CT: Yale University Press, 2003), 59.

[6] Quoted in Feldman, *Divided by God*, 66.

[7] Quoted in Sydney Ahlstrom, *A Religious History of the American People* (New Haven, CT: Yale University Press, 1972), 828.

[8] Quoted in David L. Weaver-Zercher, "Theologies," in *Themes in Religion and American Culture*, ed. by Philip Goff and Paul Harvey (Chapel Hill: University of North Carolina Press, 2004), 24–5.

[9] Quoted in McGreevy, *Catholicism*, 131.

the Bible as a text, alienating Catholic children whom their church prohibited from reading the Bible. Debate on the issue of separate Catholic education began in the 1840s when various Catholic groups demanded public funding for Catholic schools. In response, several states passed laws limiting public support for religion, and by 1876, fourteen states had enacted laws preventing government funding of religious schools. By 1890, this number grew to twenty-nine. Popular opinion now held that the doctrine of separation of church and state prohibited the funding of Catholic schools, but not the funding of Bible reading in the public schools.

In response to Catholic solicitation for public funding, different groups of Americans sought to clarify, by means of constitutional amendment if necessary, the separation of church and state. This movement expressed itself in two distinct political efforts: one initiated by liberal secularists seeking broad prohibitions on any public endorsement of religion, and the other started by groups of Protestants asserting that the civil religion prevented aid to Catholic schools. Neither ultimately proved successful.

President Ulysses S. Grant gave impetus to a federal separation amendment in a speech in Des Moines, Iowa, on September 30, 1875. His address appealed to both liberal secularists and Protestant anti-Catholics, for both heard reference to their own antagonists in Grants words: "If we are to have another contest in the near future of our national existence, I predict that the dividing line will not be Mason and Dixons's, but between patriotism and intelligence on the one side, and superstition, ambition, and ignorance on the other." Clarifying his intentions approximately one month later, President Grant said that not one dollar is "to be appropriated to the support of any sectarian school," for the splintering of American education into sectarian divisions would destroy the public schools, which are the "promoter of that intelligence which is to preserve us as a nation."[10]

Also in 1875, Congressman James G. Blaine of Pennsylvania proposed a constitutional amendment that would (1) extend the religious protections in the First Amendment to the states and (2) prohibit any public funds from being placed "under the control of any religious sect" or "divided between religious sects or denominations."[11]

---

[10] Both quotes in McGreevy, *Catholicism*, 91.
[11] Quoted in Feldman, *Divided by God*, 75.

President Grant endorsed the idea behind Blaine's proposed amendment on December 7, 1875, adding a provision that each state be required to fund free secular public education and expressing his understanding that the proposal prohibited both teaching religion in the schools and using the Bible as classroom reading. Grant further encouraged Congress to act to tax church property. Some liberal proponents of a Blaine-style amendment were cautious in framing their support for clarification of existing law as not legally necessary but politically desirable.

The Blaine Amendment ultimately failed; the House approved it by a vote of 180 to 7, but it fell two votes short of the two-thirds majority it needed to emerge from the Senate. Opposition within the Republican Party came not only from civil religionists, but also from those who feared an unprecedented expansion of federal power at the expense of state governments. The defeat of the Blaine Amendment actually diminished the scope and influence of the Constitution's separation of church and state then and subsequently. By arguing for the need for an amendment in the late 1800s to separate church and state completely, its supporters effectively asserted that no such separation already existed in the nation's primary law. When the amendment proposals failed, Americans could legitimately believe that existing law did not require strict separation.

Mormon polygamy resulted in a reconsideration of the separation of church and state similar to that spawned by Bible reading in the schools. In both instances, law used the civil religion to marginalize people who held different beliefs. Legal persecution of the Mormons by the federal government began in 1862 with the passage of the Morrill Act, which made polygamy a federal crime. The Morrill Act raised questions not only about the government's ability to prohibit an action engaged in as part of a religious practice, but also the power of the Congress to act on conceptions of Christian morals or Christian definitions of marriage in passing laws. No prosecutions were brought under the Morrill Act until 1874. In that year, Congress considered an expansion of its power to control local practices that offended national moral norms.

The prosecution of a Mormon for polygamy produced the first case in which the Supreme Court considered the meaning of the religion clauses in the First Amendment to the Constitution. The leaders

of the Mormon Church strongly believed that the federal law prohibiting polygamy violated the Constitution in that Congress lacked
the authority to interfere with local laws regarding marriage. George
Reynolds served as the defendant in testing the law, arguing both that
the Morrill Act violated Constitutional outlines of federalism and that
his religion required him to practice plural marriage – that he would be
damned if he did not. This latter argument raised the issues of whether
the First Amendment applied to U.S. territories and, if it did, whether
the Morrill Act violated Reynolds's freedom of conscience.

The *Reynolds* decision exemplifies judicial action during this era,
as the Court recognized that Congress had no authority to act regarding matters of conscience, only to then deny Mormons their liberty
of conscience as expressed in plural marriage. Justice Waite considered bigamy a crime, and his decision held that religious belief is no
excuse for criminal behavior. The Court claimed the power of the federal government to regulate behavior compelled by religious belief,
if not belief itself. The Court ultimately endorsed the ironic conception of separation that had gained popular acceptance by the 1870s –
that American freedoms depended on a legal recognition of Christian
morality limiting the expression of those freedoms, especially in support of traditional family structures. In yet a further irony, the Court
used a law infused with the civil religion to censor a territorial government that endorsed the Mormon religion for violating the doctrine of
separation.[12]

Justice Waite could legitimately see himself as perpetuating
Jefferson's ideals; the law in question regulated behavior (the picking
of pockets or the breaking of legs), not beliefs. Accordingly, he could
cite Jefferson's letter endorsing a wall of separation while justifying
governmental use of power to impose prevailing religious values on a
group of religious dissenters. Jefferson, however, premised governmental restrictions of behavior on a showing of harm – particularly the
denial of another individual's rights. What had been lost in Waite's reasoning was Jefferson's prioritization of individual liberty, the protection of which at once served to justify governmental enactment of laws
and to limit the scope of those laws. In expanding the federal government's power relative to the individual's right of religious conscience,

[12] *Reynolds v. US*, 98 US 145 (1878).

the Court, in conjunction with the state and federal governments, redefined religious liberty as a freedom only for Protestants and furthered an unofficial establishment of nondenominational Christianity, or civil religion.

Following issuance of the *Reynolds* opinion, the United States aggressively prosecuted Mormon polygamy, and Congress even strengthened the law in the 1880s to deny polygamists the right to vote or hold office and to allow government condemnation of Mormon property; the Court upheld these actions against Mormon challenges on First Amendment grounds.[13] In 1890, the Mormon Church renounced its policy of plural marriage. The United States returned the confiscated property to the church in 1894, and Utah gained statehood in 1896.

American treatment of Catholics and Mormons in the late 1800s reflects a cultural disposition to use religion as a means of defining and organizing society. Reverend Josiah Strong, in *Our Country*, published in 1885, voiced Americans' duty to convert all the people of the world into cultural Anglo-Saxons, and turning them into Christians served as an essential part of that conversion. Domestic missions during this time, most significantly the Young Men's Christian Association and the Salvation Army, became just as important to Christian reformers as foreign missions were. Native Americans offered a wonderful first opportunity for the missionaries.

In 1869, President Grant responded to corruption within the Bureau of Indian Affairs by appointing a new commissioner, Richard Ely, himself a Native American. Ely oversaw a new peace policy that divided Indian reservations among Protestant denominations, with each given authority to set up schools and "Americanize" the Native Americans. The policy created a partnership between church and state, showing an inconsistency in Grant's thinking about the doctrine of separation. Native American religions recognized humanity as part of the natural environment, brother, in a sense, to the animals and a partner with the land, water, and flora. Religious rituals reinforced, through celebrations and traditions, this natural connectedness. American law, strongly influenced by the need to Christianize the Native Americans

---

[13] *Murphy v. Ramsey*, 114 US 15 (1885); *The Late Corporation of the Church of Latter-day Saints v. United States* 136 US 1 (1890).

and enforced by missionaries on the reservations, prohibited traditional religious practices. In so doing, the law interfered with their identities.

The reaction of the Sioux (Lakota) to the cultural impositions of Western modernity paralleled that of the Shawnee in the early 1800s – the formation of a new religion that attempted to revive old cultural values and traditions while incorporating the new understandings imposed upon them. The Ghost Dance ceremonies of the Northern Plains Indians constituted a last-chance attempt to salvage some of their cultural values and beliefs. It prompted such fears and aversions that it resulted in the massacre at Wounded Knee and the generally perceived end of Native American resistance. In 1904, the United States made it illegal for the Plains Indians to practice such dances.

Despite the growth of domestic missions, American missionary efforts in the late 1800s and early 1900s focused, to an unprecedented degree, on foreign lands. Not entirely private religious endeavors, these foreign missions posed yet another challenge to the separation of church and state. President McKinley claimed that God had answered his prayers for guidance with a directive that he "educate the Filipinos and uplift and civilize and Christianize them and by God's grace do the very best we could by them, as our fellow men for whom Christ also died." In 1898, before the Federal Council of Churches, McKinley added, "Let it be ours to sustain the flag and to see to it that wherever that flag goes our holy religion goes, in every part of the world."[14]

Protestant churches formed an ecumenical response to McKinley's plea to share "our flag and our religion."[15] Ecumenical missionary efforts expressed support for the civil religion, uniting Protestants in a cause to serve both God and country. Yet, they also resulted in cultural upheaval and untold suffering for the supposed beneficiaries. A growing sensitivity to cultural diversity, encouraged by scholars such as Franz Boas, prompted many Americans to reconsider the advisability of the Christian admonition to proselytize in search of worldwide conversion. Mark Twain, not surprisingly, gave exceptional voice to these concerns in a succinct and very pointed way in 1900: "I bring you the stately matron named Christendom, returning bedraggled, besmirched and

[14] Quoted in Sullivan, "The State," 249.
[15] Meyer, *The Protestant Search*, 8–9.

dishonored from pirate-raids in Kiao-Chou, Manchuria, South Africa and the Philippines, with her soul full of meanness, her pocket full of boodle and her mouth full of pious hypocrisies. Give her the soap and a towel, but hide the looking-glass."[16] Thoughtful Americans reconsidered, yet again, the advisability of public support of any religion.

While the domestic missions to Native Americans and the foreign missions produced largely unintended adverse effects on the people and cultures they addressed, other religiously inspired movements more directly attacked those identified as different. Cultural and ethnic diversity, resulting both from immigration and from the domestic migrations of freed slaves, produced various nativist movements in the late 1800s. While these tended to be populist movements appealing largely to poor and marginally educated Americans, some gained traction within elite social circles. Religion seemed always to be a factor.

Economic problems in the early 1890s and again in the 1930s only exacerbated American bigotry. Jews, perceived to be controlling banks and financial houses, were blamed for the economic declines. While "gentlemen's agreements" excluding Jews from private clubs and residential neighborhoods did not raise questions of equal protection, the adoption of quota systems at public universities, designed to limit the number of Jewish students at their schools, certainly did. The Ku Klux Klan (KKK), the Black Legion, and the Silver Shirt Legion, each devoted to protecting white Protestant Americans from the "dangers" of Jews, African Americans, and Catholics, claimed to be both Christian and patriotic organizations. Founded by a Methodist minister, the KKK, the largest and best known of these nativist groups, overtly used Christian symbolism in defense of its bigotry. In 1924, Reverend O.R. Miller held services in a chapel in Garber, Oklahoma, which he proudly described as "the first church to be dedicated under the fiery cross of the Ku Klux Klan." A KKK newsletter from 1929 describes the intention of the burning cross "to constantly remind us that Christ is our criterion of character and His teaching our rule of life." Klansman Walter Reasoner wrote of "the fiery cross blazing in glory with its radiance like the statute [*sic*] of Liberty, enlightening

---

[16] Mark Twain, "Greeting to the Twentieth Century," *New York Herald*, December 30, 1900.

FIGURE 3.1. Ku Klux Klan members marching down Pennsylvania Avenue in Washington, DC, in 1928. The myth of the United States as a "Christian nation" encouraged a comingling of Christianity and patriotism, social forces that could be used by some as the basis for exclusionary politics. Photographer unknown, 1928. National Archives, ID #306-NT-650–4.

the world with liberty, both civil and religious."[17] Interference with people's rights to walk on public streets, not to mention countless lynchings, constituted criminal behaviors performed in the name of God and country (see Figure 3.1). As Americans came to identify their national identity with Protestantism after the Civil War, they came to use religion as a means of judging others' patriotism and inclusion in society. To the extent that law tolerated these behaviors, it lessened the separation of church and state.

Social Reform and Contesting Images of America

Beyond the persecutions of Mormons, the ostracization of Catholics, and even the tacit acceptance of quotas and the KKK, legal support of

[17] Quoted in Hamburger, *Separation*, 420, 421.

the civil religion permitted religious ideals to permeate state and local laws. Outside of judicial dicta, it is hard to find any case law from 1865 to 1937 supporting the Jeffersonian understanding of the separation of church and state. During this era, the Supreme Court came to distinguish between regulating social behaviors derived from religious belief and regulating belief itself, at least perpetuating the doctrine of separation, if not the liberty it was designed to protect. Meanwhile, Protestant Christians undertook the enactment of legislation and even various constitutional amendments to secure, through political action, legal protection of the civil religion. Despite the temporary growth of federal power in the years of war and Reconstruction, most legal change in the late 1800s occurred at the state level. The Supreme Court assisted in this process. In a series of decisions in 1873 known as the *Slaughterhouse* cases, the Court upheld the police powers of the states to regulate people's morals and behaviors. In so doing, it declined to assert the federal powers, recognized in the Fourteenth Amendment, to protect individual freedoms from state interference through the privileges and immunities clause. The attacks by the United States Congress on Mormons and Catholics at the federal level stand in sharp contrast to the pervasive practice of deferring moral judgments to the states.

Christian Desires for Social Justice

By the early 1900s, the civil religion precipitated antagonism from both rational humanists and activist Christians. The former complained of its imposition of religious values and morals and the latter complained of its failure to adequately incorporate the true religion into the governance of the nation. Activist Christians themselves experienced huge divisions between the Civil War and World War II. Yet, despite tremendous ideological and religious differences, Christian socialists, evangelicals, and fundamentalists supported grandiose changes in American political and economic systems to pursue the new concept of "social justice." United by a communitarian ethic, they called for social and legal restrictions on individual freedoms to reinforce Christian conceptions of the family; to help the poor, the weak, and the unfortunate; and to create a more egalitarian democracy and economy.

The Social Gospel movement was at the center of the Christian push for social justice. It used Christian ethics instrumentally or as a tool to serve reformers' political goals for the nation. Although its roots lie both in the communitarian emphasis of the Puritans' efforts to build godly societies and in the social reform ministries of preachers such as Beecher and Finney in the early 1800s, it might be better understood as one aspect of a broader intellectual movement that flowered in the late 1800s and continued well into the 1920s.

At that time, both in Europe and the United States, a group of social philosophers who championed new social and economic models garnered support among various intellectuals, including many ministers. Many of these philosophers premised their outlooks on long-standing conceptions of Christian ethics and challenged Christian preachers and congregants alike to live in accordance with the moral teachings of their faith. Writers such as Randolph Bourne and Van Wyck Brooks looked to earlier forms of Catholicism that celebrated humanity's duties to community and the prioritization of spirit or soul over the natural world. One of the major literary figures in the social criticism of the late 1800s, Henry George, argued for an ethical theism in which God was understood as a spiritual reality that encouraged ethical or moral justice. Edward Bellamy, writing at the same time as George and from a very similar perspective, encouraged a rededication to the gospel meaning of love. In his utopian romance, *Looking Backward, 2000–1887*, Bellamy argued for the nationalization of all industry as a means of imposing morality on business operations. Reverend Thomas Dixon, Jr., pastor of the 23rd Street Baptist Church in New York City, wrote that *Looking Backward* "embodies the essence of Christianity."[18] Bourne, Brooks, Bellamy, and George, though ethical reformers, were not ministers. Yet, they joined with Christian leaders to demand significant changes to American society and its laws – changes that would reflect their understandings of Christian morality and social ethics.

America's mainline church ministers may have been largely theological liberals, but they inclined, until the early 1900s, toward social and political conservatism. While tolerating, if not fully preaching, the civil religion, few challenged the prevailing political and economic systems, and most comfortably relied on private charity to address poverty and other social problems. The Social Gospel attacked these mainline

[18] Quoted in James Dombrowski, *The Early Days of Christian Socialism in America* (New York: Octagon Books, 1966), 89, n. 16.

ministers for their insensitivity, especially for preaching messages
encouraging submission and the deferment of happiness to the next
world. In response to this criticism, the Episcopalian, Congregational,
and Methodist Churches established agencies to help working people in labor disputes and to promote a more activist social agenda.
By 1908, several Protestant denominations came together to address
social ills under the Federal Council of Churches.

The Social Gospel movement provided a Christian outlet for social
concern. It shared with liberal theology a diminished emphasis on the
literal text of the Bible as it encouraged a greater integration of religion and daily life. Congregationalist Minister Washington Gladden
and his ally, Reverend Theodore T. Munger, described the new theology as not too dissimilar from its predecessors, but relying on a more
historically sound reading of the Scripture and replacing an excessive
individuality with an awareness of human connectedness and social
duties. The reform-minded Federal Council of Churches, in its 1920
publication, *The Church and Industrial Reconstruction*, wrote: "For
the Christian to adopt higher social standards before others are willing
to do so may involve sacrifice, but to be ready to sacrifice for the good
of mankind is an essential part of the Christian way of life."[19]

Walter Rauschenbusch, a leader of the Social Gospel movement,
offered a new understanding of what it meant to be a Christian, arguing that social duties accompany that status. Rauschenbusch wrote of
the essential message of Christianity as prophetic, asserting humanity's
duty "to transform human society into the kingdom of God by regen-
erating all human relations and reconstituting them in accordance
with the will of God." Doing so required a radical transformation in
America's political and economic structure.

It is hardly likely that any social revolution, by which hereafter capitalism may
be overthrown, will cause more injustice, more physical suffering, and more
heartache than the industrial revolution by which capitalism rose to power.…
men learned to make wealth faster than they learned to distribute it.[20]

Rauschenbusch asserted that "the Christian Church has never under-
taken to carry out … [the] fundamental purpose of its existence." He

[19] Quoted in Meyer, *The Protestant Search*, 24.
[20] Walter Rauschenbusch, *Christianity and the Social Crisis*, ed. by Robert D. Cross
    (New York: Harper & Row, 1964, 1907), 218.

argued that the reason for this failure was that the church had been too focused on salvation, immortality, and the soul rather than on humanity's fulfillment of its duties to fellow humans on earth. American Christians sought the comfort and reassurance that belief in an afterlife provided rather than new social responsibilities. In contrasting communitarian duties from individualistic desires, Rauschenbusch reconceived of heaven as nothing more than a Christian community on earth. He declared: "The kingdom of God was a social and collective hope and it was for this earth. The eternal life was an individualistic hope and it was not for this earth."[21] Rauschenbusch argued that the Bible should awaken a sense of moral duty, and that too much attention to its litany of miracles had compelled too many Christians to ignore their social obligations in hoping for God's intervention.

Many of the clergy involved in the Social Gospel believed not only that the church should be more involved in addressing social issues, emphasizing morality more than salvation, but also that Christian morality should serve as the basis for broader government action. The Social Gospel intended to Christianize the social order, to render it less competitive, individualistic, harsh, and self-interested, and to infuse it with brotherhood and a spirit of service. This focus put its adherents at odds with much of contemporary society, especially business practices. Reverend George D. Herron wrote in 1898, "How can we obey Christ's law of love, when every industrial maxim, custom, fact, and principle renders that law inoperative?"[22]

Over time, the more radical elements of the Social Gospel movement expressed themselves in various groups advocating a Christian socialism. It is one thing for ministers to impose social duties on their congregants in recognition of religious obligations. It is another for ministers or, more generally, Christians to impose duties on all members of the society in recognition of those same obligations. The difference is rooted in recognizing limits on religion's ability to influence the public sector that do not exist in the private sector. A social policy consistent with Christian moral duties subordinates all rights and freedoms to a religiously derived communitarian ethic. The Social Gospel

---

[21] Ibid., xxiii, 162.

[22] Reverend George B. Herron, "The Social System and the Christian Conscience," in *The Kingdom*, August 18, 1898.

leaders at the turn of the century may well have transgressed the line separating church and state. Their allies, the Christian Socialists and the Pragmatists, refused even to acknowledge the continued relevance of that line.

In 1894, the editors of the *Northwestern Congregationalist*, a Christian socialist journal published in Grinnell, Iowa, asserted that the Kingdom of God is "a state in which the individual finds his salvation by losing himself for the good of others" and further contended that "the Kingdom of God meant a society upon this earth in which all human affairs exhibit the nature and spirit of God."[23] Relying on this understanding of Christian duties, Christian socialists insisted on the need for inheritance taxes to redistribute wealth, eight-hour work days, public ownership of land, cooperative banks, and public housing for the poor. They premised their arguments on ethical or moral necessity, perceiving that necessity as an absolute derived from Christian doctrine. The editors had no intention of excepting government or public policies from this moral necessity.

In 1896, Wichita Congregational Minister Charles Sheldon published his novel, *In His Steps: What Would Jesus Do?*[24] It sold 30 million copies. Sheldon, a Christian socialist who had inspired Walter Rauschenbusch, told Americans to ask what Jesus would do when confronting poverty, class conflict, and alcoholism. He saw it as government's duty to promote morality and to temper individualism. Christian socialists such as Sheldon pitted capitalism against God, sin against socialism. They argued that Christianity compelled people to live a communitarian lifestyle and to subordinate themselves to the good of the whole. Laws could compel people to move toward this goal. The Society of Christian Socialists first met in a Baptist Church in Boston in 1889 and subsequently published its "Declaration of Principles" asserting the intent "to awaken members of Christian churches to the fact that the teachings of Jesus Christ lead directly to some specific form or forms of socialism" as "economic individualism" precipitates only "commercial and industrial crisis" and concentrates power in the "hands of a dangerous plutocracy." The Society of Christian Socialists hoped to create a theocratic socialist state. The

[23] Quoted in Dombrowski, *Christian Socialism*, 112, 113.
[24] Charles Sheldon, *In His Steps: "What Would Jesus Do?"* (Chicago: Advance, 1986).

Church Social Union, organized in 1891 as the Christian Social Union, expressed a compatible goal in its statement of principles issued in 1892: "to apply the moral truths and principles of Christianity to the social and economic difficulties of the present time" and "to claim for the Christian Law the ultimate authority to rule social practice."[25]

During the early 1900s, members of the Social Gospel movement and Christian socialists openly used religion to build support for a communitarian social and political agenda. In using religion in this way, they pitted Christianity against not only the unintended cruelties of capitalism and a rampant individualism that might disrupt social harmony, but also against the "self-made man" morality of the Horatio Alger stories and Irwin A. Wylie, the confidence in the free-enterprise democracy expressed by Andrew Carnegie, and the perpetuation of Americans' Jeffersonian belief in freedom of action as an inherent right. The Social Gospel movement wedded itself to broad reform movements in the late 1800s and early 1900s and, in the process, forced Americans to rethink the integration of Christianity, American nationalism, and free-enterprise capitalism that formed the civil religion.

A Christian nationalism could not be more at odds with the cosmopolitan individualism advocated by the Jeffersonians. The humanism of the eighteenth century conceived of protecting individual rights and freedoms as consistent with the social good. Society created government to preserve individual rights – one of which was freedom of conscience to think, do, dream, and pursue whatever one wanted, free from the judgment or moral sanction of others, as long as it did not interfere with the equal rights of others. The Social Gospel movement and Christian socialism espoused humanitarianism rather than humanism and encouraged moralists and ethicists to limit the range of options of what people thought, did, dreamed, and pursued to construct a better community. They desired a government that imposed duties rather than protected freedoms. In many ways, these movements sought a society more like the early colonial model of paternalism exercised for the moral good of the community – the very model that the Revolution overthrew.

---

[25] Quoted in Dombrowski, *Christian Socialism*, 98–100.

By the 1920s, the political goals of the socially oriented ministry came to the forefront. In 1928, a group of reformers, including several ministers, formed the League for Independent Political Action, committed to witnessing to socialism as well as to Christ. Its first secretary, Howard Y. Williams, served as a Congregational minister in St. Paul, Minnesota. The Great Depression only added to the reformers' enthusiasm. The failures of capitalism provided a second chance – an opportunity to rebuild society the right way, by moving from individualism to communalism supported by an active government. In a 1934 poll of almost 21,000 members of the clergy on their ideological preferences for the American economy, 95 percent favored some form of cooperative commonwealth over capitalism, with 28 percent endorsing a state-sponsored socialism. The greatest support for socialism came from Methodist, Congregational, and evangelical preachers, though it existed in all Protestant denominations. Norman Thomas, the Socialist Party candidate for the presidency, had been a Presbyterian minister. His candidacy spurred talk of merging the predominantly Christian League for Independent Political Action, which at that time counted both Reinhold Niebuhr and John Dewey as members, with the Socialist Party.

The Social Gospel of the 1930s fostered a new ecumenism that restructured the duties of all participating Christians. It encouraged proselytizing, not to gain conversions to God's truth, but to work for social justice in God's name. In this activity it found common cause not only with fundamentalists who hoped to restrain Americans' freedom to sin, but also with communitarians outside the faith on whom they would have to rely in promoting social change.

Politicizing Morality If Not Religion

It was noted earlier that the Social Gospel movement must be contextualized within a broader intellectual movement. Western theorists of the late nineteenth century challenged both human reliance on reason and human individualism. By the early twentieth century, many intellectual leaders held that people behave on the basis of irrational and self-interested impulses rooted in group dynamics to create tentative and relative truths that are used by empowered groups to explain that which cannot be understood. In this context, ideas can easily be tools of manipulation, and truth can be seen as a fungible entity used to serve immediate goals. Much of twentieth-century history seems, to many, to validate these conclusions of nineteenth-century thinkers. The ideas of Marx, Freud, and several cultural anthropologists challenged not only assumptions of human reason and individuality but also the purpose and scope of philosophy. To the extent that philosophy is a quest for truth, these people implied that the truth that philosophy finds or asserts is constructed by individuals or communities. It is therefore subjective, not objective. It exists in the consciousness of individuals or groups of people as a basis for making sense of the world and their place in it. Truth does not exist apart from humanity, but is its creation.

The rise of collectivist thought in the United States may well owe its greatest debt to Pragmatists William James and John Dewey. While many of the Pragmatists were themselves agnostic or atheistic, they recognized the relevance of Christian ethics to their societal goals and the power of religion in working to achieve them. Even fundamentalist preacher E. Y. Mullins, president of the Southern Baptist Seminary, argued that Christianity and Pragmatism shared the same goal of "sav[ing] men from pessimism."[26] To do so, like the socially concerned Christians, the Pragmatists diminished the importance of individual rights by prescribing proper thoughts and feelings necessary for the good of the whole.

In *Pragmatism*, William James cites Charles Saunders Pierce for the relatively uncontroversial proposition that "beliefs are really rules for actions." He then proceeds to explain, however, that the idea or thought supporting a belief is of no real value – the value of a belief is solely in the action it produces: "to develop a thought's meaning, we need only determine what conduct it is fitted to produce: that conduct is for us its sole significance." Later in the same text, he issues a value-laden critique of rationalist philosophy:

A pragmatist turns his back resolutely and once [and] for all upon a lot of inveterate habits dear to professional philosophers. He turns away from abstraction and insufficiency, from verbal solutions, from bad a priori reason, from fixed principles, closed systems, and pretended absolutes and origins. He

---

[26] Quoted in Michael Lienesch, *In the Beginning: Fundamentalism the Scopes Trial, and the Making of the Anti-Evolution Movement* (Chapel Hill: University of North Carolina Press, 2009), 21.

turns toward concreteness and adequacy, towards facts, towards action and towards power. That means the empiricist temper regnant and the rationalist temper sincerely given up.[27]

Truth, James argues, is clearly not a product of human reason as exercised in thinking, reading, and dialectic, nor is it objective. Truth is formed only through the experiences of people, acting in groups, as a means of producing value or serving the good. Using an inductive-reasoning model, James argues that people must come to moral judgments from specific social experiences. These moral judgments form the basis for constructing truths that are nothing more than tools used to justify social actions productive of a good consistent with morality. Morality does not derive from truth, nor from the belief in it; rather, it serves as the basis for creating truth and belief. James states that a Pragmatist "talk[s] about truths in the plural, about their utility and satisfactoriness, about the success with which they work.... Truth, for him, becomes a class-name for all sorts of definite working-values in experience."

The goal, as James identifies it, is to create a generally accepted truth within society that is the product of a moral code – a moral code that was largely consistent with the Social Gospel's conceptions of social justice. As he states, "[T]ruth is one species of good, and not, as is usually supposed, a category distinct from good." Truth must result from morality – from conceptions of good and bad. It is a value-laden, subjective creation. Ultimately, it must serve as the basis for people acting in service of the social good. It is a tool used to motivate. James writes of truth: "[I]t is true because it is useful means the same as it is useful because it is true."[28] Expressing the same idea in somewhat more traditionally Christian terms, Reverend John Haynes Holmes found "all work for human betterment [to be essentially] religious work."[29]

Though far more accepting of spiritualism than many of his fellow Pragmatists, James joined them in using popular understandings of religion in pursuit of society's needs. He argues for the "will to believe," a psychology of religion that relied on humanity's desires for

---

[27] William James, *Pragmatism*, ed. by Bruce Kuklick (Indianapolis, IN: Hackett., 1980), 26.

[28] Ibid., 28, 34, 37, 93.

[29] John Haynes Holmes, *I Speak for Myself: The Autobiography of John Haynes Holmes* (New York: Harper, 1959).

transcendental understandings to further social justice. In response to the spiritual crisis of the age, he writes, "religion and morality ... become true insofar as they contribute to the psychological and social well-being of believers."[30]

John Dewey, often recognized as the father of contemporary American education, endorses James's inductive and value-laden approach to the construction of truths. Knowledge, or belief in a truth, he argues, must be "a product of the cooperative and communicative operations of human beings living together. Its communitarian origin is an indication of its rightful use." Dewey writes that what he advocates "is the emancipation of elements and outlooks that may be called religious from religion itself." Advocating the need for a communitarian ethic, he urges the development of a religiosity rooted not in doctrine or belief in the supernatural, but rather in "the attachment of emotion to [realizable social] ends." He wants this religious zeal to mobilize people in the pursuit of a social ideal rooted in morality: "All modes of human behavior are affected with a public interest; and full realization of this interest is equivalent to a sense of a significance that is religious in its function."[31]

Dewey asserts the need to impose social controls to encourage cooperation. Though holding relativist positions on truth, Dewey and James argue for a normative, and even universal, conception of morality. James even writes of a universal moral understanding forming the basis of a different type or "better" truth – "an ideal ... at which all our temporary truths will one day converge."[32] The Pragmatists are comfortable, to an extent that no rights-oriented theorist ever could be, with a third party, even one possessing the power of an educator, a governor, or a social leader, prescribing moral judgments for others. James and Dewey assert that people "should" feel, react, think, or even believe certain things in response to stimuli rooted in social experiences. To the degree that these experiences become shared, morality becomes more universal and more likely to function, in Dewey's terms, as a "common faith." Pragmatism shared much with the Social Gospel

---

[30] German, "Economy," in Goff and Harvey, *Themes in Religion and American Culture* (Chapel Hill, NC: University of North Carolina Press, 2004), 280, quoting James.

[31] John Dewey, *A Common Faith* (New Haven, CT: Yale University Press, 1934), 8, 79, 80.

[32] James, *Pragmatism*, 95, 100–1.

movement: a search for the common good, a rejection of individual-istic morality, and a call for legal change. Just over a hundred years after the founders limited courts of equity and attempted to minimize the role of moral judgment in law through professionalizing the bar and limiting the role of juries to fact finding, the Pragmatists sought to return popular conceptions of morality and the public good to legal adjudication. Supreme Court Justice Louis Brandeis exemplified the Pragmatist in law – considering sociological evidence and conceptions of social good to be as important as law in judicial decision making. Similarly, members of the Social Gospel movement encouraged the incorporation of Biblical morality into American law.

However, a common understanding of social goals and a shared interest in incorporating morality into law do not make the Pragmatists into Christian reformers. Gerald Birney Smith from the University of Chicago Divinity School used language strikingly similar to that of James and Dewey: "Modern religious thinking is learning to draw its inspiration from the world in which we live."[33] But, Smith and his ilk, contrary to most of the Pragmatists, remained believers in God and his active role in the world. It is one thing to accept religion as a means of inculcating moral values; it is another to believe that God dictates human acceptance of those values. Yet, despite differences, the Pragmatists and the Christian reformers combined to challenge American understandings of both the separation of church and state and the separation of law and moral judgment. In this way, they formed an alliance in a turn-of-the-century crusade to redesign the nation.

The Crusade for Social Change

Secular and religious reformers shared an antipathy to the growth of large corporations wielding unprecedented power, urban centers spawning poverty and crime, and tremendous fluctuations in the econ-omy, all of which fueled calls for reform in the early 1900s. Even secu-lar scholars relied on Christian morality as the basis of social criticism. In his discussion of the absence of societal checks on socially corrosive behavior in the industrialized society of 1907, Edward A. Ross noted the decline of the "old regulative system" provided by Christian beliefs

---

[33] Quoted in Martin E. Marty, *Modern American Religion*, Vol. 1: *The Irony of It All, 1893–1919* (Chicago: University of Chicago Press, 1986), 26.

and the need for law to assume greater authority in its place. More Christian-minded reformers persisted in denying the need for a substitution, offering instead the need for law to reinforce Christian ideals.

A different conception of the role of the individual in society than that expressed in American law formed at the root of both Christian and secular reform initiatives. In 1934, Father Coughlin, a Catholic priest who reached millions of Americans through his radio show, "The Golden Hour of the Shrine of the Little Flower," and his newspaper, *Social Justice*, condemned the "anarchistic individualism both in morality and philosophy, and in civilization," and argued that it must give way to the collectivist morality taught by Jesus.[34] Reformers concerned about the living conditions of wage earners found the legal ideals of contract law at odds with Christian morality and ideas of social justice. Catholic reformer Matteo Liberatore called "free enterprise" a "terrible weapon most effectual to crush the weak."[35]

Christian reformers recognized that a broad conception of the doctrine of religious freedom, one embracing the separation of law and religion, would frustrate them in achieving their goals. As early as 1875, the National Reform Association, involved in a wide range of Christian lobbying from Sabbath-day protection to labor legislation, announced its goal to Christianize the government. Reform depended on recognition of Christian morality as the basis for new laws that would redefine the social relationships of employer-employee, husband-wife, and benefactor-recipient. Contract law, protecting individual freedoms by strictly circumscribing the nature of any social duties one person has to another, would in the reformers' plans be jettisoned for a law rooted in moral obligation and the social good. Strict contract law principles relied only on the market to determine the cost of goods and labor and when, where, and to whom alcohol would be sold or loans would be given. Recognizing each individual as a reasonable, rational, and competent legal equal prohibited a legislator, minister, or well-meaning neighbor from substituting his or her judgment for that of any party to a contract, whether for purchase, employment, or mortgage. The same principles of equality and personal freedom underlay laws granting

---

[34] Charles J. Tull, *Father Coughlin and the New Deal* (Syracuse, NY: Syracuse University Press, 1965), 49 (quote).

[35] Quoted in McGreevy, *Catholicism*, 130.

divorces and society's tentative toleration of abortion, pornography, and sexual promiscuity as long as they occurred out of public view. Christian reformers, committed to protecting people from themselves and society from sin, tackled each of these concerns and in the process succeeded, to a substantial degree, in changing America's laws.

In the late nineteenth century, Christian moralists continued their assault on the legal individualism of the founding era that they had begun in the antebellum era. Liberal conceptions of marriage and the family came under increasing attack. James Schouler and Joel Prentiss Bishop, authors of two important property law treatises of the 1870s, argued that protecting personal property within a marriage threatened both marriage and society. Attacking the women's property acts of the 1840s, Schouler asserted that laws giving independent property rights to women "weaken the ties of marriage, by forcing both sexes into an unnatural antagonism; teaching them to be independent of one another." Conversely, "God's law points to family and the mutual intercourse of man and woman as among the strongest safeguards of human happiness."[36] Bishop further contended that society was a third party in any marriage and therefore also a party to consider in any divorce proceeding. As the number of divorces increased in the late nineteenth century, Christian reformers mobilized by founding the National Divorce Reform League to pursue a Constitutional Amendment recognizing marriage as indissoluble but for unusual circumstances. In the 1870s, evangelical Anthony Comstock succeeded in gaining passage of the first national censorship law prohibiting the use of the mail system to distribute "obscene, lewd, or lascivious" materials, including contraceptives.

Bible reading in schools was not only tolerated but required by law in some states, especially in the South. The Supreme Court's decisions in the *Slaughterhouse* cases in 1873 seemingly endorsed the practice through their recognition of the growing police powers of state governments. Yet, some state courts sought to address First Amendment issues even as the Supreme Court tried to avoid them. In 1921, the Georgia Supreme Court upheld an ordinance of the city of Rome requiring each school principal to begin the day by reading the Bible

---

[36] Quoted at Sehat, *Myth of American Religious Freedom*, 144 (quotes).

and leading prayers. The court held that the separation of church and state does not require the "separation of state from Christianity."[37]

This invocation of morality, rooted strongly in popular Christian understandings, expressed itself in a wide range of communitarian initiatives. Reverend Josiah Strong argued for the "Christianization of all social institutions ... through the 'unbounded influence' of the church upon the conscience of the social organism."[38] Similarly, the Southern Baptist Convention, in its 1915 annual report, after noting "crowded [urban] tenements" and "heartless [corporate] greed," contended that true Christians cannot ignore social injustices even when their government appears inclined to do so.[39]

By far the greatest moral crusade addressed prohibition, the movement to limit or eliminate the sale of alcoholic beverages. As noted earlier, Christian reformers such as Finney and Beecher had taken strides toward temperance in the early 1800s. However, by 1865, only Massachusetts and Maine remained as dry states. During the 1870s, Frances Willard, a Methodist moralist who would become a "Gospel Socialist" devoted to Henry George and Edward Bellamy, epitomized the evangelical embrace of the Social Gospel. She envisioned the Women's Christian Temperance Union (WCTU) as a vehicle to reform society through Christian philanthropy. Despite the WCTU's tireless efforts in public demonstrations and legislative lobbying, prohibition gained little traction before 1900. The temperance campaign gained momentum only after the mainline Protestant churches, including Methodist, Baptist, and Presbyterian, made its cause a priority. Only North Dakota passed new legislation prior to 1908. Yet, by 1916, two-thirds of the states, encompassing nearly three-quarters of the American population, had prohibition laws, and the campaign for a national law was well under way (see Figure 3.2). The Eighteenth Amendment proved to be a pyrrhic victory for the Christian reformers. Prohibition culminated decades of moralistic fulmination, but once it found its way into the Constitution, prohibition

---

[37] *Wilkerson v. City of Rome*, 152 Ga. 762, 769 (1921).

[38] Wendy J. Deichmann Edwards, "Women and Social Betterment in the Social Gospel Work of Josiah Strong," in *Gender and the Social Gospel*, ed. by Wendy J. Deichmann Edwards and Carolyn De Swarte Gifford (Urbana: University of Illinois Press, 2005), 40 (quote).

[39] Quoted in Hamburger, *Separation*, 381.

FIGURE 3.2. Carrie Nation (1846–1911), American temperance advocate, with Bible and hatchet. Temperance workers, like Carrie Nation, used both the Bible and violence, often in combination with each other, to compel their fellow citizens to give up alcohol. They succeeded in passing the Eighteenth Amendment in 1919, ushering in the Prohibition era. Photographer: Philipp Kester, 1910. ullstein bild/The Granger Collection, New York. Image #0231209. All rights reserved.

only highlighted Americans' aversion to government-imposed moral restraints. Americans flocked to illegal speakeasies, readily supported known criminals and gangland killers plying the liquor trade, and took to unlawfully producing their own liquor in order to have their drinks (see Figure 3.3). In the process, they developed and encouraged a widespread disrespect for the nation's laws and governing institutions. The flapper era and the jazz age of the 1920s, with their flouting of sexual mores and social conventions, arose within a larger context of disrespect for authority, custom, and law catalyzed by the government's enforcement of an unpopular law that sought to proscribe personal behaviors.

In nearly every one of the reformists' campaigns, the essentially liberal or individualistic quality of America's culture served as an impediment to radical or permanent change. To many, this quality derived from America's laws, starting with its Constitution, prompting calls to amend the primary law. The idea of an amendment to establish the country as a Christian nation and repudiate the doctrine of separation of church and state had been proposed as early as 1863, but it sputtered then and only gained traction near the turn of the century. As the issue gained support in the early 1900s, most ministers contended that the problem existed not with the Constitutional separation of church and state but with what this meant. Ministers told congregants the partial truth that the founders separated religion from politics so as to preserve dissenters' rights to practice their religious beliefs on an equal basis with others, but they left out the liberal arguments that all religious belief, as a matter of conscience, remained speculative and beyond the purview of law. In short, the ministers credited the dissenters for passing the First Amendment and ignored the liberals and their intentions. In redefining separation as primarily addressing the need for toleration, ministers implicitly narrowed the limitations imposed on government by the doctrine of separation. As a group of more than a hundred Protestant ministers expressed during a meeting in Washington, DC, in 1912, their endorsement of the principle of separation meant only separation of church and state, not the separation of Christianity and the law. This tepid endorsement of the doctrine of separation of church and state temporarily muted Christian calls for a "Christian amendment." The campaign to amend the Constitution produced a greater degree of antipathy from liberals. Leading liberal

FIGURE 3.3. Speakeasy: Texas Guinan, Queen of the Nightclubs, in one of the New York City speakeasies that she operated in the 1920s. Prohibition produced a strong reaction against moralistic legislation; free thought, social acceptance of a wider range of female behavior, and disrespect for the law increased. Photographer and exact date unknown. The Granger Collection, New York, Image #0012787.

Francis Abbott considered it the Christian lobby's "opening salvo in the coming 'war against republican liberty.'"[40] The debates over the bill furthered the redefinition of what the primary law really meant given the increased role of Christian morality in American society. According to the redefinition of the early 1900s, governments could act on Christian morality in legislating behaviors and provide tacit support of the Christian religion.

Fundamentalism and the Scopes Trial

Though they worked together in many of the campaigns for reform in the early 1800s, fundamentalists shared little with their more socially conscious Christian brethren other than a desire for legal change consistent with Christian morality. Fundamentalism rose as a reactionary defense of traditional Christian values and asserted that conversion, the act of accepting Christ as one's savior and entrusting the future to God, promised to allay the discontent that was widely felt as the century neared its end. From its beginnings, fundamentalism was driven by conservative ministers. Reverend Dwight L. Moody began preaching in Chicago during the 1870s that while Western society was succumbing to heresy and apostasy, a golden age, marked by the return of Jesus, was imminent. Turning to a literal reading of Biblical passages that more liberal Christians viewed as allegorical, Moody and his cohorts developed a radical new theology that they promoted with no sense of irony as "Old Time Religion" rooted in premillennialist doctrine. It focused on the belief that Jesus would return to claim his saints, or true believers, prior to a period of tribulation, or rule by the Anti-Christ. The problems of the day served as indicia of the Anti-Christ's strength and portended the intervention of God to save some of his saints from the coming tribulation. This doctrine offered both a new interpretation of Christian faith and optimism formed in special knowledge and the promise of escape from the evils of this world. Most significantly, though, it offered the means by which to perceive and criticize those evils: liberal religion, greed and economic

---

[40] Quoted in Gaines M. Foster, *Moral Reconstruction: Christian Lobbyists and the Federal Legislation of Morality, 1865–1920* (Chapel Hill: University of North Carolina Press, 2002), 29.

inequality, and the falsehoods of science and rational humanism that had produced this confusing new world.

By the early 1900s, many conservative Christians recognized a broad-based threat not only to their beliefs but also to their ways of life in the social acceptance of liberal messages. William Graham Sumner celebrated a moral alternative to Christianity in his espousal of social Darwinism and "the survival of the fittest." Other secularists openly criticized Christian morality as a type of social theocracy inconsistent with democratic ideals. Businesspeople seemed to deny the relevance of religion in their professional lives, and young people eagerly embraced new fashions by the 1920s, expressed in jazz, fast cars, and changing sexual attitudes. Conservative Christians felt the need to respond. They turned to Princeton's Presbyterian Seminary, the intellectual center of Christian fundamentalism, from where Professor Charles Hodge had earlier published the first volume of a two-volume work entitled *Systematic Theology*. In it he contended that the Bible is the word of God and is literally true. Those who saw it as allegory or metaphor distorted God's message.

The fundamentalists, both in and outside of Princeton, sought to transform their society into a Christian community. Their criticism of liberal theology as expressed in the civil religion was not only that it was doctrinally wrong but also that it was morally bankrupt, contributing to drunkenness, divorce, infidelity, crime, graft, and corruption. Liberal theology, its critics charged, tolerated and even encouraged moral weakness, physical indulgence, and selfishness and ignored the discipline and attention to duty that humanity required.

The liberal-fundamentalist conflict of the late 1800s tore apart churches in much the way the Old Light–New Light divide did in the eighteenth century. As would occur again from 1980 to the early 2000s, conservative members of mainstream denominations left their churches for nondenominational or Baptist fundamentalist alternatives. The liberal-fundamentalist theological divisions manifested in the narrow debate over evolution. The two Christian groups that had worked together on the reform programs of the late 1800s divided over doctrine.

By 1920, fundamentalists consciously organized themselves into a movement for religious and societal change focused on God. Reverend William B. Riley, one of the founders of the World's Christian

Fundamentals Association (WCFA), said, "When the Church is regarded as the body of God-fearing, righteous-living men, then, it ought to be in politics, and as a powerful influence."[41] The WCFA worked to secure not only social justice for the poor, but also a reinvigoration of America's reverence for God and a nationwide ban on the teaching of evolution. Reverend Riley called the WCFA's crusade for restructuring American society "a war from which there is no discharge."[42]

When Christian fundamentalism arose in the second half of the nineteenth century, it only peripherally addressed evolution. By the 1920s, evolution and fundamentalism had become aligned in the minds of the public largely because of the crusading of William Jennings Bryan. An avowed "supernaturalist," Bryan used his acceptance of the literal truth of the Bible to reject evolutionary theory as dangerous. Bryan expressed the fears of many conservative Christians of his time in seeing evolutionary theory as a manifestation of an atheistic culture and in presuming that disaster might result from unrestrained human freedom. He wrote: "I object to Darwinism theory because I fear that we shall lose the consciousness of God's presence in our daily life, if we must accept the theory that through all the ages no spiritual force has touched the life of man and shaped the destiny of nations." As early as 1904, Bryan said that Darwinism was merely "the merciless law by which the strong crowd out and kill the weak."[43]

Bryan's attacks on evolution formed only a part of a widespread, well-organized campaign by fundamentalists to reform education in the United States that exposed great divisions among Americans on matters of faith. As fundamentalists sought to remove modern science from classrooms, liberal Christians and secularists wondered whether conservative Christians could fairly teach America's youth. Social critic H.L. Mencken wrote for many cosmopolitan Americans in contending that fundamentalists "are everywhere [that] learning is too heavy a burden for mortal minds to carry, even the vague, pathetic learning on tap in the little red schoolhouse."[44]

---

[41] Quoted in Edward J. Larson, *Summer for the Gods: The Scopes Trial and America's Continuing Debate over Science and Religion* (New York: Basic Books, 1997), 36.

[42] Quoted in Karen Armstrong, *The Battle for God: A History of Fundamentalism* (New York: Random House, 2000), 174.

[43] Quoted in Larson, *Summer for the Gods*, 39, 27.

[44] Quoted in Armstrong, *The Battle for God*, 177.

Americans in the late 1800s and early 1900s generally succumbed to the use of law to restrict human activities based on conceptions of religious truth and values. However, calls for greater reliance on faith in education led academics and businesspeople to challenge the propriety of law's use in this way. The American Association of University Professors (AAUP), in its first annual meeting in 1915, recognized a distinction between public and private (often religious) schools. Public schools, it offered, "have no moral right to bind the reason or conscience of any professor." In contrast, church-affiliated schools found a ready moral basis for doing so. The association concluded that, historically, the chief menace to academic freedom was ecclesiastical. But, Victorian-era Christians were not content to espouse their doctrines simply in Christian schools. Contests over the teaching of evolution, prayer in classrooms, and the universality of Christian values polarized Americans and earned the scorn of academics. In 1924, Joseph V. Dennis, president of the AAUP, said in his presidential address that "[f]undamentalism is the most sinister force that has yet attacked freedom of teaching."[45] That same year, the relatively new American Civil Liberties Union (ACLU) expressed its view of academic freedom as both an important right of college professors and a necessary condition for education at any level and promised to aid any teachers or professors denied this freedom by force of law.

If science constituted the major source of tension between Christians and nonbelievers, history came in a close second. History arose as a professional discipline in the last decades of the nineteenth century and offered the past as a product of human choices rather than God's providence. The actions, thoughts, and concerns of earlier people produced the world both they and contemporary Americans lived in. While historians writing in the nineteenth century (e.g., Fiske, Marx, and Bancroft) could still argue for a deterministic or purposeful trajectory within history, their fatalism was rooted in understandings of human nature and the inevitability of certain human behavioral patterns, not in God's active involvement. Science and the professionalization of the humanities both encouraged a new generation of Americans to believe only that which could be proven factually or persuasively argued. This new academic style, at least as much as the substantive curriculum,

---

[45] Quoted in Larson, *Summer for the Gods,* 77, 80.

challenged both the acceptance of the Bible as the word of God and the verity of the moral teachings that word contained. Faith, as a basis of knowing, came under its greatest attack.

The natural philosophy of the eighteenth and early nineteenth centuries generally recognized God as the "First Cause," that is, that natural laws governed the world but that they were God's creation. Newtonian science had challenged God's active providence, but not his role as creator. Darwin challenged God's role in creation and, in the process, pitted science against religion. Darwin posed several problems for Christians. First, if all existing species are the product of evolution through mutation of earlier life forms, were those earlier life forms mistakes? Does God make mistakes? If not, why would he make something that needs to die and be replaced? Second, can the Bible be read as literal truth? Once it becomes clear that the world was not created in six days and that man and woman were not formed as isolated beings and placed in Eden, what else in the Bible cannot be understood literally? Third, can humans be the only animal possessed of a soul if they are related to other animals? Can humans still claim to be created in God's image? Yet, perhaps the most difficult challenge to Christian doctrine posed by Darwinian evolution was the inevitable conclusion that humans, like all life on earth, continue to evolve. *Homo sapiens*, far from being a final or ultimate species, is simply part of an evolutionary continuum, as likely to face extinction, mutation, or evolutionary change as any other species. Darwin published *Origins of Species* in 1859 and *The Descent of Man* in 1871. However, not until the late 1890s and early 1900s did scientists find strong fossil evidence to support the idea of human evolution. This evidence proved to be so convincing to a majority of Americans that it sparked a reaction from religious fundamentalists to prohibit the teaching of evolution in the schools.

Expressing fundamentalists' social concerns, Tennessee State Senator John Butler believed that the public schools should "promote citizenship based on biblical concepts of morality" and that evolutionary theory, by challenging Biblical truth, undermined that responsibility. The bill that bore his name, making it a felony to teach evolution in Tennessee's public schools, passed the state's House of Representatives by a 71 to 5 vote on January 27, 1925, just a week after its introduction. The state Senate passed the bill on March 21, by a vote of 24 to

6 and sent it to Governor Austin Peay. He signed it as, in his words, "a distinct protest against an irreligious tendency to exalt so-called science, and deny the Bible in some schools and quarters – a tendency fundamentally wrong and totally mischievous in its effects on our children, our institutions, and our country."[46] At the same time, many citizens within and outside of Tennessee worried that the law undermined the Constitutional idea of religion as a private right of conscience and its derivative policy of separating church and state. The law clearly dictated that a Christian truth be taught to the exclusion of one rooted in science and provided for punishment of anyone who might do otherwise.

Legal challenges to the legitimacy of the law began almost before it was passed. Although the Supreme Court had yet to apply the establishment clause of the First Amendment of the U.S. Constitution to the states, the Tennessee state constitution protected individual rights to both speech and free religious belief. John Scopes, a high school biology teacher, volunteered to test the statute in a case to be defended by the American Civil Liberties Union (ACLU). The prosecution made it very clear, from attorney Tom Stewart's opening statement, that it wanted the issue in the case to be whether the people of Tennessee could recognize the Bible as true in framing public education for children in their state.

The trial is best remembered not for the decision it rendered, a guilty verdict against Scopes attendant with a *de minimis* fine, but for lead defense counsel Clarence Darrow's examination of Bryan that lampooned the fundamentalist position. The national press covered the trial, creating widespread awareness of the power of fundamentalism in the South. Bryan's defense of Jonah living in a whale for three days, woman's creation from Adam's rib, and Noah's herding of all living creatures onto an ark provoked howls of laughter in the courtroom, but anguish and bewilderment outside of it. This man had been the Democratic candidate for the presidency of the United States. While mainline seminarians and ministers repudiated Bryan's positions, northern liberals used them as a call to action. Shailer Mathews, of the University of Chicago Divinity School said: "We have to live in the universe science gives us. A theology that is contrary to reality

---

[46] Ibid., 50, 56, 58.

must be abandoned or improved." Unitarian Minister Charles Francis Potter, from New York, warned: "[W]e are just beginning to hear the fundamentalist advance – the Tennessee trial is the opening barrage." The northern press referred to Tennessee's prosecution of Scopes as an "inquisition."

Ultimately, the Tennessee Supreme Court, on appeal, upheld the statute on the grounds that because the law required no positive teaching of any doctrine, it did not prefer, endorse, or establish any religion. But, the court shrewdly overturned the conviction of Scopes on procedural grounds and urged the attorney general to dismiss the prosecution without retrial, avoiding any appeal to the U.S. Supreme Court. On appeal, Darrow had raised the old Jeffersonian–Madisonian argument that religion was a private matter "that ought to be the affair of the individual."[47] No evidence suggests that a court would have accepted Darrow's argument in the 1920s.

Certainly, at the time, fundamentalists perceived the trial to end in victory. They used the energy that it produced to introduce more than twenty antievolution bills in state legislatures across the country. Empowered by the victory at trial, many parents eschewed legal action for vigilante forms of justice and burned classroom texts that presented evolutionary theory as true. In a similar vein, conservative college students built bonfires of lip stick, jazz records, cigarettes, silk stockings, novels, and photos of prurient interest.

Like Prohibition, the Scopes trial culminated decades of conflict among liberal and fundamentalist factions within American Protestantism. Certainly, it provided both a conclusion to one of the last moral crusades of the preceding century and an insight into the religious polarities that would surface near the end of the next one. The trial marked only one of several high points in the cyclical reinvigoration of fundamentalism in twentieth- and twenty-first-century America. Viewed solely as a historical event, it demonstrates the strength of fundamentalist belief during the early 1900s, at least in the South. Northern liberals reacted with alarm, but soon dismissed the entire episode as anomalous. Yet, Tennessee's prosecution of Scopes and the enactment of subsequent legislation banning the teaching of evolution in Mississippi, Texas, Louisiana, and Arkansas, the latest of

[47] Ibid., quotes from 118, 116–17, 220, 218.

which would serve as the basis for the Supreme Court's decision in 1968 in *Epperson v. Arkansas*, were not events isolated to an earlier time or a particular place.[48] Historians during the 1950s and 1960s saw the Scopes trial as the end of the fundamentalist movement. Such expressions of the defeat of fundamentalism were more comfortably made before 1980.

Fundamentalist defenses of Biblical inerrancy became useful to religious conservatives who idealized the South not only as the home of true religion but also of genteel women, chivalric men, and laws that respected marriage, protected tranquil home ownership, and supported God. In becoming increasingly countercultural, perhaps even assuming the grotesque stereotypes offered by their critics, fundamentalists after 1926 became more radicalized and politically marginalized. Finding Republicans, mainstream Protestants, elitist intellectuals, Catholics, and Democrats in favor of repealing prohibition all to be enemies, the fundamentalist message changed from one supporting a version of Christian faith to one attacking various aspects of contemporary society understood as modernism. In this reactionary approach to American culture, fundamentalism sowed the seeds for its eventual reappearance later in the century.

Law Constricts the Private-Public Distinction

Legislation and court decisions in the late 1800s and early 1900s preserved a titular recognition of the separationist doctrine but moved the line of separation to expand public power and allow a cultural embrace of the civil religion – a liberal Protestantism. Almost all this legal change occurred at the state level. The endorsement of a more publicly recognized religion is evident in the demise of Mortmain statutes, which imposed limitations on the property religious organizations could hold, the recognition of tax-exempt status for churches, the increase in "blue laws" and Sabbath-day protections, and the proliferation of government programs employing religious institutions to serve public needs. None of these changes occurred without judicial challenges, which provided a clarification of the extent to which law separated church and state.

---

[48] *Epperson v. Arkansas*, 393 US 97 (1968).

Moral legislation undercut the rights-oriented freedoms established in the early nineteenth century. Increased police powers allowed interference with someone's right to property or contract when private contracts had effects on third parties, giving states regulatory authority over a wide range of economic activities. The expansion of regulation in the early 1900s owed as much to the Pragmatists as to the Christian reformers. Both desired a greater public-sector commitment to social justice and overcame differences in belief to work to minimize or rework Constitutional protections of individual freedoms to attain it.

The rise of police powers in promotion of the public good combined with government support of business to erode the distinction between public and private spheres. Reconstruction efforts after the Civil War relied on private endeavors to fulfill the goals of the Radical Republicans. To build the transcontinental railroad, thousands upon thousands of acres of government land, much of it taken from Native Americans despite treaty protections, were given to railroad corporations. In this context, it is less shocking that in subsequent years the Supreme Court approved the use of federal money to support both a hospital operated by Catholic nuns and a Catholic school dedicated to educating children of the Sioux Nation because their purposes were in the public interest rather than in sectarian interests.[49]

Even amid this blurring of private and public spheres, the Supreme Court recognized the need to draw a line of separation somewhere. Court decisions of the era generally used the doctrine of separation to protect churches and religious institutions, as private entities, from state interference. In 1886, the Court held that corporations are legal persons, protected not only by Article I, Section 10 of the Constitution, but also by the recently ratified Fourteenth Amendment, providing equal protection under the law. Recognizing churches or, more broadly, denominations as privately held corporations, the Court, in a series of decisions, upheld their rights to resolve property disputes internally,[50] to resolve questions of church membership or discipline without state interference,[51] to appoint clergy from abroad,[52] to hold

---

[49] *Bradford v. Roberts*, 175 US 291 (1899); *Quick Bear v. Leupp*, 210 US 50 (1908).
[50] *Watson v. Jones*, 80 US 679 (1872); *Gonzalez v. Roman Catholic Archbishop*, 280 US 1 (1929).
[51] *Bouldin v. Alexander*, 82 US 131 (1872).
[52] *Rector of Holy Trinity Church v. US*, 143 US 457 (1892).

monastic properties despite local property law prohibitions,[53] and to educate children with a religious message free from state interference.[54] However, in overturning statutes requiring attendance at public schools, which effectively banned private or parochial education, the Court relied on parental rights relative to children rather than on the free exercise clause of the First Amendment.[55] The Court also issued one last decision, in 1892, in which it referenced Christianity as a basis for American law.[56]

Decisions not specifically about religion would prove to be even more important in developing twentieth-century ideas about the separation of church and state than the aforementioned religion cases. During the early twentieth century, a growing sensitivity to racial inequality compelled a reconsideration of the origin and extent of rights. In redefining political liberty to combat a culturally entrenched racism, Americans, largely through the Supreme Court, developed new understandings of religious freedom and the separation of church and state. However, more than concern with race, the Great Depression of the 1930s accelerated the Court's redefinition of rights.

The founders conceived of rights as natural and inherent. Nobody created rights – all government could do was to recognize them. They served as limitations on government power and the range of its activities. The Constitution recognized certain rights, in the contract clause and in the amendments, as creating private spheres on which government action could not intrude.

By the early 1900s, Pragmatists, Progressives, and Christian socialists perceived the Jeffersonian conception of rights as too limiting of government – an impediment to the pursuit of social justice. Yet, national law was built on rights – they were the essence of law and of the ideology behind creating a constitutional republic. The reformers could not jettison rights, but they could expand the notion of rights so as to be more amenable to social change. New

---

[53] *Order of St. Benedict v. Steinhauseer*, 234 US 640 (1914).
[54] *Meyer v. Nebraska*, 262 US 360 (1923); *Pierce v. Society of Sisters*, 268 US 510 (1925); *Farrington v. Tokushige*, 273 US 284 (1927); *Cochran v. Louisiana*, 281 US 370 (1930).
[55] *Pierce v. Society of Sisters*, supra.
[56] *Rector of Holy Trinity Church v. US*, supra.

rights, at least equal to those that the founders argued existed in the nature of humanity, had to be created. The first step in this process involved creating a hierarchy of rights in which social utility determined value. In 1920, Zechariah Chafee, of Harvard Law School, published *Freedom of Speech*, in which he argued that freedom of speech deserved protection as essential to the creation of participatory democracy, thereby justifying a right not because of its legal and prepolitical nature but because of its instrumental value to political society. Some people, such as Senator Robert La Follette, even argued that the courts' protection of property was antagonistic to other individual rights. In this construction, the contract clause, which prohibits public interference with private contracts even to serve the social good, came under attack.

In 1905, the Supreme Court considered the constitutionality of a New York statute prohibiting employers of bakery employees from permitting or requiring their employees to work more than sixty hours per week. In its decision in *Lochner v. New York*, the Court found that the "statute ... interferes with the right of contract between the employer and the employee." The Court derived "the substantive due process argument" from the Fourteenth Amendment, contending that the due process of law protected individual rights by establishing substantive limits on the breadth of federal and state legislation. The language of the First Amendment only prevents Congress from interfering with protected rights. The Fourteenth Amendment, adopted immediately after the Civil War in the context of Americans' concerns about state actions that violated civil rights, ensures a broader protection of the "privileges or immunities of citizens of the United States," as well as their "life, liberty, and property," from any state laws or actions. In *Lochner*, the Court found no justification, such as the need to protect public health, for allowing the states' police powers to interfere with protections of private contracts. It struck down the labor legislation as violating employers' and employees' rights to contract. The majority asked: "[A]re we all ... at the mercy of legislative majorities" in having them determine for us when or the how long we can labor?[57] Yet, Justice Harlan, in a

[57] *Lochner v. New York*, 198 US 45, 53, 59 (1905).

dissent, expressed the Progressive or Pragmatic view that would soon become national law:

I think it to be firmly established that what is called the liberty of contract may, within certain limits, be subjected to regulations designed or calculated to promote the general welfare ... [or] the public morals.[58]

Harlan explicitly declared his willingness to sacrifice individual freedoms to a group's or legislature's conception of the social good. Similarly, future dean of Harvard Law School, Roscoe Pound, condemned the majority decision as based on "the same kind of wrong-headed natural rights theory that was found in the Bill of Rights."[59]

Social reformers were equally appalled by the *Lochner* decision, and the Court slowly backed away from its defense of the contract clause. In 1908, it upheld a state law limiting a woman's workday to ten hours, predicating the variation from *Lochner* on gender differences.[60] With its ruling in the *Bunting* case nine years later, the Court effectively reversed the *Lochner* decision, upholding an Oregon law limiting hours of work.[61] The *Bunting* decision began a series of cases that slowly eroded contract clause protection in recognition of expanded police powers before 1937.

Many legal historians and commentators have seen in *Lochner* and other cases upholding the contract clause an instrumentalist defense of big-business interests. Barry Friedman writes: "[T]he judiciary grew in power by offering its backing to corporate and commercial interests that exercised enormous authority throughout the country."[62] But, the *Lochner* Court saw all Americans in the way the founders did, as legal equals despite potentially huge differences in wealth and status.

---

[58] *Lochner*, supra (Harlan dissent), at 67.
[59] Quoted in Linda Przybyszewski, *Religion, Morality, and the Constitutional Order* (Washington, DC: American Historical Association, 2011), 30.
[60] *Muller v. Oregon*, 208 US 412 (1908).
[61] *Bunting v. Oregon*, 243 US 426 (1917). But see *Adkins et al. v. Children's Hospital of the District of Columbia*, 261 US 525 (1923).
[62] Barry Friedman, *The Will of the People: How Public Opinion Has Influenced the Supreme Court and Shaped the Meaning of the Constitution* (New York: Farrar, Straus, and Giroux, 2009), 13. At 137, he adds: "The Court found its way to the center of the American stage by rendering decisions that catered to the needs of those who had power over it." Justice Oliver Wendell Holmes supported the idea that the law served as a tool or instrument used to address social needs. Oliver Wendall Holmes, "The Path of Law," *Harv. L. Rev.* 10 (March 1897): 457.

It favored nobody, but enforced the law equally. By the early 1900s, men such as Dewey, Pound, and Harlan saw legal equality as a legal fiction that could no longer be sustained. They argued that when the law remained neutral, treating owners and workers alike, it inevitably perpetuated social inequalities. Succinctly, legal equality created social inequality. New rights, given just to those without social power, would have to be created to serve social justice. As Louis Brandeis wrote sixteen years prior to his appointment to the Supreme Court, "Political, Social, and economic changes entail the recognition of new rights."[63]

This new conception of rights reinforced Christian goals for social justice and was vital to the success of the New Deal. Not surprisingly, much of the impetus for the New Deal came from religious impulses. Father John A. Ryan, credited by some with initiating the idea of the living wage, accepted an invitation to serve on President Franklin D. Roosevelt's National Recovery Administration (NRA) Industrial Appeals Board. He provoked limited controversy when he said that FDR and Pius XI shared an adversity to "laissez-faire, economic liberalism and so called rugged individualism." He proceeded to describe American individualism as "perverse" and an impediment to "social cohesion."[64] The Federal Council of Churches, the National Catholic Welfare Conferences, and the National Conference of Christians and Jews all supported New Deal programs to build a new social equality rooted in moral duty.

Of course, the moralistic basis for governmental paternalism developed in the New Deal reprised the old Federalist-Republican debate of the early republic over the extent to which majoritarian conceptions of moral duty could limit individual freedoms. The Federalists in the 1790s, like the Democrats in the 1930s, argued for government to have the power to define and prescribe a certain morality and impose responsibilities on individuals to uphold it. Yet, the old Federalists recognized the cost of this power. The relationship between government power and individual rights had historically functioned much like a playground seesaw or teeter-totter with the two concerns seated at opposite ends. When government power increased, individual rights

---

[63] Samuel D. Warren and Louis D. Brandeis, "The Right to Privacy," *Harv. L. Rev.* 4 (December 1890): 193.

[64] John Higham, *Send These to Me: Immigrants in Urban America* (Baltimore: Johns Hopkins University Press, 1984), 152–3 (quoted).

decreased, and vice versa. The metaphor remained legally significant into the 1930s. Justice Sutherland, dissenting in the *Blaisdell* case in 1934, argued that economic crises did not create government power that could limit individual rights. He saw the economic problems faced by the founders in the 1780s as being at least as severe as those of the 1930s.[65] Amid economic disaster, he insisted, the founders still saw fit to bar government from interfering with private rights to contract and hold property.

Yet, by 1934, the Court had begun conceiving of rights and government power as integrated forces serving the public interest. To effectuate this new understanding of the relationship between rights and public power, the Court had to weaken the contract clause. In *Nebbia*, Justice Roberts wrote for the majority that "neither property rights nor contract rights are absolute."[66] In *Schechter Poultry*, in 1935, the Court relied on the commerce clause, permitting Congressional regulation of interstate business activities rather than the contract clause, but still struck down the National Industrial Recovery Act.[67] The last use of contract clause protections by the Supreme Court to strike down legislation came in the *Tipaldo* case of 1936. Upholding its 1923 decision in *Adkins*, the Court held:

> The right to make contracts about one's affairs is a part of the liberty protected by the due process clause.... In making contracts ... the parties have equal right to obtain from each other the best terms they can by private bargaining. Legislative abridgement of that freedom can only be justified by the existence of exceptional circumstances. Freedom of contract is the general rule and restraint the exception.[68]

President Roosevelt's landslide victory in 1936 provided him the political capital to ask Congress to allow him to add one Justice to the Supreme Court for every Justice over the age of seventy who would not retire. He promised to "pack" the Court with up to six new members. When the Court showed a willingness to compromise, Congress rejected the President's plan. Beginning with a decision upholding a minimum-wage law for women, effectively overriding both *Adkins*

[65] *Home Building and Loan Association v.* Blaisdell, 290 US 398 (1934).

[66] *Nebbia v. New York*, 291 US 502, 537 (1934).

[67] *Schechter Poultry Comp. v. US*, 295 US 495 (1935).

[68] *Morehead v. New York, ex. rel. Tipaldo*, 298 US 587, 610 (1936).

and *Tipaldo*, the Court started to reverse course.[69] On April 12, 1937, in *National Labor Relations Board v. Jones and Laughlin Steel Corp.*, the Court upheld the Wagner Act under the commerce clause and instigated a new era of rights.[70]

That new era had its roots in the ideas of the late nineteenth century, a time of tremendous conflict and change masked in part by the general acceptance of one religion. The civil religion, rooted in a liberal Protestantism, arguably represented a shared faith that united Americans from the Civil War through the Great Depression. However, the history of that period indicates that the unifying power of the civil religion was more fiction than fact. It never accepted everyone, and its underlying values – morality, liberty, individualism, and conformity – may have seemed possible of integration in 1865 but appeared irreconcilable by 1937. The civil religion did not even appeal to all Protestants. Evangelicals and fundamentalists attempted to use their religious beliefs to defend creationism from Darwinian science, to enact laws banning sin (such as drinking, pornography, and Sabbath breaking), and to urge passage of a Christian amendment. Members of the Social Gospel movement and Christian socialists justified their calls for progressive taxation, business regulations, and consumer protection by their religious beliefs. Each group, be it majority or minority, sought to enlist law on its side, recognizing that in American society law served as the final arbiter. To create a society consistent with its beliefs, each group had to claim that law served those beliefs.

Between 1865 and 1937, Americans asked law to resolve conflicts between competing worldviews. The largest of these conflicts pitted individualists against communitarians, with the latter invoking a variety of religious beliefs in support of their goals. The Social Gospel influenced cultural values and attitudes more than it influenced law. It enjoyed its greatest success in reconfiguring the church-state relationship at the state level. Just as the disestablishment battles were won state by state, so too were new laws asserting the efficacy of Christian morality and social duties won by reformers at the state level. While liberal humanist ideas served as the intellectual umbrella for disestablishment from 1776 to 1833, the Social Gospel provided an ideological

---

[69] *West Coast Hotel v. Parrish*, 300 US 279 (1937).
[70] *National Labor Relations Board v. Jones and Laughlin Steel Corp.*, 301 US 1 (1937).

uniformity for legal reform in the late 1800s and early 1900s. It created interfaith organizations working together to do good and, in bringing divergent people together, presented a ground-level example of Pragmatism at work. The federal government did little to frustrate the reformers. As in all times since the founding of the nation, law tried to avoid resolving philosophical, political, and religious debates. The Supreme Court, so afraid of expanding judicial power into a political realm, refused even to consider using the First Amendment to address government action implicating religion. Accordingly, the Amendment remained relatively poorly understood as the general conceptions of religious freedom and separation of church and state, inherited from the founding era, gained the status of cultural icons while simultaneously being radically transformed.

The intellectual movements of the late 1800s and early 1900s that culminated in the growth of the doctrine of legal positivism expressed a desire for social change emanating largely from people left of center in the American political spectrum. Yet, ironically, their ideological expressions not only freed the churches from the limitations imposed on them by disestablishment but also enabled a crusade in the late twentieth century by socially conservative evangelical Christians to reform society consistent with their religious beliefs. In a confounding twist of logic, in the early twenty-first century, these socially conservative evangelicals would argue publicly for a return to "original intent" in the adjudication of Constitutional cases while simultaneously using arguments rooted in legal positivism and postmodernism to argue for public support for Christianity as a means of protecting the interests of a distinct "minority group" within a pluralistic society.

4

The Rights Revolution, 1937–2015

It is easy to perceive the last seventy-five years as encompassing so many extreme vicissitudes in the relationship between law and religion that they are better seen as constituting several distinct periods than a continuous one. Yet, these years can largely be defined through coincident changes in cultural attitudes and law that have reshaped the country's understanding of religious freedom. A new conception of rights as both created instead of natural and communal instead of individual, deriving from various permutations of Pragmatist thought, influenced the federal law on religion. Beginning in the late 1930s and 1940s, the Supreme Court used the Fourteenth Amendment as the basis for asserting these rights to address state actions threatening First Amendment protections of religion. The Court's early decisions separated the religion clauses, creating two somewhat conflicting and specific proscriptions on government action from what had been a general affirmation of a protected right to freedom of conscience. Yet, the Court's recognition of rights as belonging to groups served as the central legal formulation in the development of its new jurisprudence. Both the Court's assertion of group rights and its separation of the free exercise and establishment clauses have created tremendous confusion and a huge increase in political concern over the nature of freedom of conscience and the extent to which separation of church and state is necessary to protect it.

In recognition of the political rights of Christians as a group, the Court from the 1940s through the end of the century gradually moved from a doctrine of neutrality between religious and secular goals for society to a position of accommodation of policies and practices endorsed by religious groups as means of achieving their societal goals. At the same time, intellectual and cultural movements within American society increased awareness of group identities as stronger and potentially more important factors than protections of individual rights in preserving democratic self-government.

New Bases for Christian Activism Emerge, 1937–1960

Economic Rights versus Civil Rights

In his 1941 State of the Union Address, President Franklin D. Roosevelt asserted the legitimacy of Americans' expectations of freedom of speech, freedom of worship, freedom from want, and freedom from fear. However inspiring Roosevelt's message may have been, it was also an ahistorical assertion. The substitution of the right to worship for the right to exercise one's freedom of conscience can be seen as merely a politically expedient and substantively unimportant linguistic artifice. Yet, freedom of conscience, in recognizing every person's innate private right to form his or her own opinion regarding religious beliefs, morals, and values, implies a greater removal of religion from governing than does freedom to worship. Freedom of conscience protects an individual's right to refrain from worship and imposes a duty on government to respect that right. More significantly, the last two of the "four freedoms" require government action to create and fulfill. There is no natural right to be free from want or fear; in fact, humanity's natural state arguably predisposes people to fears and unrealizable desires. Roosevelt therefore was implicitly arguing for both the government's creation of rights and the power to effectuate them. As alleviating "want" can only come, if at all, through a reallocation of funds within society, freedom from want necessarily involves the denial of some peoples' economic rights. Politics and law worked together during this era to reconstruct rights as serving moral and public interests, with economic rights clearly subordinate to civil rights.

The founders understood no hierarchy of rights. In fact, the founders included the protection of economic rights in the contract clause, while they reserved protecting the rights of free speech, conscience, and other civil rights until ratification of the amendments. In the late 1930s the Supreme Court not only eschewed enforcement of the contract clause to enable greater governmental participation in the economy, but also delineated civil from economic rights to give extra protection to the former. Each decision portended tremendous changes in the nation's separation of private and public realms and of church and state.

In a footnote to its decision in *US v. Carolene Products*, in which the Court articulated its policy of deferring to state legislatures in passing laws reflecting cultural value judgments, the justices reserved the power to more scrupulously review legislation that may be "directed at particular religious, national, or ethnic minorities." The Court further noted that such "prejudice against discreet and insular minorities ... tends seriously to curtail the operation of those political processes ordinarily to be relied upon to protect minorities."[1] Several aspects of this ruling, which established bifurcated review of protected rights, raise legal questions regarding the right of conscience. First, in deciding to defer to states in legislating values, the Court gives broad discretion to state and local governments to use religion or morality as the basis for law. Second, in distinguishing economic from civil rights, the Court assumes the authority to find some rights more important than others and minimizes the role of the contract clause in American jurisprudence. As the separation of church and state arose as much out of the contract clause as the First Amendment, the concept of bifurcated review divorces the separation of church and state from the legal protection of private behavior. Third, in defining rights as belonging to groups of people as well as to individuals, and particularly identifying minorities as deserving of extra protection, the Court announced a jurisprudence in which certain rights pertaining only to certain groups may serve as the basis of legitimate legislative or judicial policies.

The bifurcation of rights asserted by the Court had no basis in earlier Constitutional understandings and arose instead purely from social considerations. The Court created the preferred position of civil rights relative to economic rights in recognition of civil rights having social value. As the idea of natural rights lost favor, rights that did not have social utility lost significance relative to those that did. The Chaffee, Brandeis, and Holmes arguments for the social utility of civil

---

[1] *United States v. Carolene Products*, 304 US 144, 152–3 (1938).

rights served as the true basis of a need for a new rights jurisprudence. The Court devalued economic rights in order to place economic interests on an equal legal footing with civil rights. A new legal formulation, in which rights no longer impeded governmental action, then served as the basis for renewed judicial interest in the religion clauses after 1940.

A New Ecumenism Masks Discontent

With the bifurcation of rights, lawyers, judges, and policy makers struggled to understand the nature of religious rights. Are they civil or economic? The bifurcation of rights, adopted in the context of asserting protection for identifiable groups of people, promised a reconsideration of religion as a matter of cultural values and traditions more than beliefs or practice and as a matter of group identity more than individual conscience. Values and traditions became aspects of group identities in forging a new cultural understanding of religion for much of the twentieth century.

One prominent example of this new understanding of religion in American culture involves the term "Judeo-Christian." When first used in the 1890s, it indicated a historical connection between the two great Western faiths while preferencing Christianity: Christianity had its roots in Judaism but had evolved from and thus beyond it. By the 1940s, the term took on a new, less religiously judgmental meaning, conveying a set of sociocultural values common to people professing either religion. Use of the term signaled Americans' acceptance of a shared Western cultural tradition rooted in both faiths and the beginning of a new religious inclusiveness that prevailed in the 1940s and 1950s.

Yet, before this new ecumenism could form a variant of the civil religion, it came under attack from Christians who resented its perceived latitudinarianism. The Niebuhr brothers and Paul Tillich came to embody a new breed of religious intellectual following World War II. Reinhold Niebuhr combined the rationality and social concerns of liberal religion with an emphasis on original sin. He contended that humans are neither as wise nor as virtuous as liberals want them to be. Extrapolating from the nature of humanity to form conclusions about the most appropriate form of government, just as both the founders and earlier Christians had done, Niebuhr argued for a greater societal recognition of Christian communitarian duties. He contended that individualism surfaced in Western society during the Renaissance, both in reaction to Catholic authoritarianism and in fulfillment of classical ideas. Yet, that individualism, as ultimately expressed in free-enterprise democracies, imperiled humanity and society. Niebuhr rejected both the idealism of American liberalism and the reformers' use of religion as a tool for the social good. Convinced of the realities of human sinfulness and societal depravity, he sought a tentative integration of Marxist collectivism, as a means to counter liberal individualism, and Christian orthodoxy, as a realistic expression of human nature and the duties of humanity. He thought that liberal Christians had eschewed religious reality in pursuit of an unrealizable social utopianism. German immigrant Paul Tillich echoed the Niebuhr brothers in arguing that Western society had put too much trust in human nature and the powers of democracy and capitalism. He called for new political and economic structures to compensate for human selfishness and weakness; Christianity must underlay these new structures.

The neo-orthodox scholars argued that humanity must believe in something greater than itself. American society in the 1940s and 1950s, asserting rights to freedom and moral relativism, failed to offer anything as superior to humanity. Niebuhr criticized American Protestants for their blind support of contemporary Western society. These critiques gained considerable traction in the late 1940s as Tillich and the Niebuhrs exerted influence far beyond their academic communities. The importance of neo-orthodoxy was that it convinced some Christians that the civil religion offered a path to destruction of both religion and society. Christianity, as a form of social criticism and a means of human improvement, could never become an instrument for political or national causes. It must remain a prophetic movement, and for that it could not accommodate the societal power structure.

The issues confronting Christian theology mirrored those confronting law during the postwar years. The immediate challenge for both religion and law arose from the realization that neither a reasoned jurisprudence derived from Enlightenment principles nor a sophisticated tradition of Christian theology had prevented the rise of Nazism in Germany. American intellectuals wondered whether American law and religion, alone or in combination, had the moral, cultural, and intellectual resources to overcome a similar threat. The rise of communism in the Soviet Union, its European satellites, and China only increased Americans' concern over the continued viability of its political, legal, and religious institutions.

Law and religion each addressed the need to remain true to revered texts and established doctrines while attempting to prevent an erosion of cultural values presented in totalitarian threats. Both tentatively offered a possibility of some form of moral certainty in a legal and cultural realm that regarded morality as a private and individual concern. The legal positivist movement, employing the principles of Pragmatism to the law, must be seen in this context. The concerns of the postwar era help explain the Court's acceptance of protection for group rights and an expanded role for law in shaping society.

The ecumenical movement embracing a theological commitment to explore shared moral convictions across religious doctrines also must be appreciated in the context of postwar worries and concerns. Americans flocked to their churches in the late 1940s and 1950s as much to feel some stability, certainty, and moral reassurance as to worship. The intellectuals leading the neo-orthodox movement responded in much the same way as other Americans did, pursuing a quest for moral certainty amid a recent history of ethnic and cultural persecutions, economic collapse, and creation of the means of immediate destruction.

The ecumenism in the late 1940s and 1950s presented a false unity and masked many unresolved dilemmas by ignoring denominational traditions and broad-based cultural desires for religious inerrancy. This last concern had been met periodically by fundamentalist movements, and certainly the growth of the new ecumenism benefited from the low visibility of the evangelical movement, which, in the postwar decades, existed largely in the Old South. Yet, evangelical Christians had no intention of leaving their country to the ecumenical liberals and secularists. In 1949, a new leader from Dallas, Texas, brought southern evangelism to a national audience, tempering it with a cosmopolitan sophistication that appealed to northern and eastern Christians. Reverend Billy Graham, benefiting from the supportive coverage of his Los Angeles crusade by the Hearst newspapers, appeared more conciliatory than many fundamentalists and less racist than many southern evangelicals; he offered a calm, attractive, masculine persona for the postwar years. With its leader in place, all the conservative Christians needed was a spark to energize the faithful. The Supreme Court provided not one but two sparks.

Postwar Society Brings Legal Change

Some of the earliest Supreme Court considerations of the free exercise clause arose through cases brought by Jehovah's Witnesses. Professing their acceptance of God's true laws, they expressed disdain for many of the legal and cultural values of the United States. Ironically, in suits brought in the 1930s and 1940s, Jehovah's Witnesses relied on what they called the "Satanic Law of America" – its "Godless Constitution" – to vindicate their rights to abstain from military service or recitation of the Pledge of Allegiance.[2]

In 1939, the Supreme Court denied a town the power to prohibit Jehovah's Witnesses from proselytizing in public. But, the Court reached its decision in reliance on the First Amendment's protection of speech, not its protection of the exercise of religion.[3] Just a few months later, the Court took the important step of incorporating the First Amendment's religion clauses into the Fourteenth Amendment's protection of individual rights.

On April 26, 1938, Newton Cantwell and his two sons, Jesse and Russell, claiming to be ordained ministers in the Jehovah's Witnesses, were arrested for breaking the peace and other minor criminal offenses. The men had stopped passersby on a city street in Hartford, Connecticut, to play for them a recording that the Supreme Court refers to as "propaganda" offering "a general attack on all organized religious systems as instruments of Satan and injurious to man." The Court, on hearing the case in 1940, found that the arrests violated the defendants' right to the free exercise of religion, the protection of which from state interference existed through the Fourteenth Amendment's incorporation of the free exercise clause of the First Amendment.

The *Cantwell* decision is certainly important for its incorporation of the free exercise clause, for the first time offering federal protection of religious freedom from state and local laws. Yet, just as important is the Court's explanation of the freedom it was protecting. The

[2] Quoted in Gordon, *Spirit of the Law*, 27–30, 41.
[3] *Schneider v. New Jersey*, 308 US 147 (1939).

Court refers to the free exercise clause as protecting a "freedom of conscience," using the founder's terminology connoting not merely a freedom to believe in and practice a religion of one's choice but also a freedom to abstain from religious belief. In addition, the decision denied to state governments the power to define religion and limited states' uses of their police powers in restriction of rights of conscience to instances justified by a "clear and present danger" to public safety. Yet, as broad as this protection might appear, the Court used utilitarian language potentially minimizing its protection of individual rights and, consistent with its ruling in the *Carolene Products* case, predicated rights protection on its expressed desire for diversity in seeming to focus as much, if not more, on groups as on individuals.

The essential characteristic of these liberties is, that under their shield many types of life, character, opinion, and belief can develop unmolested and unobstructed. Nowhere is this shield more necessary than in our country for a people composed of many races and of many creeds.[4]

The factual context for the decision also raised an interesting question, not so much at the time but for later advocates for a larger Christian role in public life. The term "public" can refer to that pertaining to the government, as the Court used the word in its *Dartmouth College* decision, or to that which is available to all in an open space, as a public park or even a shopping mall. The last example indicates the nature of the problem with the term, for while a shopping mall may be public, as it is open to all, it is also private, as being privately owned and operated. The distinction of public from private spheres expressed in these early free exercise cases recognized a right to preach or leaflet on public streets or in public parks but not in a store. The subsequent broadening of the legal understanding of public spaces to include private property would reject this earlier delineation. Perhaps more important, the granting of access to public areas does not imply public, as in governmental, support for the speech or activity for which the access was granted. While allowing people to distribute handbills in a public park expresses no public endorsement of the content of the handbills, erecting a crèche or cross on that same land at public expense certainly does. This distinction would arise in later decades

4 *Cantwell v. Connecticut*, 310 US 296, 303, 310 (1940).

as a source of controversy in establishment clause cases. In the short term, the Court followed its 1940 ruling in *Cantwell* with three 1943 decisions allowing the distribution of leaflets in support of a religious belief but refusing to protect activities not specifically noted in the First Amendment and striking down the requirement of a license for protected activities.[5]

Just two weeks after issuing its decision in *Cantwell*, the Court handed down yet another opinion concerning Jehovah's Witnesses. During the 1930s, many of the roughly 40,000 members of that organization refused to pledge allegiance to the flag, considering it to be worship of a "graven image." In 1935, Lillian and Billy Gobitas, children of Jehovah's Witnesses attending school in Pennsylvania, refused to recite the Pledge of Allegiance at the start of a school day and were expelled. At this time, the Pledge did not yet contain the words "under God." The Jehovah's Witnesses objected to the Pledge because it constituted paying fealty to a human creation, be it a nation, government, or flag. This fealty violated their religious freedom, they claimed, because it failed to respect the dictates that their beliefs imposed on them not to worship graven images.

Prior to the *Gobitis* case, the Pledge was not seen as implicating religious considerations. The Supreme Court of the Commonwealth of Massachusetts held, in 1937, that the Pledge has "nothing to do with religion."[6] Courts in California, Florida, Georgia, New Hampshire, and New York came to similar conclusions, upholding the power of public schools to discipline students for refusing to salute the flag or recite the Pledge. During trial in the Eastern District Court for Pennsylvania in 1937, Lillian Gobitas clearly raised free exercise concerns when she justified her refusal to recite the Pledge by quoting from I John 5:21, "Little children, keep yourselves from idols." The trial court found in favor of Lillian and her brother, asserting that requiring a pledge to the flag "seems to me utterly alien to the genius and spirit of our nation and destructive of that personal liberty of which the flag itself is the symbol." A mandatory pledge violated the

[5] *Jamison v. Texas*, 318 US 413 (1943); *Martin v. Struthers*, 319 US 141 (1943); *Murdock v. Pennsylvania*, 319 US 105 (1943).
[6] *Nicholls v. Moyer and City of Lynn*, 7 N.E. 2d 577, 580 (Mass., 1937).

"right to freedom of conscience."[7] The state appealed, and the case reached the Supreme Court.

Justice Felix Frankfurter wrote the opinion of the Court in the *Gobitis* case. He found the Pledge to implicate matters of religious freedom, but held that the liberty to one's religious convictions is of secondary importance to the need of the state to foster patriotism and national unity. Frankfurter contended that "[n]ational unity is the basis of national security," and that to ensure the nation's security, the law may tread on protected rights of its citizens.[8] The majority's opinion provoked an outcry from defenders of civil liberties, beginning with one of Frankfurter's colleagues on the Supreme Court. Justice Harlan Fiske Stone argued in dissent that "the constitutional guarantees of personal liberty are not always absolutes.... But it is a long step, and one which I am unable to take, to the position that government may, as a supposed educational measure and as a means of disciplining the young, compel public affirmations which violate their religious conscience."[9] In his dissent, Stone, who two years earlier had written the Court's opinion in the *Carolene Products* case, with its famed footnote 4, expressed the Court's growing acceptance of rights belonging to groups. He claimed that the religion clauses protect "the liberty of small minorities" and chastised Frankfurter for "surrender[ing] ... the liberty of small minorities to the popular will."[10] Stone could easily have asserted the need to protect individual liberties, including the right to freedom of conscience, from government or the rights of every American to be free from the tyranny of the majority. But he did not, focusing instead on minority rights.

Public opinion condemned the holding in the *Gobitis* case, empowering lower-court judges to deviate from its precedential importance. In 1943, the Court took the opportunity presented by a nearly identical fact situation to reverse itself. Yet, the majority, through Justice Robert Jackson, decided the *Barnette* case not on the basis of religious expression, but instead in reliance on freedom of speech.[11] To some

[7] *Gobitis v. Minersville School District*, 21 F. Supp. 581 (D.C. Pa., 1937) and 24 F Supp. 271 (D.C. Pa., 1938). The trial court recorder misspelled the family's last name, an error which was repeated as the case was appealed.
[8] *Minersville School District v. Gobitis*, 310 US 586, 599 (1940).
[9] *Gobitis*, supra, at 602 (Stone dissent).
[10] *Gobitis*, supra, at 606 (Stone dissent).
[11] *West Virginia Board of Education v. Barnette*, 319 US 625 (1943). Ironically, in this decision also, the court reporters misspelled the plaintiff's name, which was Barnett.

degree, Jackson's opinion mirrored the thinking of the Jeffersonians, who understood religious belief as a matter of conscience. Religious belief was one form of, or perhaps a part of, one's belief system or worldview. It was not particularly special or unique. Jackson even referred to the need for the courts to protect "intellectual individualism," sounding much like Jefferson himself.[12]

Yet, Jackson's decision, too, has been the subject of criticism. By eschewing reliance on the religion clauses, Jackson rendered a less specific decision than he might have, violating a major precept of American jurisprudence. Further, by once again expressing rights protection as justified by diversity, the Court expressed a utilitarian position on rights and implied that religious freedom attaches to groups at least as much as to individuals. Jackson wrote of the importance of protecting "the rich cultural diversities" of the American people. In addition, he redefined the public role as one of "neutrality" in matters of religion or politics while setting "secular instruction" as the public's educational goal.[13] Taken together, these passages have been read subsequently as creating a governmental responsibility to be neutral in regard to the religious claims or positions of various groups – to function as a type of arbiter between groups' beliefs rather than a protector of inviolable individual rights. This interpretation provided religious minorities the chance to assert political positions in the courts that could not be won legislatively.

In acting to advance group interests rather than private rights, the Court expanded its power into a realm normally reserved for Congress. At first, the minority groups whose interests were being advanced were fringe religionists, atheists, and secularists, but over time, evangelical Christians came to assert that they too constituted a minority in need of protection. Ironically, much of the criticism of the *Barnette* decision has focused on its reversal of one of the least popular aspects of Frankfurter's decision in *Gobitis*. Frankfurter argued that the courts were not the proper forum for resolving tension between religion and governance. As the Supreme Court has struggled to form and explain a consistent jurisprudence regarding the religion clauses, more and more

---

Both Justice Douglas and Justice Black wrote concurrences arguing that the majority decision should have been rooted in the free exercise clause.

[12] *Barnette*, supra, at 642.

[13] *Barnette*, supra, at 642, 637.

Americans are thinking that Frankfurter may have been correct, if not in his decision, at least in some of his reasoning.

While the early freedom-of-expression cases caused some consternation among liberals, the early establishment clause cases provoked near-hysteria among groups of Christians. Ironically, the first of these cases actually endorsed government aid to Christian education. The first case to use the Fourteenth Amendment as a means of applying the establishment clause to the states arose from a relatively long-standing practice of indirect state support of parochial schools. Beginning in the 1920s, Catholics lobbied their state legislatures to fund books and transportation attendant to private-school education. By the late 1940s, twenty-two states provided some funding for Catholic education, with at least thirteen of those states paying for busing students to parochial schools. Both lay Catholics and Catholic educators argued that the funding, instead of undermining the separation of church and state, supported the religious liberty that separation was intended to enhance. To force Catholic parents to pay for both public education and private education constituted a form of religious discrimination, they contended. While state courts that considered public support for busing to religious schools generally held that the practice violated state constitutions, the Supreme Court endorsed using public funds to buy textbooks for Catholic schools as early as 1930, contending that the benefit of the expenditures accrued to the children, not the schools or their church sponsors.[14] This argument became known as the "child benefit theory."

The Catholic campaign for public funding of private religious schools upset large numbers of Protestants and secularists, raising some of the same antagonisms that spawned the Blaine Amendment in the nineteenth century. President Truman's announcement, in 1946, that he planned to establish an ambassadorial post at the Vatican exacerbated the public anger. Protestant ministers and seminarians united to form one of the first Protestant political organizations of the twentieth century, Protestants and Other Americans United for the Separation of Church and State (POAU), in 1947. The POAU endorsed the late nineteenth-century model of separation, in which government

---

[14] *Cochran v. Louisiana State Board of Education*, 281 vs. 370 (1930).

could recognize and support a tepidly Christian moralism, but must abstain from direct support of any specific denomination or religion.

A law in effect in New Jersey during the 1940s allowed state funding of transportation to students going to private religious schools. A suit challenging the constitutionality of that law, *Everson v. Board of Education*, came before the Supreme Court in 1947.[15] In one way, the *Everson* decision continued the Court's practice developed in a long line of nineteenth-century cases of trumpeting the separation of church and state as a vital aspect of American freedom only to ignore its meaning or relevance in resolving the case at issue. All nine justices believed that the First Amendment separated church and state, and Justice Hugo Black even invoked Jefferson's metaphor of a wall as an appropriate explanation of the principle. However, the Court ultimately relied on the "child benefit" theory, looking at the group of people helped by the law rather than at the schools, which, despite their religious nature, were positioned merely as means to accomplishing the public interest, to uphold the New Jersey law as constitutional.

Yet, in other ways, the decision departed from the jurisprudence of the preceding century. First, the *Everson* case was the first in which the Court incorporated the establishment clause into the Fourteenth Amendment, providing an additional constitutional basis for separating church and state at the state level. Second, the Court asserted its authority to enforce the doctrine of separation against states that violated it. Third, the Court defined the establishment clause as prohibiting both support of any religious organization and the preferencing of one over another, articulating the doctrine of judicial neutrality.

Justice Rutledge, joined by three of his colleagues, wrote a scathing dissent to Black's majority opinion, leading liberal disgust with the Court's approval of public support for religious schools. The American Civil Liberties Union (ACLU) criticized the child benefit theory as a pragmatic political argument not rooted in law. Notes in both the *Harvard Law Review* and the *Cornell Law Quarterly* attacked the holding.

Much as the *Dartmouth College* decision provided a short-term victory for religious schools, only to turn into long-term defeat, so too did the *Everson* case. Even in the immediate aftermath of victory, many Christians worried that the Court's embrace of separation of church and

---

[15] *Everson v. Board of Education*, 330 US 1 (1947).

state had been too broadly expressed. The Court's language in *Everson*, especially its assertion of "neutrality," seemed to destroy government's ability to offer any support for a civil religion despite the holding in the case. The Court, seemingly, could not be trusted any more than educators and other well-educated elites could. As a result, some Christians increasingly saw the world divided between believers and nonbelievers, with communists and moral degenerates among the nonbelievers. Billy Graham and his evangelical movement fueled this perception of a divided society and found support for it in the Court's next critical decision.

In 1948, the Court justified the fears that Christian activists expressed after the *Everson* decision. In another Justice Black opinion, the Court, in *McCollum v. Board of Education*, held that after-hours religious instruction in public school classrooms contravened the establishment clause of the Constitution. Justice Frankfurter expressed strong support of strict separation in a concurring opinion:

> We are all agreed that the First and Fourteenth Amendments have a secular reach far more penetrating in the conduct of Government than merely to forbid an "established church." ... We renew our conviction that we have staked the very existence of our country on the faith that complete separation between state and religion is best for the state and best for religion.[16]

In Search of a New Consensus for 1950s America

The pace of Supreme Court cases interpreting the religion clauses slowed down in the 1950s. The decade produced a couple of significant decisions, but none provoked the controversy that those of the 1940s and 1960s produced. Yet, political activity from Christians during the decade sought to clarify, or redefine, depending on one's perspective, the relationship between church and state.

In 1955, the American Law Institute declared, "We deem it inappropriate for the government to attempt to control behavior that has no substantial significance except as to the morality of the actor."[17] Pronouncements of this type combined with the Supreme Court decisions of the 1940s both to weaken the civil religion and to alert more socially active Christians to the discrepancy between their worldview

[16] *McCollum v. Board of Education*, 333 US 203, 213 (1948).
[17] Quoted in Novak, *The People's Welfare*, 149.

and that defined by the Constitution. They reacted in the same way that earlier Christians, be they in 1789, 1863, or 1905, had reacted, by calling the Constitution "Godless" and seeking to amend it. In 1954, a proposal known as the Flanders Amendment was introduced in Congress. It read: "This nation devoutly recognizes the authority and law of Jesus Christ, Savior and Ruler of nations, through whom are bestowed the blessings of almighty God." The House failed to pass the amendment but could not stifle further Christian agitation. Evangelical Protestants and conservative Catholics found common cause as opponents of communism and liberal secularism, emphasizing that these enemies each embraced atheism. Noting that communist countries banned religion, they called religion a defining characteristic of democratic states. The logic was faulty, but the politics was successful. By turning the Cold War into a battle over religion, these Christians reasserted the bonds between Christianity and patriotism, in the process putting pressure on liberal-minded Americans to support Christian social policies as part of the defense of the free world. Billy Graham said, "Only as millions of Americans turn to Jesus Christ at this hour and accept him as Savior, can this nation possibly be spared the onslaught of a demon-possessed communism." He argued that the war must be fought at home as well as abroad, asserting the dangers that atheists, liberal secularists, and communists posed to the "American way of life." He endorsed Senator Joseph McCarthy's inquisition against known or suspected communists, expressing respect for those people "who, in the face of public denouncement and ridicule, go loyally on in their work of exposing the pinks and the reds who have sought refuge beneath the wings of the American eagle."[18]

The popular opinion of evangelical revivalism was higher in the 1950s than at any time since the 1800s. Billy Graham held prayer breakfasts at the White House, and books by two clergymen, Bishop Fulton Sheen and Reverend Norman Vincent Peale, topped the best-seller lists. The *Ten Commandments* and the *Greatest Story Ever Told* sold out movie theaters. During the decade, 96 percent of Americans asserted a belief in a God, and 64 percent maintained a formal religious affiliation. Yet, polls also indicate that fewer than half the people who believed the gospels to be absolutely true could name

[18] Quoted in Sehat, *Myth of American Religious Freedom*, 231, 235, 233.

even one of the four books. This seeming paradox is actually quite indicative of the desire for consensus and affiliation that defined 1950s America. Religious life, for the twenty years after World War II mirrored American culture in its appreciation of conformity and consensus. After two world wars and the Great Depression, Americans just wanted to enjoy life and to be free from argument, strife, and division. Democratic presidential candidate Adlai Stevenson said, "It is time for catching our breath – moderation is the spirit of the times." Social critic Walter Lippman similarly found that "for the first time in history, the engine of social progress has run out of the fuel of discontent."[19]

Therefore, despite numbers showing increases in religious practice, the decade is regarded by most historians as profoundly secular. Educated elites did not deny the truth of all religious beliefs, but at least wanted them relegated to a private sphere, and the mainline denominations seemed quite comfortable in respecting this separation. A general monotheism, embracing Christians, Jews, and Muslims, enabled Americans to remain religious without showing antipathy toward or excluding anyone – save atheists and communists. In 1955, Will Herberg published *Protestant-Catholic-Jew* to both great acclaim and high sales. Subordinating each of the three belief systems to a cultural imperative, Herberg wrote:

The American Way of Life is, at bottom, a spiritual structure, a structure of ideas and ideals, of aspirations and values, of beliefs and standards; it synthesizes all that commends itself to the American as the right, the good, and the true in actual life.[20]

America's new ecumenism, broader even than the inclusiveness intended in referencing Judeo-Christian culture, coexisted harmoniously with a pervasive secularism that dominated American public life from the mid-1940s to the 1970s. President Dwight D. Eisenhower embodied the 1950s about as well as any president ever could embody any era. Of the role of religion in governing he said that "our government makes no sense unless it is founded on a deeply felt religious faith, and I don't care what ... [that faith] is." Professor William

---

[19] Quoted in Martin E. Marty, *Modern American Religion*, Vol. III: *Under God, Indivisible, 1941–1960* (Chicago: University of Chicago Press, 1986), 7.

[20] Will Herberg, *Protestant-Catholic-Jew: An Essay in American Religious Sociology* (Garden City, NJ: Doubleday, 1955), 88.

Lee Miller of Yale Divinity School said of the president: "President Eisenhower, like many Americans, is a very fervent believer in a very vague religion."[21]

The new ecumenism of the 1950s conceived of religion as derived from universal human needs – in other words, it was rooted in human psychology. The anxieties of living in suburbia alienated from family, traditional communities of support, and neighborhood meeting places; of confronting imminent destruction and death through nuclear attack; and of the Cold War that conceived of the enemy as godless and immoral all fostered an increase in religious practices. Religious leaders, both Jewish and Christian, published books integrating religious belief and psychological well-being; Rabbi Joshua Loth Liebman wrote *Peace of Mind* in 1946, and Norman Vincent Peale wrote *The Guide to Confident Living* in 1948 and *The Power of Positive Thinking* in 1952. American policy and law seemed to justify an acceptance of some religion in the public sector in recognition of society's psychological dependence on faith – a far cry from basing establishment on the truth of the doctrine being endorsed. This recognition of public-sector responsibility to fulfill psychological as well as economic needs reflected a cultural acceptance of the growth of the welfare state. Popular acceptance of governmental involvement in the economy served as a precursor to government's more active role in people's religious lives.

By far the greatest political victory won by Christian activists during the 1950s was the amendment of the Pledge of Allegiance, by Congressional action, to include the words "under God." Yet, this mid-twentieth-century endorsement of the civil religion indicates the changes in that concept; it certainly is not evocative of the Protestant hegemony of the late 1800s. The "God" of the Pledge was used in support of political ends – as a weapon against communism and as a comfort to anxious Americans. It explicitly invoked the God of Jews, Catholics, Muslims, and Protestants alike.

The Cold War produced a tremendous change in the federal government's understanding of church-state relations that resulted more from economic expediency than from religious activism. Reflecting the growing acceptance of religion as a cultural characteristic distinguishing the

---

[21] Quoted in Gordon, *Spirit of the Law*, 50, 51.

United States from totalitarian and communist regimes, the federal government in the 1950s began to rely on private providers of social services, many of them religious organizations, to meet public needs, creating what has been termed the "allocative state." Initially, religious charities provided international relief from disasters and malnutrition, medical and hospital care, and educational assistance. Ironically, many Protestant groups, previously scornful of the charitable links between Catholics and the government in education and health care, by the 1950s and 1960s hoped to form relationships with the government to increase their own coffers. Baptists, Lutherans, and even independent evangelical churches, as well as ecumenical religious groups such as the Salvation Army, participated in the allocative state.

President Johnson's Great Society built considerably on the early efforts of the allocative state. The "War on Poverty" relied on an alliance between the federal government and local community organizations, many of which were religious in nature or were organized by churches, to build community networks for economic, educational, political, and psychoemotional growth of underprivileged Americans. Yet, government officials seemed blind, at least in their public statements, to the threat these programs posed to religious freedom. In 1966, the director of the Office of Economic Opportunity, Sargent Shriver, could say that "[t]hree or four years ago it was impossible for a federal agency to give a direct grant to a religious group; today we are giving hundreds of grants without violating the principle of separation of church and state."[22] As if mocking Shriver's words, thousands of Protestant and Catholic clergymen left their pulpits to administer antipoverty programs for the government through church-related agencies.

The development of the allocative state may well have generated the revival of a form of conservatism that values, or even depends on, an active national government to support religious institutions, promote Christian morality, and protect American capital. The political neoconservatives of the late 1900s and early twenty-first century employed a utilitarianism premised on conceptions of a strong central government as necessary to protect rights and interests and

---

[22] Quoted at Axel R. Schafter, *Piety and Public Funding: Evangelicals and the State in Modern America* (Philadelphia: University of Pennsylvania Press, 2012), 41.

in so doing invoked the same ideals of the old Federalist Party in New England. Neoconservatives give power to the public sector to define and circumscribe individual rights in furtherance of the goals of religious institutions and America's corporations. Once religious institutions realized the economic windfall to be gained from government aid, their supporters had to restructure their thinking regarding the use of public power. From public cooperation in religious charitable efforts, it is but a small step to public support of religious moralism.

The Court resisted socially disruptive rulings as it seemed to endorse America's ecumenical movement and accompanying desire for social harmony in the 1950s. The normally staunch defender of civil liberties and a strict separation of church and state, Justice William O. Douglas, wrote perhaps his oddest and most troubling opinion since the *Korematsu* decision in 1944. The *Zorach v. Clauson* case concerned a New York state policy that permitted students to leave schools for religious instruction in what was referred to as "released time." Released time involved no public expense, no use of public buildings or spaces, and no endorsement by teachers or any public officials of any religion. The justices could quite easily have decided the case on grounds that the 1940 released time law contained in the Coudert-McLaughlin Religious Instruction Bill recognized a student's right to the free exercise of conscience without requiring any public pronouncement or expenditure that might implicate the establishment clause. In fact, the justices did uphold the law. Yet, Justice Douglas included extensive dicta in his opinion, confusing both his contemporaries and future generations. Douglas wrote:

There cannot be the slightest doubt that the First Amendment reflects the philosophy that church and state should be separated. And so far as interference with the "free exercise" of religion and an "establishment" of religion are concerned, the separation must be complete and unequivocal. The First Amendment within the scope of its coverage permits no exception; the prohibition is absolute. The First Amendment, however, does not say that in every and all respects there shall be a separation of church and state.

Just what did Douglas mean by the assertion that separation is not required "in every and all respects"? People are still confused by and debating those words. Compounding the problems posed by interpreting the ruling, Douglas added, "We are a religious people whose institutions presuppose a Supreme Being."[23] Clearly, Douglas excludes atheists from his conception of "We," the American people. Moreover, just what public institutions "presuppose a Supreme Being"? Three justices filed dissents to what was seemingly an easy decision. Justice Black expressed shock at Douglas's wording. Justice Jackson accused Douglas of having "warped and twisted" the wall of separation.[24] Even though Douglas later recanted the statements he made in the *Zorach* opinion, they would form the basis of powerful legal arguments by conservative religious groups for the next fifty-some years.

While liberals expressed confusion over the *Zorach* decision, conservative Christians expressed outright anger at a decision two years later, in 1954. Several New Jersey school districts allowed the Gideons, a nonprofit private voluntary association dedicated to distributing bibles, to enter school premises to hand out copies of the New Testament to students. This case, too, could have been resolved on strict public-private grounds: giving access to public buildings to a private religious group can be seen as public endorsement of religion – a form of establishment. However, the New Jersey Supreme Court found the practice unconstitutional in discriminating against non-Christians. In ruling in this way the state court accepted both the protection of group rights and the concern for social equality that the federal courts had previously expressed. The Supreme Court of the United States refused *certiorari*, for all practical purposes endorsing the state court's decision.[25] Billy Graham, implicitly recognizing public endorsement of religion as vital to democracy, called the decision "a tremendous contribution to the communist cause."[26]

The most politically significant court decisions of the 1950s concerned what were known as "captive schools" and were issued by state courts. During the 1930s and 1940s, hundreds of municipalities across the country used Catholic school buildings to teach public school students. To save money while still meeting the needs of growing populations of schoolchildren, public school districts paid rent to the Catholic churches that ran the schools and the salaries of the priests and nuns

---

[23] *Zorach v. Clauson,* 343 US 306, 312, 313 (1952).

[24] Ibid., at 325 (Jackson dissent).

[25] *Tudor v. Board of Education of the Borough of Rutherford, New Jersey,* 100, A.2d 857 (1953); cert. denied 348 US 816 (1954).

[26] Quoted in Dierenfield, *Battle over School Prayer,* 64.

who taught there rather than build and staff new schools. Following the court's decisions in *Everson* and *McCollum*, the captive-school phenomenon became legally untenable. In the early 1950s, the POAU and the ACLU combined to win court victories holding that captive schools violate both state and federal constitutions, and by the mid-1950s, states opted to build their own schools.[27]

Despite the seeming placidity of the 1950s, tensions simmered below the surface of society. Discontent among women and African Americans and an incipient frustration with conformity, as depicted in the popular book and movie, *The Man in the Grey Flannel Suit*, would erupt in the next decade. Change was coming, and many conservative Christians, especially in the South, saw it over the horizon. Prayer and Bible use in school classrooms came under increased legal scrutiny in the fifties. Early rock and roll, bebop, and jazz; experimentation with drugs; and a perceived increase in what was termed "juvenile delinquency" were seen by many as products of permissive parenting of the Dr. Spock variety or, as Billy Graham put it, "the sin of tolerance in moral issues."[28] Yet, America just was not ready for controversy over religion, morality, or much of anything else.

Consensus Is Shattered in Social Revolution

The Sixties Bring Secular Revival and New Rights Protection
The social reform movements of the 1960s largely have been understood as seeking equality from a perspective of a communitarian quest for social justice among a diverse population. Certainly the impetus for the Court to build on the idea of group rights came from legitimate concerns driven by the civil rights movement and a perception that legal equality could only be achieved through a greater degree of social equality. Yet, the era also expressed a fervent libertarianism that recognized equality as a freedom to "do your own thing." Reverend Martin Luther King Jr.'s calls for social harmony and equality can be seen as uniting these two perspectives. In his calls for civil rights, he expressed a Jeffersonian conception of individual rights and freedoms,

---

[27] *Zellers v. Huff*, 236 P.2d 949 (N.M. 1951); *Berghorn v. Reorganized School District #8*, 260 S.W. 2d 573 (Mo. 1953).
[28] Quoted in Sehat, *Myth of American Religious Freedom*, 231.

only loosely sheathed in a cloth of religious duty. Writing from a Birmingham, Alabama jail cell in 1963, King premised civil disobedience on the dictates of both God and natural law to violate unjust laws. For King, Christianity compelled an individual moral choice to seek justice, and in this conception of his religion he spoke not only for African Americans but for millions of liberal white Christians who perceived his message of human equality and peaceful protest to embody the example of Jesus. Expressing a similar conception of religious duty, the rock band Crosby, Stills, Nash, and Young, during a live concert recording in 1970, encouraged their listeners to remember that "Jesus was the first non-violent revolutionary."

Churches and courts both reconsidered the social significance of religion in American society. The Presbyterian Church declared, "[W]e have no right to claim that ours is and always has been a Christian nation."[29] Sermons of the time stressed the importance of exercising individual autonomy within a Christian context of doing good. While the Berrigan brothers and Father Groppi made national headlines, hundreds of ministers from various denominations participated in civil rights marches and protested against the war in Vietnam. The politicization of religion occurred as federal courts eliminated support for nonsectarian Christianity as the religion of the republic. Finding any public endorsement of religion constitutionally illegitimate, the courts returned to the founders' intentions to confine religious expression to the private sphere.

Both libertarianism and an appreciation of human diversity embody a respect for the rights of people to come to different conclusions regarding what the founders referred to as "matters of conscience" – religious beliefs and moral judgments. In this intellectual climate, liberal Christians stopped claiming to speak for a majority of Americans, the idea of a civil religion ceased to have any relevance, and the Supreme Court returned to treating religion as a matter of conscience. In 1964, the Court protected Black Muslims in the exercise of their religious beliefs, and that same year the Supreme Court of California protected smoking peyote as "the essence of [a particular]

---

[29] Quoted in John F. Wilson and Donald L. Drakeman, eds., *Church and State in American History: Key Documents, Decisions, and Commentary from the Past Three Centuries*, 3rd ed. (Cambridge, MA: Westview Press, 2003), 273.

religious expression."[30] In 1965, the Court interpreted a federal law granting military draft exemptions to those whose religious beliefs prevented them from taking up arms to include those whose refusal to fight was "sincere and meaningful" and rooted in a belief as important "in the life of its possessor ... to that filled by the orthodox belief in God." The decision changed the idea of "religious objection" to "conscientious objection." Justice Douglas, in concurrence, added that this right to abstain from military service applied equally to atheists and other irreligious people.[31]

Liberals probably failed to appreciate the degree to which traditional religious attitudes and beliefs defined the world for a great many Christian Americans, especially in the South. Court decisions during the 1960s that failed to respect these attitudes and beliefs seemed, to these Christians, to be impositions of a new value system, one rooted in immorality, that threatened to change their world forever. In 1961, the Court found all state requirements of test oaths or assertions of a belief in a God to violate the Constitution. In 1962, the Supreme Court banned sponsored prayer in public schools; in 1963, it banned sponsored Bible reading. In 1964 and 1967, state laws prohibiting interracial marriage were found unconstitutional. In 1965, a ban on contraceptives was likewise deemed unconstitutional. In 1969, the Court greatly limited the powers of the state to punish people for possessing pornographic materials. In 1971, the Court protected free expression even in the use of vulgarities printed on items of clothing, and in 1973, it greatly restricted the power of states to control if, when, and for what reason a woman might have an abortion.[32] Together these decisions held that the state could not impose conceptions of morality on individuals without showing an imminent danger to the health and safety of the public and that the state was similarly prohibited from using its power or money in support of a generic Christian theology.

---

[30] *Cooper v. Pate*, 378 US 546 (1964); *People v. Woody*, 394 F.2d 813 (Cal. Sup. Ct., 1964).

[31] *United States v. Seeger*, 380 US 165, 166 (1965).

[32] *Torcaso v. Watkins*, 367 US 488 (1961); re: prayer, *Engel v. Vitale*, 370 US 421 (1962); re: Bible reading, *School District of Abingdon v. Schempp* and *Murray v. Curlett*, 374 US 203 (1963); *McLaughlin v. Florida*, 379 US 184 (1964); *Loving v. Virginia*, 388 US 1 (1967); *Griswold v. Connecticut*, 381 US 479; *Stanley v. Georgia*, 394 US 557 (1969); *Cohen v. California*, 403 US 15 (1971); *Roe v. Wade*, 410 US 113 (1973).

The most controversial of these cases at the time concerned state-sponsored school prayer. During the 1950s, concern over teenage behavior, from loitering and wasting time to violent gang activities, increased tremendously. The term "juvenile delinquency" came to express a wide range of actions deemed socially unacceptable. By 1953, more than 1 million teens were being charged with crimes each year, a 45 percent increase from 1945. Plays and movies such as *West Side Story*, *The Wild One*, and *The Blackboard Jungle* depicted society's alarm over teenagers' behavior. In 1955, the New York State Board of Regents suggested that a morning prayer in the schools might reduce juvenile delinquency. The board framed a broadly ecumenical prayer worded as follows: "Almighty God, we acknowledge our dependence upon Thee, and we beg Thy blessings upon us, our parents, our teachers, and our country." The language truly was nondenominational and discriminated against neither Jews nor Muslims. Yet, it did express providential beliefs. It expressed humanity as subject to God's blessings and grace. In asserting human dependency on God, it conveyed a message of frailty, weakness, and submission – a lesson consciously to be taught relative to parents, teachers, and the country, as well as to God. In fact, the regents noted that the prayer was intended to foster "respect for lawful authority and obedience to law" through its invocation of God's blessings.[33] In this way it taught children that they do not control their own fates; they must seek help from a spiritual source.

The Herricks School Board adopted the Regents' prayer in August 1958. Lawrence Roth, a resident of the Herricks district, asserted that "religious training is the prerogative of parents and not the duty of the state." Roth, the father of two children in the district, contacted the ACLU and recruited other residents to join his cause. Monroe Lerner, in joining the suit, said that the prayer was either a "mockery" of a sacred act or an "imposition" on nonbelievers. In the aftermath of the *Zorach* decision, many in the ACLU questioned the merits of challenging the New York prayer. Leo Pfeffer, probably the leading legal scholar of the time on the issue of church-state relations, cautioned against litigating, because the prayer itself was so ecumenical that it offended only atheists. Arguing that better facts make better law, he

[33] Quoted in Dierenfield, *Battle over School Prayer*, 67.

preferred to challenge a Pennsylvania school code requiring the reading of ten or more verses from the King James Bible to begin every school day – a practice offensive to Jews, Catholics, and even some Protestants, as well as to atheists. The Pennsylvania law would, in fact, be the subject of the *Abingdon v. Schempp* case decided in 1963.

Despite Pfeffer's concern, the case of *Engel v. Vitale* challenging the New York law went to trial on February 24, 1959. Several commentators described the plaintiffs as atheists, and the evening *Long Island Post* from February 24 contained a column by George Sokolsky asking, "Why are these people in Herricks so afraid of God?"[34] He missed the point. Atheists, as many evangelicals subsequently have noted, do not fear God. Nor do they want their children to grow up fearing a figure they consider no more real than Santa Clause. Yet, they do have good reason for fearing people they consider delusional – those who ask guidance from, devote their lives to, and even make social and political decisions in accordance with the perceived wishes of an entity that, to the atheists, does not exist. However, the plaintiffs in the *Engel* case, while defending the legal rights of atheists to have their children educated in public schools without the taint of being taught from a religious perspective, were themselves not atheists. Two devout Jewish plaintiffs simply objected to praying in English without covering one's head.

The trial court issued a sixty-seven-page ruling in favor of the regents, relying in large part on language from the *Zorach* decision. The New York Supreme Court affirmed the decision in 1960, and the State Court of Appeals, the highest tribunal in New York, affirmed it in 1961. Before the US Supreme Court, William Butler, lead attorney for the plaintiffs, had to distinguish his case from *Zorach*. He argued that allowing citizens to leave a public setting to engage in private religious exercises constituted a very different practice from requiring citizens' presence in a public building while public employees oversaw or participated in the conduct of religious exercises. In a 6–1 decision (Justice Frankfurter was too ill to participate and soon left the bench, and Justice Byron White was too new to take part) issued on June 25, 1962, the Court held that any sponsored prayer in a public school violated the establishment clause

---

[34] Quoted in ibid., 91, 99, 113.

of the US Constitution.[35] In a concurring opinion, Justice Douglas corrected himself for what by 1962 seemed to be errors in judgment expressed in his *Zorach* opinion. He clearly asserted that any aid given to religion by any government in the United States was unconstitutional. He asserted that military chaplains, the printing of "In God We Trust" on money or courthouse walls, the tax exemptions given to churches and for religious donations, and congressional prayers all should be eliminated as unconstitutional actions.[36]

The Supreme Court had clarified its position on separation, returning to a judicial acceptance of Jeffersonian and Madisonian thought regarding religion as a private matter. The Court probably came closer to the founders' perceptions of religion as a private concern during the 1960s than at any other time in its history. Court members sounded much like Madison and Jefferson in expressing that the separation of church and state must be understood to protect people from any state endorsement or sponsorship of religion and, of course, also from the duty to pay for such endorsement or sponsorship. The First Amendment protects a right of conscience, and any government action endorsing even the most benign religious belief necessarily constitutes a violation of myriad individuals' rights of conscience. But law once again faced attacks from the political arena.

Liberals saw the *Engel* decision as liberating people from the tyranny of civil religion, much as the *Brown v. Board of Education* ruling had liberated people from Jim Crow. Yet, the overwhelming majority of Americans were troubled by the Court's holding. Such ideologically temperate organizations as the General Federation of Women's Clubs and the American Legion expressed formal dissatisfaction with the *Engel* decision. Somehow most Americans had not seen prayer in the public schools as violating the doctrine of separation. They could espouse the separation of church and state as an American virtue and still support school prayer. After 1963, Christian groups began arguing that the whole idea of separation was created long after the founding and should not be a basis of law.

Some Christians became so outraged over the *Engel* decision that they formed private voluntary associations to work to overturn the

[35] *Engel v. Vitale*, 370 US 429 (1947).
[36] Ibid. (Douglas conc.).

ruling. A group named Prayer Rights for American Youth sued the State of New York for "an opportunity to express their love and affection to almighty God each day through a prayer in their respective classrooms."[37] The Second Circuit Court of Appeals rejected the plaintiff's argument, asserting that the children in question have plenty of time to pray before 9:00 in the morning and after 3:00 in the afternoon.[38] Politicians nationwide reacted to the public outrage over the *Engel* decision by calling for a constitutional amendment to allow religious expression in public buildings. Every governor, except New York's Republican Nelson Rockefeller, endorsed the idea of an amendment. Southerners expressed the greatest anger. Alabama Congressman George Andrews said of the Justices of the Supreme Court, "They put the Negroes in the schools; now they take God out of the schools." Georgia Senator Herman Talmadge called the *Engel* decision "an outrageous edict [that] set up atheism as a new religion." Virginia's Democratic Senator A. Willis Robertson, father of evangelist Pat Robertson, actually threatened the Justices of the Supreme Court, telling those who side with atheists and agnostics in future cases that they do so "at your peril." Several congressmen accused the Supreme Court of making law rather than interpreting or enforcing it.[39]

Yet, the *Engel* decision serves as a reminder to Americans of the intentions behind their Constitution. Prayer and Bible reading had been removed from many public classrooms in the late 1700s and early 1800s. To the extent that any laws contravened the constitutional expressions on religion, it was those that had established a civil religion. Legal historians who see the *Engel* case and others from the same time as merely recognizing social change do the Court a disservice. Certainly, as argued in these pages, law responds to both intellectual movements and societal conditions. Yet, the Court and American law do not conform to social change so much as they moderate or govern that change by adhering to established principles, precedent, and legal history. The logical incorporation of the religion clauses into the Fourteenth Amendment inevitably would produce challenges to the states' endorsement of a civil religion. Those challenges came about

---

[37] Quoted in Dierenfield, *Battle over School Prayer*, 184.
[38] *Stein v. Oshinsky*, 348 F.2d 299 (2nd Circ., 1965); cert. denied 382 US 957 (1965).
[39] Quoted in Dierenfield, *Battle over School Prayer*, 146, 147.

in less than twenty years. When given the chance to decide them, the Court turned to the founder's intentions as much as to the prevailing ideas of the time.

No sect of Christians demands, as Islam does, that Christians pray at certain times, repeatedly during the day, or even daily. Furthermore, the Court did not ban individual prayers, whether silent or audible, at lunch, between classes, or in private areas on school property. The concern expressed by Christians does not derive from an inability to practice their religion, but rather from a disappointment that the government cannot endorse their religion – and, probably more important, teach values, morals, and social behaviors consistent with it. This is exactly what the founders did not want government to do.

Just one year after issuing the *Engel* decision, the Court banned sponsored Bible reading in public schools. Returning to the logic of the *Dartmouth* decision and the important distinction between public and private spheres, Justice Clark stated that "religious ceremonies in church-supported private schools are constitutionally unobjectionable," but they cannot be held in public schools. Any state laws addressing religion must have (1) "a secular legislative purpose" and (2) "a primary effect that neither advances nor inhibits religion."[40] In response, Reverend Billy Graham focused on societal considerations and seemed to be defending American security as much as or more so than Christianity:

At a time when moral decadence is evident on every hand, when race tension is mounting, when the threat of communism is growing, when terrifying new weapons of destruction are being created, we need more religion, not less.[41]

Graham's statement indicates the degree to which some American Christians saw their religion, their nationalism, their morals and values, and their economic well-being as all of one piece, both for themselves and for their society. A challenge to one aspect of this integrated worldview necessarily challenged every other aspect of it, much like pulling a loose thread from a woven scarf risks unraveling the entire scarf. This worldview does not confine religion to a private sphere and respects no private realm in which morals and values, as directives for life given to humanity by God, do not have relevance. The Court's

---

[40] *Abington v. Schempp*, 374 US 203 (1963).
[41] Quoted in Dierenfield, *Battle over School Prayer*, 179.

decisions dealing with privacy, perhaps even more than those addressing prayer and Bible reading in the schools, challenged that worldview.

In 1965, Justice Douglas wrote what many legal historians and commentators consider the greatest expression of his liberal rights–oriented jurisprudence. In *Griswold v. Connecticut*, the Supreme Court found unconstitutional a state law that made it a crime to use "any drug, medicinal article or instrument" to control pregnancy. It also overturned convictions of leaders of the Planned Parenthood League of Connecticut on grounds that they had provided prohibited articles to couples and thereby abetted them in the performance of a crime.[42] Douglas cited the Court's 1958 decision in *NAACP v. Alabama*, in which the Court protected "freedom to associate and privacy in one's associations."[43] Douglas then explained that the "specific guarantees in the Bill of Rights have penumbras, formed by emanations from those guarantees that help give them life and substance. Various guarantees create zones of privacy."[44] Just four years later, Justice Thurgood Marshall used the same reasoning to strike down a Georgia law that made it a criminal offense to view pornography, even in one's own home. Marshall protected "the right to be let alone – the most comprehensive of rights and the right most valued by civilized man." He added:

If the First Amendment means anything, it means that a State has no business telling a man, sitting alone in his house, what books he may read or what films he may watch.... [The state cannot attempt] to control the moral content of a person's thoughts.[45]

No decision ultimately galvanized evangelical Christians to politicize their cause more than *Roe v. Wade*, decided in 1973.[46] The Court therein found a woman's decision to have an abortion to be a private choice involving moral and considerations. Law can only interfere with a woman's choice when equal or greater rights of another individual require legal protection. Based on medical testimony, the Court found that a fetus could potentially be viable six months after

---

[42] *Griswold v. Connecticut*, 381 US 479 (1965).
[43] *NAACP v Alabama*, 357 US 449 (1958).
[44] *Griswold*, supra at 484.
[45] *Stanley v. Georgia*, 394 US 557, 564, 565 (1969).
[46] *Roe v. Wade*, 410 US 113 (1973).

conception and therefore due legal protection as of that time. Before then, a woman's right to choose what she wants to do with her body is not an appropriate realm for state regulation. The *Roe v. Wade* decision continued a line of cases recognizing women as individuals – rather than as wives, mothers, and domestic functionaries – and reasserted that morals are products of individual conscience and therefore private, not public, considerations. The abortion issue since 1973 has served as a new and bitter battleground for Americans with different worldviews.

Evangelical arguments made in the 1960s and 1970s mirrored those of the Black Muslims and the Jehovah's Witnesses in their denigration of the legal principles and institutions of the United States, seeming to encourage a form of civil disobedience. Social conservatives attacked the godlessness of the Constitution, the errors of the Supreme Court, and the permissiveness of state and local laws. Yet, given their conservative inclinations, they wanted to support the country's laws. To hold these conflicting ideas, they had to argue that the current law was a perversion of the nation's true legal principles and deserved to be rewritten. Billy Graham complained that law had come to serve the subversive goals of racial, sexual, and religious equality. Numerous Christian authors, perhaps most notably Francis Schaeffer, attempted to rewrite the history of the founding, in the process arguing against George Washington's assertion that the United States had not been created as a Christian nation. As the country reconsidered its history and values, old legal arguments resurfaced.

The Supreme Court never had a chance to consider the *Scopes* case under the religion clauses of the First Amendment. Perhaps surprisingly, the teaching of evolution versus creation remained an issue into the 1960s, finally providing the Court with that opportunity. In 1965, a biology teacher in Little Rock, Arkansas, Susan Epperson, acting for the state teachers' union, filed suit challenging a statewide prohibition on the teaching of evolution. The trial court found the statute unconstitutional, but the Arkansas Supreme Court held the law to be "a valid exercise of the state's police power to specify the curriculum in its public schools."[47] The US Supreme Court reversed the state court's opinion, in the process applying the "secular legislative

---

[47] *Epperson v. Arkansas*, 393 US 97 (1968).

purpose" test articulated in *Abington v. Schempp*. Justice Fortas, writing for the Court, considered all antievolution laws to be derivatives of Tennessee's law, which intended to make it unlawful "to teach any theory that denies the story of Divine creation of man as taught in the Bible," clearly finding their purpose in religious, not secular teachings. He added that the government must be "neutral" in matters of religion.[48]

Using both the language in the *Schempp* decision and growing popular understandings of the role of government under the First Amendment to be that of a neutral, subsequent fundamentalists have argued that public schools must assume a stance of neutrality between advancing creationism – promoting Christianity – and evolution – promoting atheism. Tennessee led the country in adopting this argument in a 1973 statute and was soon followed by six other states.[49] Afterward, evangelical Christians Henry Morris and Tim LaHaye coined the term "intelligent design" and marketed it as a means of teaching the Biblical creation story accommodated to an awareness of science. In the near future, the idea of intelligent design would be combined with the argument that secular humanism formed a religion and that multiculturalism required equal consideration of Christian doctrine. From this conceptual basis evangelicals asserted that religious nondiscrimination required the teaching of intelligent design alongside evolution in the public schools. However, by the 1970s, most evangelicals perceived the greatest threat to their worldview to come not from science but from the social sciences and humanities.

The Court's rights-based decisions dealing with religion in the 1960s produced a reactionary political movement rooted in religion similar to that which arose in the Second Awakening. This conservative politicization of religion had the effect of dividing Christians into two camps. Mainline Protestant churches lost congregants in the 1960s because their ministers failed to convince more traditional parishioners of the utilitarian construction of the Bible as moralistic

---

[48] Ibid., 108

[49] In 1982, a federal court found these legislative acts unconstitutional under the First Amendment. Judge Overton further declared that evolution is not a religion and creationism is not a science. *McLean v. Arkansas Board of Education*, 529 F. Supp. 1255, (E.D. Ark., 1982). The Supreme Court reached a similar conclusion in *Edward v. Aguillard*, 482 US 578 (1987).

parables that offered social direction in a relativistic world. Clergy within the mainline churches largely supported civil rights and environmental legislation and opposed the Vietnam War. Evangelical conservatives within these churches resented the clerical support of liberal causes and flocked to nondenominational evangelical churches in the late 1970s and 1980s.

Political realignment accompanied the religious division that arose in the late 1960s. The Republican Party had formed and prospered through a reassertion of the primacy of individual rights and an endorsement of social change. The Party, since its founding in the 1850s, had been committed not only to the protection of property rights from governmental interference but also civil rights. The Party originated, in large part, to limit or abolish slavery, and after the Civil War, it recognized the value of women's suffrage while championing voting rights for the freed slaves. The Party's assertions of racial equality so alienated white voters in the Jim Crow South that the region became known as the "Solid South" for its predictable Democratic voting patterns from the 1880s until 1968. While social equality remained beyond the purview of law, conceptions of legal equality influenced Party positions on economic issues. Theodore Roosevelt, in the early 1900s, endorsed legal limitations on trusts and monopolies, a position also taken by Adam Smith in the 1770s, to protect the economic freedoms of all Americans.

Richard Nixon began a change in Republican Party strategy while campaigning for the presidency. Nixon asserted the need for government to protect the social order through law. Inevitably, that law would limit some individual freedoms. In this reconceptualization of the Party's position on law and order, he endorsed Christian communitarian ideals that asserted citizens' duties to behave as components of an integrated social whole. Ignoring the language of the Constitution as well as the idea from social contract theory that while people have rights, states can only exercise powers, Nixon reasserted the old "states rights" argument from the antebellum era to allow state legislatures the authority to act in support of their parochial cultures without interference from the liberal, rights-oriented federal courts. He found support from Billy Graham, who encouraged Americans to turn away from dissensions and protests and to accept Jesus, law, and order. Graham's understanding of Jesus was not as "the first non-violent revolutionary," not as the man who overturned the moneylenders' tables or made a sacrilegious procession into Jerusalem on a Jewish holy day. Rather, Reverend Graham, appearing with Nixon throughout his campaign (see Figure 4.1), reminded his listeners that Jesus instructed people to obey public leaders. Much like earlier conservatives such as Edmund Burke, James Kent, or Timothy Dwight, he saw religion as a necessary part of the social order – a basis for popular acceptance of law and authority. In this framework, law, based on religious values promoting social conformity and moral behavior, worked to limit individual freedoms in order to serve the social good. In 1969, Republican strategist Kevin Phillips explained that the new Republican Party would appeal to "apprehensive bourgeois and law-and-order seeking individuals" with "a proclivity to authoritarianism."[50]

The Seventies Polarize American Cultural Politics

During the 1970s, each of the two major political parties struggled to develop its position relative to the other. The first presidential candidate to claim status as a "born again" Christian and to argue for Christian duty as a component of American citizenship, Jimmy Carter, was a southern Democrat. Meanwhile, the influence of moral conservatism remained minimal in the Republican White House of President Gerald Ford. In 1975, First Lady Betty Ford said, in a national television interview, that she condoned abortion, sex outside of marriage, and legalizing marijuana. Her public approval ratings increased after the broadcast.

Aside from the *Roe v. Wade* case, the 1970s brought little change to established legal doctrines. Despite the promises for dismantling the unofficial Protestant establishment, or civil religion, indicated by the Supreme Court's postwar decisions, the Court in 1970 let stand the tax-exempt status of churches. New Chief Justice Warren Burger wrote the opinion, agreed to by an 8–1 majority. He noted that "[t]he Establishment and Free Exercise Clauses of the First Amendment are not the most precisely drawn portions of the Constitution," and that previous decisions evinced "considerable internal inconsistency."[51] Yet, it is an accepted role of the Court to clarify imprecise language and to

---

[50] Quoted in Sehat, *Myth of American Religious Freedom*, 256.
[51] *Walz v. Tax Commission* 397 US 664–8 (1970).

FIGURE 4.1. Richard M. Nixon with Billy Graham at a Billy Graham Crusade. A new Republican Party alliance with evangelicals in 1968 gave political voice to religiously based social conservatives and ended the Democratic Party's control of the "Solid South." Photographer: Oliver F. Atkins, head of the White House Photo Office, 1970. Richard M. Nixon Presidential Library, Yorba Linda, CA. Control #NLRN-WHPO-C3587-04.

resolve inconsistencies. Burger chose not to. As Justice Douglas wrote in dissent, "I would suppose that in common understanding one of the best ways to 'establish' one or more religions is to subsidize them, which is what a tax exemption does."[52] He also asserted that since incorporation of the First Amendment into the Fourteenth, the Court had not been nearly as inconsistent as Burger claimed. Certainly, after the 1970s, that inconsistency would increase.

By the 1970s, America had entered into the beginning of what became known as the "culture wars," a period of four decades, with no real end in sight, during which opposing groups of Americans have fought over conceptions of and policies regarding family, education, morality, art, law, and political leadership. An early battle in these culture wars concerned the Equal Rights Amendment (ERA). In 1972, Congress passed what would have been, on ratification, the twenty-seventh Amendment to the Constitution. The ERA, as it became known, read: "Equality of rights under the law shall not be denied or abridged by the United States or by any state on account of sex." The ERA provoked a firestorm of opposition from conservative Christians, opposition that catapulted Protestant minister Jerry Falwell and Catholic parishioner Phyllis Schlafly into national celebrities.

Thirty states acted quickly to ratify the ERA, but the Falwell and Schlafly campaigns against the amendment began to shape perceptions of it by 1974. Only five more states ratified the ERA, and in 1978 it died, three votes short of ratification. Opposition arose from differing conceptions of the family, womanhood, and morality. Schlafly argued that the Bible taught that the family, not the individual, constituted the most basic social, political, and economic unit in society. A woman, as wife and mother, must be seen as a vital part of that unit, not as a distinct or autonomous person. In her campaign she invoked three themes that would become characteristic of the populist strategies of the Religious Right for the next thirty-some years: fear of societal change, regional and class differences, and the need for society to conform to God's truth. Regarding the ERA, Schlafly argued that the law would require women to serve in combat and would mandate unisex bathrooms (fear); that the amendment was the brainchild of eastern elites, liberals, and feminists

[52] Ibid. (Douglas dissent).

(regional and class interests); and that God's will regarding woman's place in society was expressed in the Bible, that it is valid, and everything that contravenes it is error and sin (God's truth). Reverend Falwell, with support from Beverly LaHaye, presented a similar attack on the ERA, arguing for the government to protect the biblical endorsement of the nuclear family, with its prescriptions of manhood and woman's domestic role. To combat what she perceived to be feminist influences on young women, LaHaye wrote *The Spirit-Controlled Woman*, asserting that Christian wives have a duty to "'die to oneself' and submit to their husbands."[53] She asserted that a husband's authority over his wife is second only to God's. The ERA's opponents brilliantly exploited the rising influence of religious conservatism and some procedural errors by their opponents. By 1982, when the time limit ran out, the ERA was hopelessly stalled, and the Religious Right celebrated its victory as a blow for traditional values.

The most significant Christian movement to arise from the battle over the ERA was that spearheaded by Jerry Falwell. In 1979, Falwell joined other leading conservative Christians in forming the "Moral Majority." Members saw themselves as Christ's soldiers in a holy war against secularism, specifically targeting legalized abortion, pornography, and the absence of prayer and Bible reading in the schools while also promoting a strong military and free-enterprise capitalism. Falwell contended that the Bible endorsed capitalism and that he felt no compulsion to address the needs of the poor in his ministry. Maintaining an obvious intellectual inconsistency, the Moral Majority sought to limit government's ability to interfere in the commercial realm, but to increase its powers to legislate morality and limit people's civil rights. It proposed an inversion of the bifurcation established in the *Carolene Products* case, in which legislative actions touching economic rights would be judged less critically than those impairing civil rights. The positions of the Moral Majority became the platform of a political consortium known as the Religious Right in the 1980s and afterward.

A leading intellectual of the Religious Right, Richard John Neuhaus, appears cognizant of the intellectual inconsistency with the coalition's positions. To further the societal recognition of Christian values without expanding governmental power, he advocates minimizing the

---

[53] Quoted in Gordon, *Spirit of the Law*, 136.

separation between public and private spheres. He argues that churches and other private institutions can be "mediating structures" between individuals and their government and calls for the legal "unfettering" of churches so that they can assume responsibility for social services.[54] Of course, the founders delineated the two spheres because of their preeminent concern for rights and conceived of the role of the individual within society as unencumbered by the moral dictates of a third party, either the government or churches acting with governmental authority. Softening the distinction between public and private spheres produces not only greater authority for the churches but also a correlative diminution of individual rights and freedoms. The policies of President George W. Bush ultimately relied on Neuhaus's ideas.

Recent evangelicals have struggled to integrate an opposition to much of secular society while still desiring full participation within it. For example, evangelicals once condemned beauty pageants for their tasteless and sinful display of women's bodies and their encouragement of personal exploitation of God's gifts for fame, pride, and money. By the 1990s, these pageants were dominated by evangelical contestants who unceasingly gave thanks to God for their successes in them and pledged to use the platforms the pageants gave them to further "His" work.

Perhaps more significantly, evangelicals have created their own schools to combat the secular liberalism they perceive to dominate American higher education. To pursue its social goals while also expressing a conservative message, the Religious Right had to identify its positions as consistent with America's past – even with the visions of the nation's founders. Conservatives decry the judicial activism of judges and call for original meanings of the Constitution to be their guide. But to return to original meanings of the Constitution and to preserve the founders' vision of the country while still imposing Christian evangelical beliefs, values, and moral teachings on the American public requires, if not a total rewriting of history, at least the exclusion of the Jeffersonians. Accordingly, the state of Texas has largely written Jefferson out of its textbooks. Ministers Jerry Falwell, Pat Robertson, and Tim LaHaye, among others, each founded a university in part

[54] Peter L. Berger and Richard John Neuhaus, *To Empower People* (Washington, DC: American Enterprise Institute, 1977), 33.

to further their educational mission. Liberty University, founded by Falwell, and Regent University, started by Robertson, also have law schools.

Legal Confusion Results from Christian Assertiveness, 1980–2014

Conservative religionists of the late twentieth century found their enemy in secular humanism, which Tim LaHaye explained as a philosophy of "amorality, evolution and atheism."[55] Holding no disillusion as to the scope of the challenge, Reverend Falwell, sounding much like Lyman Beecher in 1812, called for "a disciplined charging army" that Paul Weyrich said would "overturn the present structure in this country – we're talking about Christianizing America."[56] Commitment to this goal encouraged a new ecumenical movement. Orthodox Rabbi Moses Feuerstein, Cardinal Spellman, and Reverend Billy Graham joined together to criticize the secularization of American law. In 1984, the National Council of the Churches of Christ in the United States called for a greater attention to morality in the nation's laws.

Much like the classical republicans in the Revolutionary era and the Federalists in the early republic, social conservatives in the 1980s argued that religion, expressing moral standards, served as the best means of instilling virtue. In this ideological context it was sometimes easier to understand what the Religious Right opposed than what it favored. Its complaints grouped numerous policies and practices as evidence of degeneracy by design. The *Christian Times*, in June 1980, provided a list of adverse social and legal developments resulting from secular humanism: "To understand humanism is to understand women's liberation, the ERA, gay rights, children's rights, abortion, sex education, the 'new' morality, evolution, values clarification, situation[al] ethics, the separation of church and state, and the loss of patriotism."[57] Reprising an evangelical approach from the nineteenth century, the Religious Right generally sought to win legislative victories at state and local levels and judicial victories at the federal level, attacking each of the despised policies one at a time.

---

[55] Tim LaHaye, *The Battle for the Mind* (Old Tappan, NJ: Revell, 1980), 59.
[56] Quoted in A. James Reichley, *Religion in American Public Life* (Washington, DC: Brookings Institution, 1985), 331.
[57] Quoted in Wills, *Head and Heart*, 485.

An increase in evangelical devotion in and of itself might have meant little to the law and social institutions of the United States, but for a widespread social commitment to undo the cultural revolution of the 1960s through the creation of a newly energized community. A new communitarianism arose in the late 1970s, rooted in two different bodies of ideas: (1) the postmodern de-emphasis of individual rights relative to group identities and interests and (2) a Christian emphasis on social morality and its corresponding invocation of duties. To implement this communitarianism, reformers had to extrapolate from the reconceptualization of rights offered by Chaffee, Brandeis, Holmes, and Harlan to form a rights-based argument suited to the political and social context of the late twentieth century, the key aspect of which was the recognition that different people could have different rights. Once again, Christian reformers found an unusual ally in battling for social change.

An unprecedented number of cases addressing the relationship of religion to public policy have come before the Supreme Court since 1980. As the degree to which religion may shape government policy or to which churches may even be vehicles for instituting that policy became contentious political issues, Americans looked to law to resolve the political impasse. The Court, seemingly, has wanted to oblige. However, far from being above the political maelstrom, it has become enmeshed within it – repeatedly changing course, modifying legal tests, and redirecting arguments. Confusion and social division have been the results as the culture wars have only increased in ferocity. In response, legal scholars of all persuasions seem to be speaking for large numbers of the American people in criticizing the Court and calling for a more reasoned and stable jurisprudence.

Despite all this confusion, certain explanatory themes can provide some understanding of this contemporary era. First, the traditional division between public and private sectors has been greatly diminished – to an extent unprecedented since the colonial age. Second, opponents of a strict separation of church and state have used language and ideas from decisions of the Court reached in the 1960s and 1970s to advance arguments that Christians, as a group, deserve the same legal protection and political representation as other "minorities" and that Christianity deserves the same public support as secular humanism, which they argue is but a different religion. Third, the sharp divide in worldviews among Americans has produced opposing views of the role of the individual within society, implicating morals, values, and issues of authority that have been increasingly subject to legal as well as political attention.

A Divided America Reconsiders the Importance of Community

Christians have found support for greater communitarianism from unlikely sources. Academia's desire for a stronger public community, since 1980, is evident in its reconsideration of the idea of civil society. This scholarship has contributed to a decline in the relevance of the public-private distinction by arguing that the extension of rights undermines or devalues civic responsibility and moral duty, in effect promoting self-interested individualism at the expense of the social good. This conclusion has led some to encourage public support for churches serving a pragmatic role in building community from the bottom up. However, for religion to serve as the basis of community, it must once again become public. The prospect of a public religion raises the same issues that confronted the founders. The concerns are not merely how to resolve tensions or conflicts between various beliefs or how to recognize a public faith without violating the rights of dissenters; the issue is whether or not any religious belief can be substantiated sufficiently so as to serve as a basis for public morals and laws. If not, it must be solely a matter of individual conscience.

This problem has been addressed by a late twentieth-century variation of Pragmatism that has exerted a tremendous influence on America's political and intellectual life. Contemporary thinkers of this perspective largely ignore legal principle, ideology, and intellectual consistency as semantics easily eschewed for pragmatic benefit. They argue, in effect, that if people need religion, and government can use it to meet social needs, then nothing should stand in government's way of doing so. From this perspective, the objective truth of the religion or the right of the people to accept or reject a particular faith becomes largely irrelevant. Terms such as "truth" and "rights" are fungible creations to serve certain interests; language becomes less a representation of ideas than a tool for manipulating thought.

In this context, perhaps the greatest debate is over what is meant by the word "public." Father Richard John Neuhaus uses the word expansively as meaning "out in the open" in calling for a "public piety" and "public discourses" on religion and morality. In calling for public recognition of the importance of religion, he conflates the two meanings of the word "public," encouraging both the very reasonable right of people to speak proudly and openly about their beliefs and the more contentious role for government to endorse those same beliefs.[58]

The term "religion" has proven equally problematic. Scholars such as David Hall and Robert Orsi have identified a "lived religion" as a form of belief that arises from "being in an ongoing dynamic relationship with the realities of everyday life."[59] It arises, as does "truth" for Dewey and James, inductively from experience, as a way of validating or explaining one's life. Winifred Fallers Sullivan argues "that 'religion' is not a useful term for United States law today, because there is no longer any generally accepted referent that is relevant for defensible political reasons"; the multifarious forms of religion existing today defy categorization or description by use of the term "religion" – at least in a legal context.[60]

The Supreme Court has recently shown signs of encouraging the cultural inclinations for a greater sense of community by adopting this more postmodernist orientation, especially in broadening law's definition of religion and in ignoring individual rights–based arguments to justify greater government involvement in supporting and disseminating religious ideas. In so doing the Court addresses the same issue that has confronted Americans since the founding: the proper role of the individual within society. Only recently have individual rights not been the paramount concern in its resolution.

Christianity and, in fact, all religions express their own judgments on the proper role of the individual in society. Christianity has a long history of telling people what they can and cannot do, what they should feel, and how they should think. Few intellectual endeavors are both as prescriptive and proscriptive as religion is. The legitimate scope

[58] Richard John Neuhaus, *The Naked Public Square: Religion and Democracy in America* (Grand Rapids, MI: Eerdmans, 1984).

[59] Robert Orsi, "Everyday Miracles: The Study of Lived Religion," in *Lived Religion in America: Toward a History of Practice*, ed. by David D. Hall (Princeton, NJ: Princeton University Press, 1997), 7.

[60] Winnifred Fallers Sullivan, *Prison Religion: Faith-Based Reform and the Constitution* (Princeton, NJ: Princeton University Press, 2009) 18.

of Christianity's ability to prescribe and proscribe must necessarily involve considerations of what is meant by public dissemination of religious tenets. Significantly, none of the initiatives of the Religious Right concern its own members' freedoms to worship or to live in accordance with their own beliefs. Christians in the United States have always had a right to pray, to read the Bible, to put up crèches or crosses, to carry babies to full term, and to do anything else their religion demanded of them. What ardent Christian activists wanted, and still want, is for the government to help them impose these practices as norms for others. Evangelical Christianity, after 1970, politicized the moral imperatives of Christian belief, transformed evangelical and other conservative Christians into a significant political force, and helped erode the distinction between public and private realms and limit the separation of church and state in order to build a Christian community.

Contesting understandings of the public realm and the place of religion within it have played out in national conflicts over the "right to life." In 1976, Congress responded to evangelical appeals to limit the *Roe v. Wade* decision by enacting the Hyde Amendment, prohibiting federal funds to be used in abortions. The Supreme Court upheld the legislation, asserting that the statute was not rooted in religion but in "traditionalist values."[61] More recently, the *Schiavo* case provoked national attention. Both President George W. Bush and his brother, Governor Jeb Bush of Florida, sought to sustain artificially the life of a woman whose irreversible brain damage rendered her incapable of mobility, thought, or emotion. In these right-to-life disputes, conservative Christians argue that moral issues are not the province of individuals, but rather are expressions of public values that need to be informed by religion. Moreover, they argue that the proper position for government to take on moral issues is already known as it has been dictated by God. The 1987 nomination of Robert Bork to the Supreme Court turned this very issue into a political debate with very high stakes. In his 1984 publication, *Tradition and Morality in Constitutional Law*, Bork despaired that legal recognition of individual autonomy had led to "the privatization of morality," or state-sponsored "moral relativism."[62] While the Senate's rejection of Bork followed by the loss

---

[61] *Harris v. McRae*, 448 US 297, 319–20 (1980).
[62] Robert H. Bork, *Tradition and Morality in Constitutional Law* (Washington, DC: American Enterprise Institute, 1984).

of the *Schiavo* case convinced most evangelical leaders of the political difficulty of imposing Christian morality through national legislation, pragmatic and postmodernist arguments for a greater public role for religion have increasingly served as the basis for litigation strategy and nonlegislative policies. Meanwhile, the Religious Right has argued that morality is a political concern best left to state and local governments and has focused its legislative efforts on prohibiting same-sex marriage and limiting abortions.

Faith-Based Initiatives Reward the Efforts of the Religious Right

Despite the Religious Right's glorification of the presidency of Ronald Reagan, he devoted no real attention to the agenda sought by conservative Christians. The Reagan White House pushed no federal programs to limit abortion, secure school prayers, or provide funding to parochial schools. In fact, in greatly reducing social welfare expenditures, the Reagan administration cut off or reduced the flow of federal funds to many religious organizations benefiting from the allocative state, prompting protests from the Salvation Army and Lutheran Services. Personally, Reagan was an odd hero for evangelical groups; he was divorced, seldom attended church, and maintained close personal friendships with numerous homosexuals.[63] Much like Andrew Jackson and his followers developed a grotesque caricature of Thomas Jefferson and used it to claim consistency between their populist positions and the ideas of a respected statesman, so too have "Tea Partiers" and members of the Religious Right distorted Reagan's image for populist appeals. In fact, presidents did little to support activist Christian goals for communitarian change until 2000. Reagan's successor in 1988, George H.W. Bush, largely continued to ignore the agenda of the Religious Right while still blurring the line between public and private spheres in invoking his "Thousand Points of Light." Democratic Party President Bill Clinton revitalized religion's role in the allocative state by creating "Charitable Choice," prohibiting discrimination against religious providers in awarding federal contracts for delivery of public services.

[63] This idea and some of the supporting materials are expressed in Sean Wilentz, *The Age of Reason: 1974–2008* (New York: Harper Collins, 2008), 282.

George W. Bush, son of the forty-first president, claims to have accepted evangelical Christianity from Reverend Billy Graham at the family compound in Maine. He has said that subsequently God called him to run for the presidency in 2000 in order to do his will. On his first day of office, Bush issued an executive order prohibiting any international organization receiving funds to counsel women about abortions. Perceiving conception to be an act of God's will, he later substantially limited the use of stem cells in medical research funded by the federal government as a means of protecting fetuses.

President Bush spoke openly about the religious influences on his policies, particularly noting that he and God were working toward the same goals, even in going to war against Iraq. He remarked that he was not convinced of Darwinian science and supported the teaching of intelligent design. During his administration, the National Park Service carried a book at its bookstores in which it was asserted that the Grand Canyon was formed by Noah's flood. While in office, Bush supported a Constitutional amendment to ban same-sex marriage. For a man who advocated Constitutional originalism and returning power to state governments, an amendment of this type, much like the federal government's intrusion in the *Schiavo* case, indicates his subordination of legal principle, ideology, and intellectual consistency to his religious goals.

However, President Bush's major contributions to the cause of the Religious Right and erosion of the doctrine of separation came in his placement of conservative Christians in his administration and in his faith-based initiatives. In 1996, Congress passed the Personal Responsibility and Work Opportunity Reconciliation Act as part of President Clinton's welfare reform legislation. A brainchild of the Religious Right, it allowed religious organizations to receive block grants from state governments to use in providing public welfare services. As Governor of Texas, George W. Bush was one of the first governors to take advantage of the program, distributing millions of dollars to churches in his state. During his first term as president, Bush expanded this idea by introducing faith-based initiatives, in which religious institutions received federal funds to address public needs. When Congress defeated Bush's proposal, he implemented it through executive order. Under the program, an abstinence-only sex education course received $170 million in 2005 alone, and Pat Robertson's ministries received $1.5 million.

The faith-based initiatives obviously raise serious First Amendment questions. They greatly expanded the policy used since the 1950s in privatizing governmental responsibilities. The privatization of government functions challenges the legal distinction between public and private spheres that was asserted in the contract clause and served, even more than the religion clauses, as the legal rationale for separating church and state. Moreover, it evinces the acceptance of pragmatic expediencies to shape policies that stood little chance of popular support even within the president's own party.

Not all the recent privatization involved religious organizations. Perhaps the most celebrated use of private contractors performing governmental responsibilities is the hiring of private security firms, such as Halliburton, to carry guns and engage in military operations on behalf of the United States in wars in Iraq and Afghanistan. As of 2011, for-profit corporations operated more than 700 public K-through-12 schools paid for with tax dollars. Whether military actions or education is involved, as the public sector subcontracts its social duties to the private sector, the public loses its ability to manage and direct the services being provided. Certainly Americans' antipathy to taxes, government growth, and budget deficits has fueled some of the privatization, but the Religious Right's demands for a political voice and Bush's receptivity to those demands served as major factors in the formation of policy on privatization.

While all the programs administered under the umbrella of faith-based initiatives have raised Constitutional and social policy objections, by far the loudest and most complex concerns have been voiced in protest over programs that focus on "religious technologies of the self": family counseling, substance abuse counseling, and prison rehabilitation. These programs encourage aid recipients to develop "new selves" from explicitly Christian influences.[64] An example is the InnerChange Freedom Initiative, a subsidiary of Prison Fellowship Missionaries. It offers a Christ-centered Bible-based course intended to reduce criminal recidivism through personal transformation. Societal concerns for a greater sense of community and for lowering criminal recidivism combined with a cultural increase in spiritualism since

[64] Sullivan, *Prison Religion*, 15. The term "technologies of the self" derives from an essay by Michael Foucault published in Luther Martin, Huck Gutman, and Patrick H. Hutton, *Technologies of the Self: A Seminar with Michael Foucault* (Amherst: University of Massachusetts Press, 1988).

1980 to render Christian teachings of submission and obedience to authority acceptable to large segments of the American public.

Although many Americans expected President Barack Obama to discontinue the faith-based initiative programs, he has failed to do so and has actually increased aid to religious agencies. As government looks to do more with less, religious organizations may become increasingly involved in areas of community need, and states may well further their relationships with religious organizations. Contemporary Americans seem more pragmatic than idealistic, and as the Court becomes more conservative, it seems less inclined to protect freedoms from institutional powers. Yet, the issue is far from resolved.

Supreme Court Decisions Endorse Limited Separation

For much of the twentieth century, various political leftists and social reformers challenged not only free-enterprise capitalism, but also the rights-oriented philosophies that created it. While Enlightenment-era thinkers perceived rights as a natural indication and expression of human equality, subsequent theorists have posited that the emergent commercial class in Western Europe in the seventeenth century created the idea of rights as a means of gaining political power. Once entrenched, that commercial class used rights, as the basis of law, to secure both its economic and political power and, in effect, as a tool for preserving social and economic inequality. From this perspective, individual rights and the autonomy they provide are artificial creations used to empower some people while marginalizing others. Michel Foucault, expressing this postmodernist way of thinking, "criticized rights as a language of humanism in which the image of the sovereign individual is invoked to serve the needs of sovereignty itself."[65] In one of the many ironies in American political history, the Religious Right, after 1970, formed an intellectual and even a political alliance with leftists and postmodernists who shared an understanding of rights that championed community ethics over individual freedoms and group rights as the basis of political power.

The roots of the Religious Right's acceptance of a new formulation of rights began in response to the 1961 decision in *Torcaso* prohibiting

---

[65] Austin Sarat and Thomas R. Kearns, eds., *Identities, Politics, and Rights* (Ann Arbor: University of Michigan Press, 1995), 10–11.

the use of test oaths. Once again, dicta, in a footnote, proved to be problematic. The Court noted that "among the religions in this country which do not teach what would generally be considered a belief in God are Buddhism, Taoism, Ethical Culture, and Secular Humanism."[66] In this assertion the Court appeared to suggest that secular humanism might be a religion.

In 1933, a small group of thirty-four people, mostly academicians, had announced their support for a "Humanist Manifesto" in which they asserted that secular humanism constituted a religion and that it would replace earlier religions rooted in superstition and mysticism. After the *Torcaso* decision, evangelicals pointed to the Humanist Manifesto as the basis for legal arguments claiming that government protection or support of secular humanism is as much an establishment of religion as prayer in public schools or the erection of a cross in a public park. They began to assert that secular humanism constituted the religion of liberalism and that governmental support of it was both a form of religious discrimination and a violation of the First Amendment. By the 1970s, religiously conservative lawyers and scholars, such as John Whitehead, began to argue that the founders, by treating religion as a nonprivileged form of belief, intended the First Amendment to protect all matters of conscience or forms of belief equally. Secular humanism could be no more favored than Christianity.

As early as 1960, ecumenical Professor Wilfred Cantwell Smith at Harvard Divinity School asserted that all aspects of human life are "cast in a multicultural context." He added: "Every community on earth is becoming a minority in a complexity of diverse groups."[67] White Protestant Christians therefore composed a minority, and Smith encouraged them to recognize their status and adapt to it. In advocating this position he hoped to encourage a broader Christian embrace of diversity – an ecumenism founded not only on basic Christian values and beliefs but also on an acceptance of different religions, races, and cultures. Yet, in asserting the minority status of white Christians in a multicultural world he presaged a new legal doctrine that would be

---

[66] *Torcaso v. Watkins*, 367 US 488, 495, n. 11 (1961).
[67] Quoted in David A. Hollinger, "After Cloven Tongues of Fire: Ecumenical Protestantism and the Modern American Encounter with Diversity," *Journal of American History* (June 2011), 21.

used by right-wing evangelicals. As a minority group, Christians could claim legal protection of their unique beliefs.

By the 1980s, Christian activists had combined the idea that secular humanism constituted a religion with the argument that Christians, as an identifiable group, deserved equal governmental respect of their beliefs and practices. Alabama Federal District Court Judge W. Brevard Hand accepted this position of the Christian activists in 1987 in *Smith v. Mobile*, finding secular humanism to be an atheistic form of religion.[68] However, the decision was overturned on appeal.

Supreme Court decisions upholding civil rights legislation from the 1960s and 1970s accepted the argument for group identities as a means of creating a more just society and upheld the bifurcation of rights developed in the *Carolene Products* decision preferencing civil rights over property rights. The Court repeatedly found no equal protection violations in laws creating group rights that protected or favored certain groups at the expense of others. Simultaneously, a new term, "empower," came into common usage, indicating the advisability of laws, policies, and even outlooks that create opportunities allowing people previously hindered by social convention to fulfill their personal goals. The idea of group identity, and hence of group rights, arose from a burgeoning school of social psychology that postulated that one's identity is composed as much from the various groups to which one belongs – defined by such markers as race, sex, religion, and class – as from one's own individual thoughts and experiences. Yet, as the Constitution made no mention of group rights, these rights had to be created by statute. In creating group rights individual rights necessarily have been diminished. The legal recognition of group rights has fostered a new legalistic communitarianism rooted in psychological theories that proved helpful to activist Christians.

Playing to the popular acceptance of multiculturalism in the late 1970s and early 1980s, members of the Religious Right came to see themselves as a persecuted minority in need of legal protection as a group. Because 85 percent of the American people defined themselves as Christian, religious leaders had to construct a theory of persecution to justify their assertion for the need of protective laws to empower

---

[68] *Smith v. Mobile*, 655 F. Supp. 980 (Ala., 1986); overturned at 827 F. 2d 684 (11th Cir. 1987).

their people. They asserted that the laws of religious neutrality and separation of church and state established secular humanism as a de facto national religion, ironically transforming Christians into dissenters within what some Christians had long argued was a Christian nation. Asserting secular humanism to be a religion, Rousas John Rushdoony argued that every state depends on laws, and those laws express particular religious perspectives. The laws of the United States expressed an acceptance of secular humanism.[69] This conclusion served as the foundation of a new legal theory – that of "accommodation" – by which minority and special interest groups are not merely tolerated by law, but accommodation is made for them.

In the 1970s, the Religious Right became active in religious clause litigation as counsel or through the filing of *amicus* briefs. In the process it formed a legal theory from the assertions that secular humanism constitutes a religion and that Christians, as a group, have a right equal to that of secular humanists to public support of their religion. The Supreme Court paid surprising attention to these arguments while still attempting to enforce both the free exercise and establishment clauses. Considerable confusion has been the result.

In its 1971 *Lemon* decision, the Court clarified establishment clause protections by requiring a challenged law or action to (1) have a secular purpose, (2) not to advance or inhibit religion, and (3) not to foster government's entanglement with religion.[70] While *Lemon* remains law, it has not been consistently applied in adjudicating subsequent cases. In 1981, the Court allowed state universities to permit religious groups to meet in school buildings. Decisions in 1983 and 1988 endorsed nonpreferential government recognition and support of religious groups. Perhaps most significant, in 1987, Justice Brennan, most likely unintentionally in a decision generally repudiating the argument of the Religious Right, reopened the door to the teaching of creationism in asserting that religious beliefs might be taught in public schools if they had a "clear secular intent."[71] This case law, generally expressing a "benevolent neutrality," indicated early movement toward the accommodationist jurisprudence.

---

[69] Rousas John Rushdoony, *Law and Liberty* (Vallecito, CA: Ross House, 1984), 4.

[70] *Lemon v. Kurtzman*, 403 US 602 (1971).

[71] *Widmar v. Vincent*, 454 US 263 (1981); *Mueller v. Allen*, 463 US 388 (1983); *Bowen v. Kendrick*, 487 US 589 (1988); *Edwards v. Aguillard*, 482 US 578 (1987).

In 1987, the Court expressly adopted the doctrine of accommodation as a means of limiting the intrusiveness of the establishment
clause, permitting a far greater degree of public support for religion
as a means of building a community.[72] "Accommodation" has been
defined as the legal recognition that "religion should maintain at least
a symbolic presence in most areas of public life."[73] However, the development of the doctrine since 1985 indicates its dependence on recognition of Christians as an interest group that deserves a place at the
table in American political discussions. The Court has noted that "[a]t
some point, accommodation may devolve into an unlawful fostering
of religion."[74] This conceptual "point" has seldom been found.

The Court modified the *Lemon* test in 1997 through *Agostini
v. Felton* and again in 2000 through *Mitchell v. Helms*. Yet, well after
each of these decisions, the *Lemon* test has been applied by lower
federal courts and even the Supreme Court.[75] In *Agostini*, Justice
O'Connor, writing for the court, formally incorporated certain principles articulated in intervening cases to change the second prong of
the *Lemon* test from "neither advancing nor inhibiting religion" to not
"advancing religion through indoctrination," a much harder standard
for plaintiffs to meet to show a violation of the establishment clause.
Specifically, the Court found that public use of religious school classrooms, staffed by public teachers, does not in and of itself "create the
impression of a 'symbolic union' between church and state" so as to
constitute a type of indoctrination. The court thereby reversed earlier
case law in which such an impression was held to "advance religion."[76]
Three years later, Justice Thomas further revised the *Lemon* test. In the
Mitchell decision, Thomas rejected the formalistic distinction between
public and private realms as relevant to questions of federal aid to religious schools. He wrote that the law's "hostility to aid to pervasively

---

[72] *Hobbie v. Unemployment Appeals Commission of Florida*, 480 US 136, 144–5
(1987); *Locke v. Davey*, 540 US 712 (2004).

[73] Reichley, *Religion in American Public Life*, 3.

[74] *Corp. of Presiding Bishops of Church of Jesus Christ of Latter-day Saints v. Amos*,
483 US 327, 334–5 (1987).

[75] Recent applications of the *Lemon* test include *Kitzmiller v. Dover School District*,
400 F. Supp 2d. 707 (M.D. Pa., 2007) and *McCreary v. ACLU*, 545 US 844 (2005).

[76] *Agostini v. Felton*, 521 US 203, 227, 226 (1997), reversing *Aguilar V. Felton*, 473 US
402 (1985), and *School District of Grand Rapids v Ball*, 473 US 373 (1985). The
decision also presented a second question as part of the second prong of the test, that

sectarian schools has a shameful pedigree that we do not hesitate to disavow."[77] The Court found that if aid is determined to serve a secular need and is allocated on the basis of neutral criteria that neither favor nor disfavor religion, it is permissible. Thomas reintroduced the term "neutrality," once so antagonistic to Christian activists, to legitimize public aid to religion. This irony, as well as judicial reaction to Thomas's opinion, only increased confusion. Justice O'Connor, even in concurrence, voiced concern that the proposition that "government aid to religious schools ... [will not be deemed to] have the effect of advancing religion so long as the aid is offered on a neutral basis and the aid is secular in content" forms a rule with "unprecedented breadth for the evaluation of Establishment Clause challenges to government school-aid programs."[78] Justice Souter, in dissent, noted the problem in applying a Constitutional test of neutrality, or nondiscrimination, among groups.

Evenhandedness in distributing a benefit approaches the equivalency of constitutionality in this area only when the term refers to such universality of distribution that it makes no sense to think of the benefit as going to any discrete group. Conversely, when evenhandedness refers to distribution to limited groups within society, ... it does make sense to regard the benefit as aid to the recipients.[79]

Applying the establishment clause has led to tremendous inconsistency. Some of this inconsistency is attributable to Justices who prefer certain words over others in framing the revised *Lemon* test. While Justice O'Connor looked for "endorsement" or "indoctrination," Justice Kennedy looked for "coercion" to find prohibited conduct. Yet, language alone cannot explain all the inconsistencies. In 1980, the court found displays of the Ten Commandments in schools to violate the *Lemon* test as having "plainly religious" intent.[80] Four years later, Justice Burger, in a 5–4 decision, allowed public funds and land to be used to display a nativity scene during December. Burger called the display "passive symbols" respecting Christmas as a secular as well as

---

being whether or not an aid program "defines its recipients by reference to religion." It is arguable, after *Agostini*, whether the third prong of the Lemon test remained.

[77] *Mitchell v. Helms*, 530 US 793, 822, 828 (2000).
[78] Ibid. at 837 (O'Connor conc.)
[79] Ibid. at 884 (Souter diss.).
[80] *Stone v. Graham*, 449 US 39 (1980).

a religious holiday. He also referred to Douglas's regrettable language in the *Zorach* case, adding that the Constitution "affirmatively mandates accommodation, not merely tolerance, of all religions and forbids hostility to any." Even more surprising was his contention that the history of official acknowledgment of religion in America was "unbroken" since 1789.[81] In fact, the history of public recognition of religion is one of great vacillation and is anything but unbroken or consistent, as Burger himself noted in the 1970 *Walz* decision upholding the tax-exempt status of churches. In dissent, Justice Brennan, joined by Justices Marshall, Blackman, and Stevens, vehemently attacked Burger's reasoning. He asserted that if the crèche is seen as secular, or void of religious content, it is offensive to Christians; if not, "the symbolic reenactment of the birth of a divine being who has been miraculously incarnated as a man stands as a dramatic reminder of ... [nonbelievers'] differences with Christian faith." Brennan called the decision "a coercive ... step toward establishing the sectarian preferences of the majority at the expense of the minority" and said that the "Court ... [took] a long step backwards to the days when Justice Brewer could arrogantly declare that 'this is a Christian nation.'"[82]

Only five years later, the Court required removal of a nativity scene, but not a Christmas tree, from government buildings in Pennsylvania. In her opinion for the Court, Justice O'Connor somehow reasoned that displaying religious symbols in the building constituted a public endorsement of religion, but placing them in a public park in front of a building did not. Yet, even in enforcing the establishment clause, the Court in 1989 contended that the Constitution requires "a respect for religious pluralism," rooting its decision in respect for various group beliefs rather than in protection of individual rights.[83] Finally, on one day in 2005, the Court ruled in opposite ways on very similar cases.

---

[81] *Lynch v. Donnelly*, 465 US 668, 673, 674 (1984). Burger was at least consistent in his reasoning from the previous year. In *Marsh v. Chambers*, 463 US 783 (1983), upholding the use of a prayer to open Congress, he wrote: "In light of the unambiguous and unbroken history of more than 200 years, there can be no doubt that the practice of opening legislative sessions with prayer has become part of the fabric of our society." To invoke Divine guidance on a public body entrusted with making the laws is not, in these circumstances, an 'establishment' of religion or a step toward establishment" (p. 792). Brennan, also consistent in dissent, called the decision a "betrayal of the lessons of history" (p. 817).

[82] *Lynch*, supra, at 711, 718–19, 725 (Brennan diss.).

[83] *Allegheny County v. ACLU*, 492 US 573, 610 (1989).

It allowed display of the Ten Commandments on the grounds of the Texas state capital but ordered them removed from inside a Kentucky courthouse. Not only is the inconsistency troubling. Logic dictates that any use of public funds or public property by public officials in promotion of Christianity violates the right of conscience, especially of atheists and non-Christians who have not endorsed the action. Use of public funds or property to support a religion must necessarily be an establishment of that religion.

Just as disturbing as the inconsistent and illogical legal reasoning in establishment clause cases is the refusal of some state legislators, and even some courts, to follow existing precedent. In 1982, Alabama Governor James signed an act requiring classroom prayer, stating that he knew the bill violated federal law and challenged authorities to "fire me.... I dare them to do that." On review of the act in a case brought by Ishmael Jaffree, an atheist and a parent of a student in the Alabama schools, Judge W. Brevard Hand, for the Alabama Federal District Court, called the *Engel* and *Schempp* cases wrongly decided, saying that the Court "erred in its reading of history." Arguing that the misreading of history left the matter one of first impression, he upheld the statute.[84] During the 1990s, public schools in Alabama forced Jewish students to pray and to write essays on the topic of "Why Jesus Loves Me"; ministers led prayers before football games, pep rallies, graduations, and band concerts; a minister "condemned to hell," during a school assembly, students who had not accepted Jesus Christ as their lord and savior; missionaries distributed bibles within schools; and school officials justified mandatory prayer and Bible reading on grounds that "teachers must save children's souls if their parents did not."[85]

In 1990, the Third Circuit accepted the Religious Right's calls for judicial recognition of pluralism, initially asserted by the LaHayes, in striking down as invalid discrimination against religion a school district's ban on all religious expressions on school property, including prohibiting an overtly Christian performance by an entertainer.[86] The

---

[84] *Jaffree v. Board of School Commissioners*, 554 F. Supp. 1104 (S.D. Ala. 1983). On appeal, the case was overturned, a holding endorsed by the Supreme Court in *Wallace v. Jaffree*, 472 US 38 (1985).

[85] Dierenfield, *Battle over School Prayer*, 2–3, 182–3.

[86] *Gregoire v. Centennial School District*, 907 F.2d 1366 (3rd Circ., 1990). See also Gordon, *Spirit of the Law*, 141.

Supreme Court had earlier acknowledged, without endorsement, the LaHaye argument when Justice O'Connor, in 1988, stated that groups of people holding different beliefs often made "competing demands on government, many of them rooted in sincere religious belief[s], that inevitably arise in so diverse a society as ours."[87] After the *Agnostini* ruling, O'Connor further developed her legal focus on pluralism as a social reality in developing a jurisprudence of "equal access," in the process subordinating individual rights to, at best, a secondary concern. In *Allegheny County v. ACLU*, she wrote, in concurrence, that the Constitution requires "a respect for religious pluralism." She explained: "We live in a pluralistic society. Our citizens come from diverse traditions or adhere to no particular religious beliefs at all."[88] In *Kiryas Joel Village School District v. Grumet*, she asserted that "government may generally not treat people differently based on the God or Gods they worship or don't worship."[89] And in a concurring opinion in *Wallace v. Jaffree*, she quoted her earlier opinion in *Lynch v. Donnelly*:

> Direct government action endorsing religion or a particular religious practice is invalid ... because it sends a message to nonadherents that they are outsiders, not full members of the political community, and an accompanying message to adherents that they are insiders, favored by the community.[90]

Throughout these opinions, rights are not absolutes, but tools to serve social considerations. They are formed and shaped to address social group membership and psychological needs or concerns.

In support of these concerns, the Court has used the "equal access" argument to overcome the limitations imposed by the establishment clause; instead of limiting government's address of religion, the clause has been used to compel it. In 1995, the Court required the University of Virginia to fund a voluntary religious group of students on terms equal to those applied to other student organizations. The group's publication, *Wide Awake*, an overtly religious periodical, could not constitute a basis for the administration's denial of funding. Justice

---

[87] *Lyng v. Northwest Indian Cemetery Protective Association*, 485 US 439, 452 (1988).

[88] *Allegheny County v. ACLU* 492 US 573, 627, (1989) 610 (conc.). See also *Westside Community Schools v. Mergens*, 496 US 226 (1990).

[89] *Kiryas Joel Village School District v. Grumet*, 114 S. Cf. 2491, 2487 (1995) (conc.).

[90] *Wallace v. Jaffree*, 472 US 38, 69 (1985).

Souter, in another dissent, argued that the majority was using the equal access argument to distort the meaning and intention of the establishment clause: "[I]f the Clause was meant to accomplish nothing else, it was meant to ban this use of public money in support of religion."[91] The school's founder, Thomas Jefferson, would have agreed.

In 2001, Justice Thomas wrote an opinion for the Court ruling that a public school could not exclude a religious organization from using its building after hours when it allowed other local groups to use it. The Good News Club taught Christian morality and practical observances to children aged six through twelve. Thomas wrote that "[t]he Good News Club seeks nothing more than to be treated neutrally and given access to speak about the same topics as other groups."[92] The dissent, however, found a problem in approving this access:

[Good News will be conducting an] evangelical service of worship calling children to commit themselves in an act of Christian conversion. [The Thomas opinion] stand[s] for the remarkable proposition that any public school opened for civic meetings must be opened for use as a church, synagogue, or mosque.[93]

By 2000, evangelical Christian students had formed 15,000 religious clubs in public schools.

Since the 1980s, some conservatives have trumpeted the voucher system as a means of both limiting government and improving the quality of American education. The voucher system allows tax monies to be used, in the form of vouchers, to pay for private school education. Of course, the system undermines the public school system by taking money from it. If education is truly a responsibility of government, then logically all taxpayers should support public education, and the public should determine educational policy. Vouchers allow some taxpayers to avoid their democratic duties and some governments to delegate control of an important concern to private entities. The system, however, has gained the support of many Christian parents who want to send their students to Christian schools at public expense. The Court upheld the Ohio voucher system in a 2002 decision precisely

---

[91] *Rosenberger v. Rector and Visitors of the University of Virginia*, 515 US 819, 115 S. cf. 2510, 2535 (1995).
[92] *Good News Club v. Milford Central School*, 533 US 98 (2001).
[93] Ibid. at 138–9 (Souter diss.).

because it protected private choice without discriminating, despite the fact that 95 percent of the funding benefited religious schools.

After the *Agostini* ruling, the Justices have continued to grapple with the phraseology and legal emphasis of the test to apply to establishment clause cases. Clearly, the Court's endorsement of neutrality in recent years is more accommodating of religion in the public sphere than the secularist jurisprudence that prevailed for much of the preceding 40 years.

Justice Souter noted the confusing changes in the Court's use of the concept of neutrality in establishment clause cases: "[N]eutrality originally entered this field of jurisprudence as a conclusory term, a label for the required relationship between the government and religion as a state of equipoise between government as ally and government as adversary.... Our subsequent re-examination ... [has] recast neutrality as a concept of 'evenhandedness'" between competing ideological perspectives or interest groups. In other words, the concept has been redefined from prohibiting government action to aid or hinder religion to permitting it as long as the aid is not made discriminatorily.[94]

The various problems identified in the Court's recent applications of the establishment clause came together in 2014 in *Town of Greece, New York v. Galloway*. The Court ignored 2,000 years of history in which Christianity has provided the rationale for persecutions, wars, and discriminations to continue its endorsement of religion as a means of building community.[95] Celebrating the role of religion as a means of bringing people together while avoiding any mention of an individual's right to be free from funding or hearing public-sector pronouncements of religion, the Court upheld a city's use of an overtly Christian prayer to open its town board meetings. In neither the majority opinion nor the dissent is any argument for the protection of individual rights even mentioned. Justice Kagan's dissent addresses religious pluralism, exclusion, and discrimination, but not the idea that religion is a private matter and the freedom to exercise or refrain from it is an individual right. The majority opinion again viewed prayer and religion less as indicia of belief than as components of a national culture or expressions of history and traditions: "[O]ur history and traditions

94 *Mitchell v. Helms*, 530 US 793, 883 (2000) (Souter diss.).
95 *Town of Greece, New York v. Galloway*, 572 US 134 S.Ct. 1811 (2014).

have shown that prayer in this limited context could 'co-exist with the principles of disestablishment and religious freedom.'"[96] The Court subsequently defined that limited context as

[a] place at the opening of legislative sessions, where it is meant to lend gravity to the occasion and reflect values long part of the nation's heritage. Prayer that is solemn and respectful in tone, that invites lawmakers to reflect upon shared ideals and common ends before they embark on the fractious business of governing, serves… [a] legitimate function.[97]

In focusing on the psychological and utilitarian benefits of prayer and its promotion of an appropriate state of mind, the Court further extended the degree to which the public sector can accommodate a specific religion. A specific religion can foster an appropriate state of mind just as well as a vague one can. The Court even asserted that "[g]overnment may not mandate a civic religion that stifles any but the most generic reference to the sacred any more than it may prescribe a religious orthodoxy."[98] Yet, in asserting that Christianity, in particular, invokes "values long part of the nation's heritage" and "shared ideals" the Court raises a question as to whether any other religious message or prayer could be tolerated. The delegates to the Constitutional Convention in 1787 rejected the idea of opening prayers out of respect for the private right of individual conscience. This respect is largely absent from the Court in the twenty-first century.

The major test for the establishment clause in recent years has been the federal government's program of faith-based initiatives. To date, judicial consideration of the program has come through the prison ministry initiative, which has not yet gone before the Supreme Court. At the trial court, Judge Pratt, of the Federal District Court for the Southern District of Iowa, found a contract between the State of Iowa and the Inner Change Freedom Initiative (IFI) to counsel prisoners to violate the establishment clause. Judge Pratt, in reference to the *Lemon* test, noted that while the contract had a secular purpose, its effect was to promote the Christian religion.[99] On appeal to the Eighth Circuit, the case came before a panel that included recently retired

---

[96] 134 S.Ct. 1820 (2014).

[97] 134 S.Ct. 1823.

[98] 134 S.Ct. 1822.

[99] *Americans United for Separation of Church and State v. Prison Fellowship Missionaries*, 432 F. Supp. 832 (S.D. Iowa, 2006).

Justice O'Connor, serving by designation. Accordingly, the appellate court's decision carried extra significance.

The Eighth Circuit recognized that IFI used its contract to proselytize to the prisoners: "biblical principles are integrated into the entire course curriculum of [Inner Change], rather than compartmentalized in specific classes. In other words, the application of biblical principles is not an agenda item – it is the agenda."[100] The issue was whether governmental sponsorship of this agenda violated the establishment clause. The court found, in using the *Agostini* test, that Iowa had a secular purpose in hiring IFI, leaving only a question of whether in doing so it "advanced religion." To find that it did required proof that the program resulted in "governmental indoctrination." The panel found that the program did result in indoctrination of Christian beliefs; therefore, it had "the effect of advancing or endorsing religion." The panel accordingly held that "the direct aid to Inner Change violated the Establishment Clauses of the United States and Iowa constitutions."[101] Yet, confusion has still resulted from this decision, causing some scholars even to see it as an endorsement of faith-based initiatives. In the last paragraph of its opinion, the Eighth Circuit disputes IFI's assertion that it is barred from future contracts with the Iowa Department of Corrections, noting that the case prohibits only management, direction, and funding of IFI by the state.[102] The Supreme Court has heard one challenge to the faith-based initiative program. However, the justices avoided addressing the merits of the establishment clause challenge by ruling, in a 5–4 decision, that the plaintiff, Freedom from Religion Foundation, a private, voluntary association dedicated to atheistic concerns, lacked standing to bring a taxpayer suit.[103]

Some legal scholars see the Court's restructured conception of neutrality as reflecting the need for law to comply with popular understandings of the Constitution, national values, and public goals. From their perspective, the people determine, through majority will, what the law will be; America's recent embrace of evangelical Christianity

---

[100] *Americans United for Separation v. Prison Fellowship Missionaries* 509 F. 3d 406, 414 (8th Circ., 2007).

[101] Ibid. at 425.

[102] Ibid. at 428.

[103] *Hein v. FFRF*, supra.

cannot help but influence law as well as policy. Conversely, the law can be seen as derived from the ideological perspectives and patterns of reasoning of the lawyers and judges who subtly shape it in working within the restraints imposed by precedent, constitutionality, and deference to statutory policy. From this latter perspective, the intellectual influences of Pragmatism, modern psychology, and postmodernism have restructured our law to devalue individual rights to serve group and social interests. The restructuring of the principle of neutrality can be seen from this intellectual context as politics masquerading as law.

Just as Enlightenment-era ideas shaped the Constitutional and legal thought of the founders, so too have more contemporary ideas influenced the legal thinking of the twentieth century. The Court's endorsement of value-oriented legislation in restriction of contract rights evinces an acceptance of the Pragmatists' critique of classical liberalism. Moreover, the policy expressed in the *Carolene Products* decision persisted until the 1980s, when new academic models explaining interest group affiliation and public choice forced a reconsideration of what constituted a minority. Such reasoning allowed any interest group to be considered a minority, including a church group or religious body, and to press for law to recognize its position.

Since the work of Randolph Bourne in the 1920s, if not before, Pragmatism has been linked to social engineering. The underlying assumption supporting social engineering is a belief that experts are best able to determine policy, even policy that depends on moral choices. Pragmatists express tremendous confidence in the willingness of the masses to follow the elite. The Pragmatists' argument for creation of a usable truth implies both (1) that the created truth will encourage certain forms of thinking and behaviors and (2) that the created truth supports the sociopolitical goals of its creators. These implications subordinate the exercise of individual rational judgment to an elite conception of the social good. Moreover, since the 1960s, Pragmatism has largely deviated from its roots in science and positivism, each of which imposed a rational framework on Pragmatists' thought, toward a postmodernist humanism. In fact, many contemporary scholars find the roots of postmodernism in classical Pragmatism. Its recognition of emotional response as a means of knowing, its rejection of value in rational contemplation, its embrace of plural and relative truths, its call for morality to govern the conceptions and administration of

justice, and its emphasis on language as a means of shaping perceptions all resonate with postmodernist thought's diminution of reason
and rationality. Both schools of thought attempt to impose a moralistic
system of values as parameters on individual thought and action. This
imposition relies on the reconceptualization of rights that occurred in
the late 1930s, augmented by the ideas of neutrality and accommodation that have emerged since 1980. The new communitarianism is a
product of Christian and postmodern thought.

Once rights become enmeshed with politics, or policy formation,
they lose their power to restrict government action. The liberal theory
of rights recognized by the founders assumed rights to vest equally in
people, supposing all people to be legally alike. From this perspective,
legal scholar Ronald Dworkin argued that "rights stand outside of,
and above, politics," serving as a type of "trump card" to deny government the power to act.[104] Conversely, postmodernist thinkers argue
that rights are context-specific and emphasize not their legal power,
but rather their social influence and effect. Rights, as a linguistic tool,
express society's understanding of group or individual identity and of
society's policy goals. Ironically, church groups, professedly conservative in outlook, have adopted a postmodernist view of rights to build
legal arguments.

Even though the doctrine of accommodation has eroded separation of church and state, it has not completely destroyed it. In 1992,
the Court upheld a ban on public prayers at public school graduations.[105] In fact, the court has been remarkably consistent in ruling
on state-sponsored prayer in schools since the *Engel* decision. In the
last school prayer case before the Court, it ruled that student-led public prayers violated the establishment clause.[106] In condemning school
prayers while endorsing legislative prayers, the Court seems to priori-
tize the sensitivity of children to indoctrination. Yet, do children have a
greater right to freedom of conscience than adults do? By focusing on
the societal effects of the use of prayer in the public sector the Court
reasserts its utilitarian and postmodern jurisprudence in lieu of true
rights protection.

---

[104] Ronald Dworkin, *Taking Rights Seriously* (London: Duckworth, 1977), xi.
[105] *Lee v. Weiseman*, 112 S. Ct. 2649 (1992).
[106] *Santa Fe Independent School District v. Doe*, 530 US 290 (2000).

In 2003, the Court overturned its decision in *Bowers v. Hardwick*, issuing another of the few secularist victories since 1980 and confirming the jurisprudence of the 1960s. The court found that the Texas law punishing sodomy violated the right of privacy. In making this finding it argued that the fact that homosexuality offends many Christians cannot be the basis for criminalizing the behavior. In dissent, Justice Scalia, joined by Chief Justices Rehnquist and Justice Thomas, asserted that the Court's prohibition of "laws based on moral choices" also threatened "laws against bigamy, same-sex marriage, adult incest, prostitution, masturbation, adultery, fornication, bestiality and obscenity."[107] No doubt many liberals would argue that, but for the bestiality laws protecting innocent animals, those laws regarding private behavior by sole or consenting adults should be repealed.

Most of the confusion over the establishment clause cases must derive from the Court's attempt to use it as a prohibition of discrimination. The Amendments comprising the Bill of Rights were framed and ratified to protect individual rights, and the religious clauses, taken together, were intended to protect the individual right to freedom of conscience. If the establishment clause is meant to protect individuals in their right to be free from any imposition of religion by government, it makes no sense to enforce it as prohibiting discrimination against various religious groups.

The free exercise clause has been the subject of less litigation since 1980 but nearly as much controversy. The Court's greatest protection of rights under the free exercise clause came during the 1960s. In *Sherbert v. Verner*, the Court applied the "compelling state interest test," requiring a high standard of any state trying to use its police powers to restrict religious exercise.[108] The Court applied that test ten times thereafter, the last time in 1989.[109] Since then, several variations on the test have been applied, leading once again to some confusion.

---

[107] *Lawrence v. Texas*, 539 US 558, 590 (2003) (Scalia diss.). For more on the decision and its cultural context, see Dale Carpenter, *Flagrant Conduct: The Story of Lawrence v. Texas: How a Bedroom Arrest Decriminalized Gay Americans* (New York: W.W. Norton, 2011).

[108] *Sherbert v. Verner*, 374 US 398 (1963). The test requires a compelling or overriding state interest and a law narrowly tailored to that interest.

[109] *Gillette v. US*, 401 US 437 (1971); *Wisconsin v. Yoder*, 406 US 205 (1972); *McDaniel v. Paty*, 435 US 618 (1978); *Widmar v. Vincent*, 454 US 263 (1981); *Thomas v. Review Board*, 450 US 707 (1981); *US v. Lee*, 455 US 252 (1982) *Bob*

The *Smith* case came before the Court in 1990. It concerned a man discharged from his employment for using peyote. He acknowledged the use as part of his religious exercise and applied for unemployment compensation from the state of Oregon. The state denied the benefits because Smith admitted to using peyote, a criminal offense in Oregon, and people discharged for committing crimes were ineligible for benefits. In deciding the case the Court turned to the accommodation principle articulated in earlier establishment clause cases. Writing for the Court, Justice Scalia rejected the idea that government needed a compelling or overriding interest to intrude on religious exercise: "Any society adopting such a system would be courting anarchy."[110] The Court would not step in to secure religious freedoms limited by laws that did not discriminate and that served even a valid state interest. Scalia left the accommodation of religious beliefs to the democratic processes of the various states, acknowledging but dismissing the risk in doing so:

It may fairly be said that leaving accommodation to the political process will place at a relative disadvantage those religious practices that are not widely engaged in ... [but, this result is an] unavoidable consequence of democratic government.[111]

Americans generally greeted the *Smith* decision with alarm. Did not the Constitution, recognizing the fallibility of democracy to protect rights, set parameters on public power in respect of personal rights, one of the chief rights being that of religious freedom? To submit the protection of rights to the political process was to offer no protection at all. Moreover, in limiting protection of civil rights through application of the "rational basis test," in which a law is found legitimate if it is in pursuit of a legitimate state interest and reasonably related to serving that interest, the Court rejects the reasoning of the *Carolene Products* decision, in which civil rights were to be accorded extra protection. In response to the *Smith* ruling, Congress passed the Religious

James University v. US, 461 US 574 (1983); *Hobbie v. Unemployment Commission*, 480 US 136 (1987); *Frazee v. Illinois Department of Employment Security*, 489 US 829 (1989); *Hernandez v. Commissioner of Internal Revenue*, 490 US 680 (1989). However, several lower courts continue to use the "compelling state interest" test. *Warner v. City of Boca Raton*, 64 F Supp. 2d 1272 (N.D. Fla., 1999).

110 *Employment Division v. Smith*, 454 US 872, 888 (1990).
111 Ibid. at 890.

Freedom Restoration Act (RFRA) in 1993 to "restore the compelling state interest test" in free exercise cases.[112] However, in 1997, the Court found the RFRA unconstitutional when applied to state legislation. Congress was held to have power, under the Fourteenth Amendment, to enforce protections of individual freedom against the states, but not to alter the meanings of those freedoms. The Court implicitly ruled that it, not Congress, is the only body able to interpret the meaning of Constitutional protections: "Legislation which alters the meaning of the Free Exercise Clause cannot be said to be enforcing the Clause."[113] Ironically, in exercising its unique powers, the Court largely deferred to state legislatures to determine the limits of religious freedom. After 1997, federal legislation would be subjected to a higher standard from federal judges than would state legislation. The Republicans on the Court seemed to return to a new version of federalism reminiscent of old states' rights arguments. In so doing they empowered state legislatures at the expense of individual rights – another indication of the increasingly communitarian priorities of contemporary Republicans.

Most recently, in *Burwell v. Hobby Lobby*, the Court allowed closely held corporations owned by people whose religious beliefs preclude their use of birth control to legally refrain from providing health insurance covering contraception to their employees, even though such insurance is required by federal law.[114] The decision recognizes, in effect, a religious belief of a corporation. It ignores that the First Amendment, as part of the Bill of Rights, secures individual rights from governmental interference. A corporation may be a legal individual, but one struggles to understand how it possesses a mind or a conscience. An individual has a recognized right to conscience, but a corporation cannot. Corporations can have property rights, but not rights of conscience. The argument supposes a public duty to protect religion and the institutions that express it, whereas the First Amendment, at least at the time of its drafting, protected individuals in the exercise of their private consciences. Religion per se was neither protected nor preferred in the Constitution.

---

[112] Witte, *Religion and the American Constitutional Experiment*, 150.
[113] *City of Boerne v. Flores*, 521 US 507, 117 S. Ct. 2157, 2164 (1997).
[114] *Burwell v. Hobby Lobby*, 573 US 134 S.Ct. 2751 (2014).

The argument that religious individuals and organizations that pursue religious ends can be exempted from federal laws that intrude on religious beliefs likely will surface again in the context of same-sex marriage. As this book goes to print, social conservatives are raising political arguments concerning their rights, under the free exercise clause, to dissent from endorsing or even recognizing same-sex marriages, now granted status under the law equal to that of male-female unions.[115]

Several scholars have argued that the confusion in the Court's decisions since 1980 arises from difficulties in defining religion. The willingness of the Religious Right to portray secular humanism not as an antireligious ideology but as constituting a religion itself has only added to the difficulty. Linguistic and definitional problems are, of course, to postmodernist thought like pollen to a bee. Professor Sullivan, expounding a postmodernist critique of the American law on religion as too individualistic, asserts that isolating religion to protect both its free exercise and its imposition in contravention of the establishment clause is impossible.[116] The recognition of rights as belonging to groups is, for her, only a halting halfway step. She encourages a total reconsideration of "the nature of the state and its relation to the individual ... [in the] evolving cultural politics of religion."[117] She sees this evolution primarily in anthropological and psychological terms as Americans "naturalize" and "reintegrate" religion into their society. She writes:

> By naturalizing I refer to a legal and social process by which religion and spirituality are increasingly seen in the U.S. to be a natural, and largely benign – if varied – aspect of the human condition, one that is to be accommodated rather than segregated by government.[118]

This anthropological and psychological approach to religious accommodation as a means of building a community is reminiscent of the Roman Empire's accommodation of Roman religion. Few, if any, of Rome's leaders accepted Zeus and his extended family and friends as living deities, yet their presence was everywhere, and frequent

---

[115] *Obergefell v. Hodges* 2015 WL 213646 (S. Ct. 2015).
[116] Sullivan, *Prison Religion*, 8–9.
[117] Ibid., 9.
[118] Ibid., 2.

governmental deference was made to them as benign encouragements of deference and morality. As of 2005, the words "religion" or "religious" appeared more than 14,000 times in the laws of the United States and its states. In the early twenty-first century, American law recognizes religion as an influence on morals, politics, and jurisprudence even if it has trouble defining what it is.

Epilogue

The Significance of History and a Reconsideration of Original Intent

The battle over the role of religion in American society forms the longest-running debate in the nation's history. Since the mid-1700s, it has pitted two opposing worldviews, humanism and Protestant Christianity, as competitors for the values, beliefs, and attitudes of the American people and the laws and institutions they create. The political battlegrounds over which law and religion have contested have seldom been over religion itself, focusing instead on morality or values. The conflict between law and religion generally has been expressed in Americans' efforts to grapple with inequalities in wealth, limits on personal freedoms, and the powers of private associations and corporations. As a result, law's consideration of religion has been as much a matter of contract law, police powers, and corporate law as of the First Amendment.

In the recurring battles between Christian communitarians and secular individualists, the former have formed a series of alliances intended to advance their political causes. Whether fighting for disestablishment, abolition, Sabbath-day protection, prohibition, bans on abortion, or in the various movements for public recognition of Christianity, Christian activists have found momentary common cause with others who shared their immediate political goals, if not their long-term religious aspirations. Each of these movements has resulted in some degree of legal change, but never the total societal recognition of the Christian activists' position. Still, the multiple legal changes have, over time, eaten away at the strict separation envisioned by the founders and the public-private distinction that was essential to creating it.

People struggle to maintain two inconsistent ideas simultaneously; so too must societies. American culture is rooted in two conflicting idea systems that can roughly be expressed as Enlightenment humanism and Christian moralism. For most of American history, certainly from the colonial era until the middle of the twentieth century, Christianity has been a voice of protest against individualism and its humanistic expressions in free-enterprise capitalism and democracy. To a large extent, the civil religion, at once both a betrayal of each idea system and an integration of the two, has allowed Americans to hold onto their inconsistent ideologies while largely ignoring their irreconcilability. Formed in the mid-nineteenth century in the heat of Christian activists' crusade to reform America, it muted the ardent Christians' communitarian challenge while lessening the harshness of liberalism. Further modifications to the liberal system of laws, in the 1930s in particular, occurred largely in response to new forms of the civil religion. President Roosevelt's assertion of the "Four Freedoms" expressed Americans' conceptions of rights and freedoms as inclusive of communitarian duties. But, the breakdown of the civil religion in the second half of the 1900s left Americans aware of the intellectual inconsistency in the cultural worldview they had relied on since the Civil War. While opposition to the civil religion had previously come largely from extremists, by the 1970s few Americans could see Christianity as supporting free-enterprise capitalism, democracy, and environmental despoliation and exploitation as well as justifying militaristic imperialism and gross inequalities in wealth. Ironically, those who did were conservative evangelical Christians and their Mormon and Catholic allies who rejected not only their own church histories but much of a broader American history as well to assert an especially virulent form of the civil religion that asserts that God has chosen Americans and privileged them with a republican government and free-enterprise capitalism that they must now protect as a sacred duty to him.[1]

---

[1] It must be noted that while American Catholics have largely adopted a conservative social and political agenda, the Vatican and Catholics worldwide have not. In 2015, Pope Francis reiterated his predecessor's complaints against the free market and a "culture of relativism" in seeking a global consensus to address climate change and human suffering. Papal Encyclical *Laudato Si*, 2015.

Much of the recent historiography on church and state relations has been largely driven by those who oppose a strict separation and has focused on dissenters as expositors of the founders' intentions. Historians who emphasize the role of the dissenters relative to liberals in disestablishment generally minimize the extent of separation. Recent work also has argued, quite contrarily to the positions asserted in the preceding text, that the First Amendment itself controls the relationship between church and state and that a precise reading of its language either (1) prohibits the federal government from exercising jurisdiction over religion while allowing the states the autonomy to endorse religion at their will or (2) only prohibits governmental preference for one denomination over another, allowing nonpreferential support of a general Christianity or of all religions equally. Still others argue that the Constitution never disestablished religion at all and that separation arose only in the late nineteenth century as a means of protecting the civil religion. In making these arguments historians who endorse a larger role for religion in society have kept the Constitution and original intent in the center of the discussion. The reason for this is that social conservatives generally are disinclined to want drastic revision to the Constitution or to see it as subject to radical change arising from popular political movements. They see the Constitution as being difficult to revise and as a force preventing, or at least curtailing, radical political innovation. They want to see the Constitution as still controlling the policies of the nation in the twenty-first century. To do so, though, they have to argue that the Constitution accepts the public support or even endorsement of religion. Accordingly, conservative historians appear consumed with reinterpreting the founding era so as to render it less liberal, less individualistic, and more religious. They excise from the Constitution the secular, rational values that its framers and ratifiers embedded in it.

The foregoing text has argued that ideas and politics have exercised at least as much influence over the form of church-state relations as has the Constitution. The American system requires law to be consistent with the Constitution, but changing ideas influence not only legislation but also interpretations of Constitutional language. The black-letter text of the Constitution has always been understood not only in the context of the ideas percolating among the founders at the creation, but also in the context of contemporary thoughts and political needs.

This is not to say that the founding era is not important to constitutional interpretation – it is. But so too are the late nineteenth century, the 1960s, and the contemporary era. Ironically, the social conservatives, wedded as they are to "original intent," must look to perhaps the most secular, humanistic, and individualistic era in 400 years of American history to make an argument for the founders' endorsement of a public religion. Unfortunately for them, the argument that Americans supported a public religion could well be made at almost any other time in American history, but is difficult to sustain for the founding era.

Recently, some legal historians, quite apart from any consideration of church-state relations, have argued that interpretations of the Constitution have always been subject to popular, as opposed to judicial, conceptions of its meaning. Consistent with the broad conceptions of this "popular Constitutionalism," some scholars have made arguments that popular understandings of the religion clauses largely eroded whatever separation might have been intended by the founders. But, social conservatives cannot accept these arguments, as they tend to undermine both the integrity of the Constitution as a written document and the controlling influence of its black-letter text on the present. Just as important, the proponents of popular constitutionalism discount the vital influence of law, and especially of the Constitution, in controlling political discourse and placing some parameters on political majorities.

The entire idea of a constitution, or social contract, is that it articulates certain inviolable ideals that form the basis of society. These ideals must, of course, be compatible with prevailing attitudes, values, and beliefs, or the social contract becomes a source of discontent or even revolution. But a constitution articulates ideals that are by their nature sustainable over time, perhaps even permanent. Majoritarian sentiment at any single point in time cannot form the only basis for repudiating constitutional ideals; the founders made it difficult to amend the Constitution in recognition of this premise. The founders overtly considered the protection of conscience in this political and philosophical context. Jefferson wrote that while the spirit of the times in which he lived would not tolerate criminal convictions or civil limitations placed on disbelievers, "the spirit of the times may alter, will alter," and concluded that "the time for fixing every essential right on a legal basis is while our rulers are honest and ourselves united."[2] Original intent cannot be subordinated to majoritarian sentiment insufficient to amend the Constitution.

Yet, what is meant by "original intent"? Perhaps it is best to regard original intent as expressing essential first principles that shape the law. The First Amendment embodies the principle that government may not intrude on any individual's freedom of conscience, as religious truth is a speculative matter best left to individual judgments. In order to secure this right, the founders prohibited government action that they perceived could threaten it: an establishment of religion or an impairment of any individual's free exercise of religion. In Constitutional jurisprudence, sometimes the Court has given greater significance to these means of protecting the right of conscience than to the right itself. A proper regard for the Constitution as a statement of principles requires a greater attention to the individual right of conscience and a subordination of both the establishment and the free exercise clauses to that principle. Doing so not only defeats the proposition that government can support a general Christian religion, because as the founders noted in the 1780s, such a policy would contravene a right of conscience, but it also repudiates the argument that states may promote religion. As Justice William O. Douglas stated in another context, "In our federal system, we are all subject to two governmental regimes, and freedoms of speech and of the press protected against the infringement ... [by] only one [of them] are quite illusory. The identity of the oppressor is, I would think, a matter of relative indifference to the oppressed."[3]

Constitutional protection of the freedom of conscience rests on a conception of rights as individual and a delineation of public and private spheres that have been much eroded by the twenty-first century. As the founders created the private sphere to protect all rights, the erosion of the distinction between public and private spheres threatens them all. So, too, does the assertion that rights are based in societal or psychological needs and belong to groups. Yet, the idea of group rights is not going away, and the contract clause's separation of public and private realms is not returning. Accordingly, the protection of

---

[2] Thomas Jefferson, "Query VII" in *Notes*, 213.
[3] *Gertz v. Robert Welch, Inc.*, 418 US 323, 359 (1974).

the right of conscience has to be recognized as a principle distinct from the pillars on which it was initially raised. Strict reliance on original intent fails if the reliance depends on ideological conceptions of a proper society in the late 1700s that have been rejected in the twenty-first century. Recent jurisprudence on the First Amendment has created the accommodationist theory by focusing on the two religion clauses of the amendment and by trying to force them into prevailing ideas recognizing group rights and vital public-sector responsibilities. Confusion and inconsistency have been the result. Instead, the Court must articulate the right of conscience as a first principle protected by the First Amendment – the historical record provides overwhelming evidence for this. This principle, standing apart from the clauses that express means of protecting it, can then be understood as rooted solely in individuals, for certainly the judicial recognition of group rights has not yet eviscerated the legal protection of individual rights. This individual right must once again form a barrier to any government action that compels or expresses support of religion in the public sector or tolerates criminal prosecution or the limitation of civil rights on a morality justified by its derivation from religious teaching.

Bibliographic Essay

This book had its origins, unrecognized at the time, in classes I took from Professor Robert Wiebe at Northwestern University in the late 1970s. Professor Wiebe contended that American society experienced periodic fluctuations in tolerating and inhibiting dissent. Our history, he argued, could be understood, in part, by an appreciation of the cyclical fluctuations through which we shaped the cultural parameters defining acceptable beliefs, behaviors, and values. As a student interested as much in philosophy as in history, I spoke at some length with Professor Wiebe about the intellectual sources of those parameters. We discussed the possibility that the country's dual intellectual roots in Protestant Christianity and Enlightenment humanism created a tension within our intellectual culture that precipitated the cyclical fluctuations he had identified. One or the other of these idea systems temporarily gains relative dominance, only eventually to be tempered or even supplanted by the other. Together the two idea systems functioned to organize American cultural beliefs and values around a mean, mitigating the tendencies toward more extreme expressions of either worldview. Interestingly, when Mike and Chris invited me to write this book, they referred to Wiebe's *A Search for Order* as the best example of a synthetic history.

As a synthetic work, this book attempts to analyze the historical relationship between law and religion from a near-total reliance upon secondary sources. The format used for works in this series requires a strict limitation of footnotes. This essay credits authors whose insights and ideas have shaped my own.

While I was a graduate student, Professor Larry Friedman recognized a strong similarity between my thinking and that of Sidney Mead and introduced me to his work. I owe a significant debt to Mead, who alerted me to the alliance between pietists and liberal rationalists at the time of the nation's founding and the subsequent breakup of this alliance in the early 1800s. His three books describing the historical tensions between American versions of Christianity and humanism have served as the greatest single influence on the development of the thesis of this book. Sidney Mead, *The Lively Experiment: The Shaping of Christianity in America* (New York: Harper & Row, 1963); *The Nation with the Soul of a Church* (New York: Harper & Row, 1975); *The Old Religion in the Brave New World* (Berkeley: University of California Press, 1977).

The following narrative highlights other important, sometimes crucial, contributions on more specific aspects of this text.

I. Christian History and Theology

A. *General Surveys*
A recent popular history provides strong general introductions to Christianity as an idea system and its tensions with classical Western thought: Charles Freeman, *The Closing of the Western Mind: The Rise of Faith and the Fall of Reason* (New York: Alfred A. Knopf, 2003). Subsequent ideological conflict between Christianity and Enlightenment-era thought is developed in Michael Burleigh, *Earthly Powers: The Clash of Religion and Politics in Europe from the French Revolution to the Great War* (New York: Harper Perennial, 2005); R. R. Palmer, *The Age of the Democratic Revolution: A Political History of Europe and America, 1760–1800* (Princeton, NJ: Princeton University Press, 1959); Henry F. May, *The Enlightenment in America* (New York: Oxford University Press, 1976); Lefferts A. Loetscher, *Facing the Enlightenment and Pietism: Archibald Alexander and the Founding of Princeton Theological Seminary* (Greenwood, CT: Greenwood Press, 1983); Theodore Dwight Bozeman, *Protestants in the Age of Science: The Baconian Ideal and Antebellum American Religious Thought* (Chapel Hill: University of North Carolina Press,

1977); Charles Taylor, *A Secular Age* (Cambridge, MA: Belknap Press, 2007).

Garry Wills has recently provided a uniquely American history describing this ideological tension in a very wide-ranging and readable book, *Head and Heart: American Christianities* (New York: Penguin, 2007). Anne Norton noted the dual intellectual heritage of the American people in 1986 in *Alternative Americas: A Reading of Antebellum Political Culture* (Chicago: University of Chicago Press, 1986). Earlier, John Thomas asserted that American expressions of Enlightenment thought were Christianized by strong evangelical forces arising in the nineteenth century in *Alternative America: Henry George, Edward Bellamy and Henry Demarest Floyd and the Adversary Tradition* (Cambridge, MA: Belknap Press, 1983).

Histories of Christianity focusing more specifically on Reformation theology and its various forms and expressions in Europe and America include Martin E. Marty, *The Christian World: A Global History* (New York: Modern Library, 2007); Patrick Collinson, *The Reformation: A History* (New York: Modern Library, 2003); Diarmaid MacCulloch, *Christianity: The First Three Thousand Years* (New York: Viking Press, 2009); John Witte, Jr., *Law and Protestantism: The Legal Teachings of the Lutheran Reformation* (Cambridge: Cambridge University Press, 2002). An old classic, Harold J. Grimm, *The Reformation Era, 1500–1650* (New York: Macmillan, 1954), remains a helpful introduction to the Reformation in Europe.

B. American Religious History

The best general history of religion in America is still Sidney E. Ahlstrom, *A Religious History of the American People* (New Haven, CT: Yale University Press, 1972). More recent works appropriate for classroom use as well as academic study include Harry S. Stout and D. G. Hart, eds., *New Directions in American Religious History* (New York: Oxford University Press, 1997); Amanda Porterfield, ed., *American Religious History* (Malden, MA: Blackwell, 2002); John Corrigan and Winthrop S. Hudson, *Religion in America*, 7th ed. (Upper Saddle River, NJ: Pearson Prentice Hall, 2004). A nice collection of original documents that is suitable for classroom use is Robert R. Mathisen, ed., *Critical Issues in American Religious History* (Waco, TX: Baylor University Press, 2006).

II. Colonial American History

A. *Religious History*

The field of colonial religious history has been dominated for decades by studies of New England Puritanism. A large body of literature supports the assertion of colonial-era Calvinism imposing communitarian duties upon American colonists. Any study of New England Puritanism must start with Perry Miller, *Orthodoxy in Massachusetts, 1630–1650* (Cambridge, MA: Harvard University Press, 1933); *The New England Mind: The Seventeenth Century* (New York: Macmillan, 1939); *The New England Mind: From Colony to Province* (Cambridge, MA: Harvard University Press, 1953). During the seventeenth century, Puritanism transformed from a trans-Atlantic ideology of universal reform to a local and domestic orientation of salvation and self-governance. Adherents to New England's variation of Puritanism adapted socially and ideologically to the unique circumstances of life in America. In *From Colony to Province*, Miller argues that Puritanism was forced to address unexpected manifestations of American exceptionalism in the presence of increased religious diversity, growing Enlightenment ideologies, an intellectual and social valuation of science, and greatest of all, the increasing pressures of a market economy.

Despite Miller's arguments about the untenability of Puritanism in confronting social and intellectual change in the eighteenth century, Puritanism's real crisis occurred in the seventeenth century. Miller's two key theses, American exceptionalism and declension, both address developments prior to 1700. Miller depicts Puritanism as an ideological bridge from the medieval to the modern minds, significant for its ability to accommodate change in its doctrinal balance of piety (salvation by grace) and works (temporal behaviors and values). Doctrinal accommodation brought decline in the second half of the seventeenth century. Cultural change brought defeat in the eighteenth century. Through his study of Puritanism, Miller denigrates ideology as the basis of a society. Puritans tried to base a society on ideology and failed. A new society developed in its place based not on ideas but on experience.

Edmund S. Morgan, a student of Miller's, has been more prolific and nearly as influential as his mentor. Morgan, troubled by the doctrinal inconsistencies of the Puritans, expanded his investigation from intellectual history to cultural and social histories. The inability of the Puritans to realize the judgment of God compelled a greater emphasis on "works" than on "grace." Morgan accordingly asserts that internal inconsistencies in the Puritan doctrine led to a reformulation of that doctrine as early as the 1630s. Doctrinal problems only increased in later years when social pressures confronted Puritanism. The absence of ties between the church and the unregenerate community resulted in unprecedented purity within the church but also in unprecedented isolation of the church. Edmund S. Morgan, *Visible Saints: The History of a Puritan Idea* (New York: New York University Press, 1963); *The Puritan Family: Religion and Domestic Relations in Seventeenth Century New England*, rev. ed. (New York: Harper & Row, 1996).

Both Miller and Morgan stressed the communitarian nature of Puritan society, derived from the doctrinal commitment to build a Godly community. The family served as the basic unit of this society. In *The Puritan Family*, Morgan attempts to resolve some of his concerns with Puritan doctrine through an examination of social relationships. In their zeal to combat declining piety, maintain a Godly community, and insulate their children from "bad company," late seventeenth-century Puritans created institutions that made it easier for certain "core" families to remain affiliated with the church. Such policies transformed the "visible" Puritan churches into societies populated by the children of elite families who no longer practiced the same kind of rigorous piety as did their parents and grandparents. In a statement that echoes Miller's "declension" thesis, Morgan concluded, "When theology became the handmaid of genealogy, Puritanism no longer deserved its name." Ibid., 186.

Morgan's work should be considered with that of David D. Hall, who sees family commitments as the strength of Puritanism and not as a cause of its decline. David Hall, *Worlds of Wonder, Days of Judgment: Popular Religious Beliefs in Early New England* (New York: Alfred A. Knopf, 1989). Barry Levy has conducted a study of Quaker family life similar to that of Morgan's on the Puritans. Levy finds that over time, Pennsylvania's Quakers lacked the religious and political institutions necessary to build their moral society. Quaker domesticity functioned as a substitute, with the home serving as a haven. Barry Levy, *Quakers and the American Family: British Settlement in the Delaware Valley* (New York: Oxford University

Press, 1988). Further examination of familial relations within Puritan society has arisen in the context of social and women's histories. The legal and social acceptance of the male head of the household making all political, economic, and religious decisions for the family has been well documented. Elaine Forman Crane, *Witches, Wife-Beaters, and Whores: Common Law and Common Folk in Early America* (Ithaca, NY: Cornell University Press, 2011); Mark McGarvie and Elizabeth Mensch, "Law and Religion in Colonial America," in *Cambridge History of Law in America*, Vol. 1: *Early America 1580–1815*, ed. by Michael Grossberg and Christopher Tomlins (New York: Cambridge University Press, 2008): 324–64. Tapping Reeve, a lawyer in Connecticut who wrote a treatise on domestic law, understood domestic order as Blackstone did, recognizing the powers of masters over servants, husbands over wives, parents over children, and guardians over wards. In many colonial households, one man held each of those powerful roles. His powers declined during the eighteenth century. Holly Brewer, "The Transformation of Domestic Law," in Grossberg and Tomlins, *Cambridge History*, I: 288–9. Both Amanda Porterfield and Laurel Thatcher Ulrich confirm a decline in Puritan communitarian values in the adoption of more capitalistic and individualistic values. Amanda Porterfield, *Female Piety in Puritan New England: The Emergence of Religious Humanism* (New York: Oxford University Press, 1992); Laurel Thatcher Ulrich, *Good Wives: Image and Reality in the Lives of Women in Northern New England, 1650–1750* (New York: Alfred A. Knopf, 1982).

The general conclusion of more recent historians focusing on Puritan theology is that Puritan culture was much more diverse than Miller assumed. Ultimately, this conclusion leads to a refutation of Miller's declension thesis, for if Puritan society was not monolithic and ideologically pure, from what did it decline? There can be no declension from a nonexistent ideal. Paul Lucas, Janice Knight, and Baird Tipson have shown that disputes over doctrine and social practice divided New England's churches. Conflict over the balance of works and grace produced sectarian differences within the theocracy. Disagreements over the control of doctrine and discipline, the evangelical role of the church, the relationship of the church to the civil government, and the degree of toleration acceptable in a godly community further fractured any supposed consensus. Paul R. Lucas,

Valley of Discord: Church and Society along the Connecticut River,
1636–1725 (Hanover, NH: University Press of New England, 1976);
Janice Knight, *Orthodoxies in Massachusetts: Rereading American*
Puritanism (Cambridge, MA: Harvard University Press, 1994);
Baird Tipson, "Samuel Stone's Discourse Against Requiring Church
Relatives," *William and Mary Quarterly* (October 1989), 786–99.
See also David D. Hall, "On Common Ground: The Coherence of
American Puritan Studies," *William and Mary Quarterly*, 3rd Series,
44(2) (April 1987); 193–229. Hall writes that a significant historiography disputes Miller's assertion of consensus, what Hall terms
"monolithic unity," finding instead "multiple voices in dialogue" as
well as cultural "ambivalence." Hall also asserts that Miller's "artificial dichotomy" between intellect and piety (new and old, reason and
faith, works and grace) trapped him into seeing in the rise of one the
decline of the other. To some degree, however, Hall may miss Morgan's
argument of the importance of the balance between mutually inconsistent beliefs being essential to a perpetuation of a worldview.

As historians have discovered New England's diversity, Puritanism
is seen as even more repressive and authoritarian. Miller presents the
Puritans as a vanguard of seventeenth-century theology and civil society, while Theodore Bozeman perceives them as doctrinally regres-
sive and socially parochial. Theodore Dwight Bozeman, *To Live*
Ancient Lives: The Primitivist Dimension in Puritanism (Chapel
Hill: University of North Carolina Press, 1988). Kai Erikson contends
that by the 1690s, New England ceased to be "Puritan." Puritans confirmed God's election of those who conformed to social norms by
punishing those who did not. Recognition of deviant behavior as wor-
thy of punishment established conforming behavior as deserving of
salvation. In their definition of dissent, Puritans also defined themselves. The Antinomian Controversy of 1636, the Quaker Persecutions
of the 1650s, and the witchcraft hysteria of 1692 each questioned
the Puritan limits of tolerance. In reforming the acceptable parameters of dissent, society diminished identities negatively formed. Kai
T. Erikson, *Wayward Puritans: A Study in the Sociology of Deviance*
(New York: Wiley, 1966).

Andrew Delbanco removes American Puritanism from its
Augustinian and Calvinist context and asserts that its essence is in
Manichaeism. Manichaeism asserted a bipolar world of good and evil

and that good people experience evil because of the sin of others. The decline noted by others in increasingly condemnatory sermons and diaries was nothing more than the self-excoriation of later Puritans who believed that they could not live up to the ideals of the first generation. Andrew Delbanco, *The Puritan Ordeal* (Cambridge, MA: Harvard University Press, 1989). Delbanco writes in the genre of literary criticism and forms his views on Puritanism as much from the works of Hawthorne as from Winthrop, a questionable premise.

Writing in the same year as Delbanco, James Hoopes finds Puritan theology premised on an awareness of salvation (grace) through a means other than conscious thought. The entire Puritan cosmological understanding was challenged with the publication of John Locke's *Essay Concerning Human Understanding* in 1690. Puritanism accordingly had to adapt to the new knowledge of the Enlightenment. Hoopes argues that the work of Charles Morton in 1693 develops a Puritan accommodation of Enlightenment thought in its articulation of sensory awareness that reached fruition in the Great Awakening. Puritanism did not so much decline as change during the eighteenth century. James Hoopes, *Consciousness in New England: From Puritanism and Ideas to Psychoanalysis and Semiotic* (Baltimore, MD: Johns Hopkins University Press, 1989). A more recent work on Puritanism's confrontation with the Enlightenment argues that an acceptance of empiricism and natural philosophy transformed Puritanism in the seventeenth century. Sarah Rivett, *The Science of the Soul in Colonial New England* (Chapel Hill: University of North Carolina Press, 2011).

Numerous scholars have attempted to understand the nature of New England Calvinism amid the transformative influx of economic freedom. Perhaps the best recent work in this field is Mark Valeri, *Heavenly Merchandize: How Religion Shaped Commerce in Puritan America* (Princeton, NJ: Princeton University Press, 2010). Valeri argues that tremendous changes in the thinking of ministers and laypeople near the end of the seventeenth century and through the eighteenth century not only accommodated capitalism and economic prosperity but also imbued them with providential purpose. Capitalism did not triumph over Calvinism; rather, it encouraged a reconsideration of Calvinist doctrines. Valeri's conclusions lend support to the idea that by 1750, a market economy that had become well integrated with American religious culture provided motives for rebellion against England. See also T.H. Breen, *The Marketplace of Revolution: How Consumer Politics Shaped American Independence* (New York: Oxford University Press, 2004); Margaret Ellen Newell, *From Dependency to Independence: Economic Revolution in Colonial New England* (Ithaca, NY: Cornell University Press, 1998). These recent works diminish the conflict between Calvinism and economic individualism by stressing the transformation of Calvinism into a liberal Protestantism that redefined the idea of communal good, morality, and freedom and echo, to an extent, the earlier argument in Stephen Innes, *Creating the Commonwealth: The Economic Culture of Puritan New England* (New York: W. W. Norton, 1995).

Most earlier scholars, perceiving Calvinism as less flexible, found greater inconsistency between colonial religion and the free market. Bernard Bailyn, *New England Merchants in the Seventeenth Century* (Cambridge, MA: Harvard University Press, 1959). The new social historians of the 1960s, 1970s, and 1980s paid greater attention to common people and small towns than did Miller or Bailyn, yet confirmed, almost in spite of themselves, their predecessors' conclusions. Kenneth Lockridge, *A New England Town: The First Hundred Years* (New York: W. W. Norton, 1970, 1985); John Demos, *The Unredeemed Captive: A Family Story from Early America* (New York: Vintage Books, 1994); J.R.T. Hughes, *Social Control in the Colonial Economy* (Charlottesville: University of Virginia Press, 1976); Darrett B. Rutman, *Winthrop's Boston: Portrait of a Puritan Town, 1630–1649* (Chapel Hill: University of North Carolina Press, 1965); Summer Powell, *Puritan Village: The Formation of a New England Town* (Middletown, CT: Wesleyan University Press, 1963). In a largely Marxist interpretation void of theological inquiry, Gary Nash asserts that the development of a distinctly American culture began in the eastern seaboard cities and that capitalism largely defined that culture. By the mid-eighteenth century, urban societies had been transformed from corporate commonwealths dedicated to mutual support into communities of self-interest. Gary B. Nash, *The Urban Crucible: The Northern Seaports and the Origins of American Revolution* (Cambridge, MA: Harvard University Press, 1979).

Doctrinal diversity and change do not necessarily preclude the maintenance of a strong communitarian ethic within colonial New England. The historiography is nearly unanimous in asserting this communitarian character. Sacvan Bercovitch finds New England's use of jeremiads, scripture lessons establishing communal norms, to place social concerns in the context of person's duty in support of the Godly community. Sacvan Bercovitch, *The American Jeremiad* (Madison: University of Wisconsin Press, 1978). Christine Heyrman asserts that the transition to a market-driven economy in the late 1600s only triggered a conservative impulse to preserve traditional communitarian values. Puritan doctrine served as the means to counter liberal economic tendencies. Christine L. Heyrman, *Commerce and Culture: The Maritime Communities of Colonial Massachusetts, 1690–1750* (New York: W.W. Norton, 1984). Stephen Innes finds a persistence of Calvinist communitarianism well into the 1700s, as economic expansion led to greater political and social equality rather than to fragmentation. Stephen Innes, *Labor in a New Land: Economy and Society in Seventeenth-Century Springfield* (Princeton, NJ: Princeton University Press, 1983). Bruce Daniels builds on Miller's findings of spiritual communitarianism in asserting that theology and a social vision reinforced each other in early New England's regulation of behavior. Bruce C. Daniels, *Puritans at Play: Leisure and Recreation in Colonial New England* (New York: St. Martin's Press, 1995). David Hackett Fischer characterizes New Englanders as people sharing a religious sensibility manifested in their desire for a distinct society noteworthy for its communitarian ethic. David Hackett Fischer, *Albion's Seed: Four British Folkways in America* (New York: Oxford University Press, 1989). The integration of Puritanism, family, and a communitarian society at the dawn of the eighteenth century is well presented in the highly readable book, John Demos, *The Unredeemed Captive: A Family Story from Early America* (New York: Alfred A. Knopf, 1995).

Though using different terms in describing the phenomenon, historians are nearly as uniform in their recognition of a breakdown of the communitarian ethic during the eighteenth century. Jack P. Greene, *Pursuits of Happiness: The Social Development of Early Modern British Colonies and the Formation of American Culture* (Chapel Hill: University of North Carolina Press, 1988); Jon Butler, *Becoming America: The Revolution Before 1776* (Cambridge, MA: Harvard University Press, 2000). Various factors contributed to this development: greater diversity of immigrants, introduction of new ideologies, and the imposition of religious toleration from England. Yet, most of the histories of New England's colonies in the first half of the eighteenth century have focused on the tensions between economic expansion and Calvinism as the root of the loss of community.

Recent work focused on the colonies south of New England has indicated the pervasiveness of Calvinist thought and its prescription of communitarianism throughout English America. Alan Taylor, *American Colonies* (New York: Viking Press, 2001); Stephen Botein, *Early American Law and Society* (New York: Alfred A. Knopf, 1983); Kathleen McCarthy, *American Creed* (Chicago: University of Chicago Press, 2003); Erskine Clarke, *Our Southern Zion: A History of Calvinism in the South Carolina Low Country* (Tuscaloosa: University of Alabama Press, 1996); Jon Butler, *The Huguenots in America* (Cambridge, MA: Harvard University Press, 1983); David D. Hall, "Narrating Puritanism" in *New Directions in American Religious History*, ed. by Harry S. Stout and D.G. Hart (New York: Oxford University Press, 1997). On the prominence of communitarian values in the southern colonies, including Virginia, see D.B. Rutman and A.H. Rutman, *A Place in Time: Middlesex County, Virginia, 1650–1750* (New York: W.W. Norton, 1984); Allan Kulikoff, *Tobacco and Slaves: The Development of Southern Cultures in the Chesapeake, 1680–1800* (Chapel Hill: University of North Carolina Press, 1986); J.G. Kolb, *Gentlemen and Freeholders: Electoral Politics in Colonial Virginia* (Baltimore, MD: Johns Hopkins University Press, 1998); and James R. Perry, Jr., *The Formation of a Society on Virginia's Eastern Shore, 1615–1655* (Chapel Hill: University of North Carolina Press, 1990). The similarity of the struggles faced by residents of New England and Virginia in reconciling pious parochialism and striving cosmopolitanism is developed in Kenneth Lockridge, *Settlement and Unsettlement in Colonial America* (Baton Rouge: Louisiana State University Press, 1981). The extent to which deference to a local elite, often reinforced by religious doctrines and institutions, frustrated individualism and democracy throughout colonial America is examined in a series of essays in Michael G. Kammen, ed., *Politics and Society in Colonial America* (Chapel Hill: University of North Carolina Press, 1967).

The complex interaction between religion and cultural change in colonial Pennsylvania is especially accessible through an influential study: Barry Levy, *Quakers and the American Family: British Settlement*

in the Delaware Valley (New York: Oxford University Press, 1988).
Other treatments include Frederick B. Tolles, *Meeting House and
Counting House: The Quaker Merchants of Colonial Philadelphia,
1682–1763* (New York: W.W. Norton, 1963); Dietmar Rothermund,
*The Layman's Progress: Religious and Political Experience in Colonial
Pennsylvania, 1740–1770* (Philadelphia: University of Pennsylvania
Press, 1961); Stephanie Grauman Wolf, *Urban Village Population,
Community and Family Structure in Germantown, Pennsylvania,
1683–1800* (Princeton, NJ: Princeton University Press, 1976);
Aaron Spencer Fogleman, *Hopeful Journeys: German Immigration,
Settlement, and Political Culture in Colonial America, 1717–1775*
(Philadelphia: University of Pennsylvania Press, 1996); and Michael
Zuckerman, ed., *Friends and Neighbors: Group Life in America's First
Plural Society* (Philadelphia: Temple University Press, 1982). Several
authors have described Pennsylvania and the mid-Atlantic states, in
contrast to New England, as developing an early emphasis on indi-
vidualism and a market economy because of heterogeneous popula-
tions and a devaluation of religion: Gary Nash, "Social Development,"
in *Colonial British America: Essays in the New History of the Early
Modern Era*, ed. by J.P. Greene and J.R. Pole (Baltimore, MD: Johns
Hopkins University Press, 1984), 233–61, esp. 235–9; and James
T. Lemon, *The Best Poor Man's Country: A Geographical Study of
Southeastern Pennsylvania* (Baltimore, MD: Johns Hopkins University
Press, 1972). A.G. Roeber, *Palatines, Liberty, and Property: German
Lutherans and Colonial British America* (Baltimore, MD: Johns
Hopkins University Press, 1993), shows the important role of German
immigrants in shaping innovative conceptions of public and private
realms in this cultural context.

New York, like New England, experienced strong early influences
from Calvinist thought that shaped its early society. Randall H. Balmer,
*A Perfect Babel of Confusion: Dutch Religion and English Culture
in the Middle Colonies* (New York: Oxford University Press, 1989).
John Webb Pratt, *Religion, Politics and Diversity: The Church-State
Theme in New York History* (Ithaca, NY: Cornell University Press,
1967). Yet, the colony quickly became culturally and religiously
diverse and embraced a quite secular market economy before its
neighbors. A number of books provide a general background on the
politics of colonial New York in relation to its social and economic

life. Examples include Patricia U. Bonomi, *A Factious People: Politics and Society in Colonial New York* (New York: Columbia University Press, 1971); Michael G. Kammen, *Colonial New York: A History* (New York: Charles Scribner's Sons, 1975), and Milton M. Klein, ed., *The Politics of Diversity: Essays in the History of Colonial New York* (Port Washington, NY: Kennikat Press, 1974). George L. Smith, *Religion and Trade in New Netherland: Dutch Origins and American Development* (Ithaca, NY: Fall Creek Books, 1974) describes religion in relation to law, politics, and the economy in the early years. For the effects of the Glorious Revolution on domestic rebellion and its aftermath, see Jerome R. Reich, *Leisler's Rebellion: A Study of Democracy in New York 1669–1720* (Chicago: University of Chicago Press, 1953). Books covering the more immediate pre-Revolutionary period include Edward Countryman, *A People in Revolution: The American Revolution and Political Society in New York, 1760–1790* (Baltimore, MD: Johns Hopkins University Press, 1981) and Dorothy Dillon, *The New York Triumvirate: A Study of the Legal and Political Careers of William Livingston, John Morin Scott and William Smith, Jr.* (New York: Columbia University Press, 1949).

Any work on the religious and legal culture in colonial Virginia should begin with Rhys Isaac, *The Transformation of Virginia 1740–1790* (Chapel Hill: University of North Carolina Press, 1982), and Edward L. Bond, *Damned Souls in a Tobacco Colony* (Macon, GA: Mercer University Press, 2000). Timothy Breen has written excellent works distinguishing colonial Virginia from colonial Massachusetts: see his books, *Puritans and Adventurers: Change and Persistence in Early America* (New York: Oxford University Press, 1980), and *Tobacco Culture: The Mentality of the Great Tidewater Planters on the Eve of Revolution* (Princeton, NJ: Princeton University Press, 1985). The growth of dissenting sects in Virginia after the Great Awakening is available in Jewel L. Spangler, *Virginians Reborn: Anglican Monopoly, Evangelical Dissent, and the Rise of the Baptists in the Late Eighteenth Century* (Charlottesville: University of Virginia Press, 2008). Good summaries of early Virginia legal culture can be gained from A.G. Roeber, *Faithful Magistrates and Republican Lawyers: Creators of Virginia Legal Culture, 1680–1810* (Chapel Hill: University of North Carolina Press, 1981), and George L. Chumbly, *Colonial Justice in Virginia* (Richmond, VA: Dietz Press, 1938). The extent to which religion and the authority of the church influence criminal prosecutions in colonial Virginia is available in Arthur P. Scott, *Criminal Law in Colonial Virginia* (Chicago: University of Chicago Press, 1930).

Maryland, like Massachusetts, had religious toleration imposed upon it by England. A contrast between colonial Puritan and English Anglican enforcement of Christian ethical prescription can be found in David Underdown, *Revel, Riot, and Rebellion: Popular Politics and Culture in England 1603–1660* (New York: Oxford University Press, 1987). David Lovejoy, *The Glorious Revolution in America* (New York: Harper & Row, 1972), provides an account of the interplay between religious/political conflict in England and in the colonies.

Maryland's colonial history describing the influences of religious strife and ultimate Anglican establishment upon the colony is available in Gregory A. Wood, *The French Presence in Maryland, 1524–1800* (Baltimore, MD: Gateway Press, 1978); Lois Green Carr and David Jordan, *Maryland's Revolution of Government, 1689–1692* (Ithaca, NY: Cornell University Press, 1974); M. Graham, "Meetinghouse and Chapel: Religion and Community in 17th Century Maryland," in *Colonial Chesapeake Society*, ed. by Lois Green Carr, Philip D. Morgan, and Jean B. Russo (Chapel Hill: University of North Carolina Press, 1988), 242–74; A.E. Matthews, "The Religious Experience of Southern Women," in *Women and Religion in America*, Vol. 2: *The Colonial and Revolutionary Periods*, ed. by Rosemary Radford Ruether and R. S. Keller (New York: Harper & Row, 1981), 193–232; J.D. Krugler, "Lord Baltimore, Roman Catholics, and Toleration: Religious Policy in Maryland during the Early Catholic Years, 1634–1649," *Catholic Historical Review* 65 (1979), 49–75; T.P. Pyne, "A Plea for Maryland Catholics Reconsidered," *Maryland Historical Magazine* 92 (1997), 163–81; B.B. Hardy, "Roman Catholics, Not Papists: Catholic Identity in Maryland, 1689–1776," *Maryland Historical Magazine*, 92 (1997), 139–61; E.A. Kessel, "A Mighty Fortress Is Our God: German Religious and Educational Organizations on the Maryland Frontier, 1734–1800," *Maryland Historical Magazine* 77 (1982), 370–87.

The extent to which Christian ideology subordinated women to male authority and limited their social opportunities is further developed in Cornelia Hughes Dayton, *Women before the Bar: Gender, Law, and Society in Connecticut, 1639–1789* (Chapel Hill: University of North Carolina Press, 1995); Ann Braude, *Sisters and Saints: Women and American Religion* (New York: Oxford University Press, 2008); Kathleen M. Brown, *Good Wives, Nasty Wenches, and American Patriarchs: Race, Gender, and Power in Colonial Virginia* (Chapel Hill: University of North Carolina Press, 1996). Laurel Thatcher Ulrich, *Good Wives*, develops the idea that women did occasionally defy religiously justified patriarchal conceptions of women's duty to submit. The persistence of religious attitudes compelling female submission despite occasional moments of female ascendency within churches is developed in Catherine Brekus, *Strangers and Pilgrims: Female Preaching in America, 1740–1845* (Chapel Hill: University of North Carolina Press, 1998).

The Great Awakening has been the subject of a large and contentious body of literature. Historiographic disputes focus on whether the Awakening constituted a conservative reaction to religious change or an expression of that change as well as the evaluation of the movement as a religious, cultural, or political expression of discontent. Key readings include Jon Butler, "Enthusiasm Described and Decried: The Great Awakening as Interpretative Fiction" *Journal of American History* 69 (September 1982), 306–9; Joseph A. Conforti, *Jonathan Edwards, Religious Tradition and American Culture* (Chapel Hill: University of North Carolina Press, 1995); Darrett Rutman, *The Great Awakening: Event and Exegesis* (New York: Wiley, 1970); Frank Lambert, *Inventing the Great Awakening* (Princeton, NJ: Princeton University Press, 1999); Harry S. Stout, *The New England Soul: Preaching and Religious Culture in Colonial New England* (New York: Oxford University Press, 1986); Alan E. Heimert, *Religion and the American Mind from the Great Awakening to the Revolution* (Cambridge, MA: Harvard University Press, 1966); David Hall, *Worlds of Wonder, Days of Judgment: Popular Religious Belief in Early New England* (New York: Alfred A. Knopf, 1989); and Nathan O. Hatch, *The Sacred Cause of Liberty: Republican Thought and the Millennium in Revolutionary New England* (New Haven, CT: Yale University Press, 1977) and *The Democratization of American Christianity* (New Haven, CT: Yale University Press, 1989).

Significant works interpreting the intellectual and cultural significance of Jonathan Edwards reproduce the larger historiographic arguments over the Awakening itself. Perry Miller, *Jonathan Edwards* (New York: William Sloan Associates, 1949), contended that Edwards articulated a modern theology at odds with much of Puritan thought. George Marsden, *Jonathan Edwards: A Life* (New Haven, CT: Yale University Press, 2003), offers a repudiation of Miller by placing Edwards in an international Calvinist attempt to secure the "universal and exclusive truth" of Christianity in a world of diverse intellectual and religious opinions. Two excellent collections of essays on Edwards include Stephen J. Stein, *Jonathan Edward's Writings: Text, Context and Interpretation* (Bloomington: Indiana University Press, 1996), and Nathan O. Hatch and Harry S. Stout, *Jonathan Edwards and the American Experience* (New York: Oxford University Press, 1988). Less attention has been paid to James Davenport, a contemporary of Edwards who arguably contributed at least as significantly to the theological changes at midcentury, but that will soon be rectified with the publication of Douglas Winiarski's book on Awakening preaching. Until then, see Harry Stout and Peter Onuf, "James Davenport and the Great Awakening in New London," *Journal of American History* 71 (December 1983): 556–78.

B. Legal History

A growing and very good historiography on the legal history of colonial America shows how law supported patriarchy, communitarianism, hierarchy, and communal homogeneity. A good overview is provided in two collections of essays. Christopher Tomlins and Bruce H. Mann, *The Many Legalities of Early America* (Chapel Hill: University of North Carolina Press, 2001); Michael Grossberg and Christopher Tomlins, *The Cambridge History of Law in America*, Vol. 1. A recent two-volume publication is indispensable for serious scholars: William E. Nelson, *The Common Law in Colonial America*, 2 vols. (New York: Oxford University Press, 2008, 2012). Early chapters of an older text provide an instrumentalist theory of law: Lawrence M. Friedman, *A History of American Law* (New York: Simon & Schuster, 1973).

Probably the leading works on the legal history of early Massachusetts are William E. Nelson, *Americanization of the Common Law: The Impact of Legal Change on Massachusetts Society, 1760–1830* (Cambridge, MA: Harvard University Press, 1975), and *Dispute and Conflict Resolution in Plymouth Country, Massachusetts 1725–1825*

(Chapel Hill: University of North Carolina Press, 1981), and David Konig, *Law and Society in Puritan Massachusetts: Essex County, 1629–1692* (Chapel Hill: University of North Carolina Press,1979). The use of criminal law to enforce religious and cultural norms and homogeneity in thought and action is presented in Edwin Powers, *Crime and Punishment in Early Massachusetts, 1620–1692* (Boston, MA: Beacon Press, 1966), and N.E.H. Hull, *Female Felons: Women and Serious Crime in Colonial Massachusetts* (Urbana: University of Illinois Press, 1987). On issues of social and religious conformity, see Louise A. Breen, *Transgressing the Bounds: Subversive Enterprises among the Puritan Elite in Massachusetts, 1630–1692* (New York: Oxford University Press, 2001). Other significant works on New England include Richard J. Ross, "The Career of Puritan Jurisprudence," *Law and History Review* 26(2) (2008): 227–59; Bruce H. Mann, *Neighbors and Strangers: Law and Community in Early Connecticut* (Chapel Hill: University of North Carolina Press, 1987); John Phillip Reid, *Rule of Law* (DeKalb: Northern Illinois University Press, 2004); Edgar J. McManus, *Law and Liberty in Early New England: Criminal Justice and Due Process, 1620–1692* (Amherst: University of Massachusetts Press, 1993); and George L. Haskins, *Law and Authority in Early Massachusetts A Study in Tradition and Design* (New York: Macmillan, 1960). On law and religious discipline in early Massachusetts, see T. Dwight Bozeman, *The Precisionist Strain: Disciplinary Religion and Antinomian Backlash in Puritanism to 1638* (Chapel Hill: University of North Carolina Press, 2004), and James F. Cooper, Jr., *Tenacious of Their Liberties: The Congregationalists in Colonial Massachusetts* (New York: Oxford University Press, 1999). The extent to which law, religious doctrine, and spiritualism were intertwined during the colonial era is developed in Douglas L. Winiarski, "'Pale Bluish Lights and a Dead Man's Groan': Tales of the Supernatural from Eighteenth-Century Plymouth, Massachusetts," *William and Mary Quarterly*, 3rd series, 54 (1998), 497–530. While most of the documentation of the change in the common law in the late eighteenth century is in Revolutionary-era and early republic scholarship, exceptions are the aforementioned works by Nelson, Mann, and Reid, as well as Peter Charles Hoffer, *Law and People in Colonial America* (Baltimore, MD: Johns Hopkins University Press, 1998).

The era of witchcraft trials has been subject to myriad interpretations, among which are Peter Charles Hoffer, *The Salem Witchcraft Trials: A Legal History* (Lawrence: University Press of Kansas, 1997); Carol F. Karlsen, *The Devil in the Shape of a Woman: Witchcraft in Colonial New England* (New York: W.W. Norton, 1987); Charles W. Upham, *Salem Witchcraft* (Mineola, NY: Dover Publications, 2000); Chadwick Hansen, *Witchcraft at Salem* (New York: George Braziller, 1969); and Marion Starkey, *The Devil in Massachusetts: A Modern Inquiry into the Salem Witch Trials* (New York: Alfred A. Knopf, 1949).

Rhode Island, always an outlier in the early history of New England, has been a focal point of scholarly attention because of its model of religious toleration implemented by Roger Williams. Several biographers of Williams have seen his society as the progenitor of the national system of religious freedom. John M. Barry, *Roger Williams and the Creation of the American Soul: Church, State and the Birth of Liberty* (New York: Penguin Books, 2012); Timothy L. Hall, *Separating Church and State: Roger Williams and Religious Liberty* (Urbana: University of Illinois Press, 1998); Edwin S. Gaustad, *Liberty of Conscience: Roger Williams in America* (Grand Rapids, MI: William B. Eerdmans, 1991). However, in doing so they implicitly champion a view of American religious freedom rooted in humanity's duty to God rather than in a liberal or rationalist conception of rights and limit the scope of the separation of church and state accordingly. Somewhat different perspectives on Williams can be found in Donald Skaggs, *Roger Williams' Dream for America* (New York: Peter Lang International Academic Publishers, 1993), and Edmund S. Morgan, *Roger Williams: The Church and the State* (New York: Harcourt, Brace, and World, 1967). The influence of religion on the laws and institutions of Rhode Island is developed in Sidney V. James, *Colonial Rhode Island: A History* (New York: Charles Scribner's Sons, 1975), and Sidney V. James and T. Dwight Bozeman, *John Clarke and His Legacies: Religion and the Law in Colonial Rhode Island 1638–1750* (University Park: Pennsylvania State University Press, 1999).

While New England has dominated the field of colonial legal history for decades, good historiographic materials can be found on the other colonies. An interesting microhistory case study of law, religion, and cultural values in colonial Virginia is John Ruston Pagan, *Anne Orthwood's Bastard: Sex and Law in Early Virginia*

(New York: Oxford University Press, 2003). Both Sung Bok Kim, *Landlord and Tenant in Colonial New York: Manorial Society, 1664–1775* (Chapel Hill: University of North Carolina Press, 1978), and Irving Mark, *Agrarian Conflicts in Colonial New York 1711–1775* (New York: Columbia University Press, 1940), describe land-grant disputes in colonial New York. Those disputes are put in the context of religious conflict in Elizabeth Mensch, "The Colonial Origins of Liberal Property Rights," *Buffalo Law Review* 31 (1982), 635, and "Religion, Revival and The Ruling Class: A Critical History of Trinity Church," *Buffalo Law Review* 36 (1987), Part II: 427. A brief legal history of Maryland is available in J.H. Smith, "The Foundations of Law in Maryland, 1634–1715," in *Selected Essays: Law and Authority in Colonial America*, ed. by George A. Billias (Barre, MA: Barre Publishers, 1965), 92–115.

III. Revolutionary War and Early Republic

A. *Thought and Culture in the Early Republic*

The field of intellectual American history experienced a rebirth in the late 1960s due considerably to the efforts of Bernard Bailyn. Bailyn considered the pamphlet literature circulating in the colonies from 1750 to the beginning of the Revolution, tracing its largely Whig ideas to the country theorists writing in England in the early 1700s and promulgated in the colonies by diverse merchants, lawyers, planters, and preachers. He published these papers in Bernard Bailyn, ed., *Pamphlets of the American Revolution, 1750–1776*, 2 vols. (Cambridge, MA: Harvard University Press, 1965). He concluded from his study of these papers that a fierce antiauthoritarianism combined with a commitment to virtue and a recognized need to protect private property to form a new American ideological perspective that prompted both the need for Revolution and the building of a new nation consistent with Revolutionary principles. Bernard Bailyn, *The Ideological Origins of the American Revolution* (Cambridge, MA: Harvard University Press, 1967).

Gordon Wood, a student of Bailyn at Harvard and then long-term professor at Brown, built on Bailyn's work. He argued in 1969 that American republicanism depended on virtue as a means of tempering individualism and promoting a commitment to the civic good.

Gordon S. Wood, *The Creation of the American Republic, 1776–1787* (Chapel Hill: University of North Carolina Press, 1969). Shortly thereafter, J.G.A. Pocock stressed the tenuous balance between power and liberty, virtue and corruption, and self-interest and the civic ideal embodied in the founding of America. John Greville Agard Pocock, *The Machiavellian Moment: Florentine Political Thought and the Atlantic Republican Tradition* (Princeton, NJ: Princeton University Press, 1975). Together these works emphasized the importance of classical republican thought, in which a virtuous citizenry subordinated self-interest to its concern for the civil society, to the founding of the republic.

However, in 1987, UCLA Professor Joyce Appleby contended that American Revolutionary-era ideology contained various threads and that the antiauthoritarianism identified by Bailyn expressed itself in a fervently libertarian individualism that overwhelmed the more civic-oriented classical republicanism in the ascendency of Jeffersonian liberalism in the 1790s. Joyce Appleby, *Capitalism and a New Social Order: The Republican Vision of the 1790s* (New York: New York University Press, 1984). Wood himself seems to have been convinced by Appleby's argument. In 1992, he asserted that liberalism expressed Americans' integration of economic freedom (capitalism) with political freedom (democracy). Gordon S. Wood, *The Radicalism of the American Revolution* (New York: Alfred A. Knopf, 1992). Appleby and Wood found Americans' views of human nature derived as much from the thinking of Adam Smith as from John Locke and that Smith's view of humanity influenced the design of the new republic. Incessant self-interested stirrings did not lead to chaos but rather to a new social order premised on freedom, equality, and the personal pursuit of happiness. That contract law served as the means of creating the new society enjoys tremendous popularity but is perhaps most strongly asserted by Jay Fliegelman: "Central to the rationalist ideology of the American Revolution was the belief that in an ideal world all relationships would be contractual." Jay Fliegelman, *Prodigals and Pilgrims: The American Revolution against Patriarchal Authority* (New York: Cambridge University Press, 1982): 123. Many historians have noted the adoption of capitalism during or after the War. See the special issue, "Capitalism in the Early Republic," *Journal of the Early Republic* 16(2) (Summer 1996): 159–308; Naomi R. Lamoreaux, "Rethinking the Transition to Capitalism in the American Northeast," *Journal of American History* 90 (September, 2003): 437–61, and Allan Kulikoff, *Agrarian Origins of American Capitalism* (Charlottesville: University Press of Virginia, 1992).

Certainly, by 1800, Jefferson's election as President signified a broad-scale rejection of the old republican model for the liberal one. James Horn, Jan Ellen Lewis, and Peter Onuf, *The Revolution of 1800: Democracy, Race, and the New Republic* (Charlottesville: University of Virginia Press, 2002); Dan Sisson, *The American Revolution of 1800* (New York: Alfred A. Knopf, 1974); Bernard A. Weisberger, *America Afire: Jefferson, Adams and the Revolutionary Election of 1800* (New York: HarperCollins, 2000); Lance Banning, *The Jeffersonian Persuasion: Evolution of a Party Ideology* (Ithaca, NY: Cornell University Press, 1978). On the conservative religious reaction to Jefferson's election, see Colin Wells, *The Devil and Doctor Dwight: Satire and Theology in the Early American Republic* (Chapel Hill: University of North Carolina Press, 2002). But see John E. Hill, *Democracy, Equality, and Justice: John Adams, Adam Smith, and Political Economy* (Lanham, MD: Lexington Books, 2007). Hill generally argues that Smith held a traditional republican perspective more similar to that of Adams and his fellow Federalists than to Jefferson. Yet, even Hill notes that his argument may be questioned. He writes: "Adam Smith is often seen as an advocate of individualism; however, because community was also very important to him, I see him as an advocate of individuality within communities."

Subsequent scholarship has deepened our understanding of liberalism's influence upon various aspects of life in the early republic. Perhaps the greatest change was the substitution of the individual for the family as the primary political, economic, and social actor. Appleby, *Inheriting the Revolution: The First Generation of Americans* (Cambridge, MA: Belknap Press, 2000); Daniel Walker Howe, *What Hath God Wrought: The Transformation of America, 1815–1848* (New York: Oxford University Press, 2007). Several authors have explored the free market as empowering individuals to pursue their personal desires for fine things as well as their commercial, financial, or status goals. Richard L. Bushman, *The Refinement of America* (New York: Random House, 1992); Paul E. Johnson, *The Early Republic, 1789–1829* (New York: Oxford University Press, 2007); A. Kristen

Foster, *Moral Visions and Material Ambitions: Philadelphia Struggles to Define the Republic, 1776–1836* (Lanham, MD: Lexington Books, 2004); Jean V. Matthews, *Toward a New Society: American Thought and Culture, 1800–1830* (Boston: Twayne, 1991). Wood himself returns to this argument in Gordon S. Wood, *Empire of Liberty: A History of the Early Republic, 1789–1815* (New York: Oxford University Press, 2009). A free economy promoted the ideal of equality as offering opportunities for all to pursue their dreams with the chance of success or failure. This understanding changed the cultural norms regarding virtue and social duty. John M. Murrin identifies this liberal ascendency as a social revolution following the political one, involving a transition from classical republicanism to vulgar democracy and materialistic individualism. John M. Murrin, "Political Development" in *Colonial British America: Essays in the New History of the Early Modern Era*, ed. by Jack P. Greene and J.R. Pole (Baltimore, MD: Johns Hopkins University Press, 1984), 414–56. See also Curtis P. Nettels, *The Emergence of a National Economy, 1775–1815* (New York: Holt, Rinehart, and Winston, 1962); Drew R. McCoy, *The Elusive Republic: Political Economy in Jeffersonian America* (New York: W.W. Norton, 1980). Most historians see the growth of political and economic freedoms as coterminous expressions of a rights-oriented ideology. Yet, this perspective has been challenged recently in Clement Fatovic, *American Founding and the Struggle over Economic Inequality* (Lawrence: Kansas University Press, 2014).

Liberal individualism influenced nearly every aspect of early American society and culture. Changes in people's manners and conceptions of social structure, noting a new openness and a decline in deference, are presented in C. Dallett Hemphill, *Bowing to Necessity: A History of Manners in America, 1620–1860* (New York: Oxford University Press, 1999). Changes in childrearing are explained in James Gilreath, ed., *Thomas Jefferson and the Education of a Citizen* (Washington, DC: Library of Congress, 1999). A greater toleration of diverse opinions and popular dissent, indicative of a growing cultural respect for each individual as an equal rational thinker, is expressed in Michael Warner, *The Letters of the Republic* (Cambridge, MA: Harvard University Press, 1990); Robert H. Wiebe, *The Opening of American Society* (New York: Alfred A. Knopf, 1984); Gilman Ostrander, *Republic of Letters: The American Intellectual*

Community, 1775–1865 (Madison, WI: Madison House, 1999); and Steven C. Bullock, *Revolutionary Brotherhood: Freemasonry and the Transformation of the American Social Order, 1730–1840* (Chapel Hill: University of North Carolina Press, 1996). The relative brevity of this cosmopolitan society is noted in Lawrence J. Friedman, *Inventors of the Promised Land* (New York: Alfred A. Knopf, 1975). The growth of romantic love, companionate marriage, and greater sexual freedom, each of which embodies recognition of freedom, autonomy, and social equality, is well documented in the literature on the early republic. Richard Godbeer, *Sexual Revolution in Early America* (Baltimore, MD: Johns Hopkins University Press, 2002); Timothy Kenslea, *The Sedgwicks in Love: Courtship, Engagement, and Marriage in the Early Republic* (Boston: Northeastern University Press, 2006); Cynthia A. Kierner, *Scandal at Bizarre: Rumor and Reputation in Jefferson's America* (New York: Palgrave Macmillan, 2004). A decline in the use of capital punishment as well as public execution of corporal punishments also reflects the early republic's respect of individual equality and a decline in public authority relative to individual rights and the secular goal of atonement for wrongs in a societal context rather than a purgation of sin. Jack D. Marietta and G.S. Rowe, *Troubled Experiment: Crime and Justice in Pennsylvania, 1682–1800* (Philadelphia: University of Pennsylvania Press, 20006); Alan J. Hirsch, *The Rise of the Penitentiary: Prison and Punishment in Early America* (New Haven, CT: Yale University Press, 1992); Louis B. Masur, *Rites of Execution: Capital Punishment and the Transformation of American Culture, 1776–1865* (New York: Oxford University Press, 1989). But, see also Michael Meranze, *Laboratories of Virtue: Punishment, Revolution and Authority in Philadelphia, 1760–1835* (Chapel Hill: University of North Carolina Press, 1996), for a more postmodernist interpretation of these developments.

Perhaps the greatest indication of the rights orientation of the early republic and its resulting protection of individual autonomy is the separation of public and private spheres. This separation produced a decline in public services, especially poor relief and education, which had been administered by the churches and paid for with taxes throughout most of colonial America. During the early republic, Americans expressed their distrust of government and dislike for taxes by limiting support for these services. Education became much more secular in nature during this time. Good primary sources on education are available in Ellwood P. Cubberly, ed., *Readings in Public Education in the United States: A Collection of Sources and Readings to Illustrate the History of Education Practice and Programs in the United States* (Boston: Houghton Mifflin, 1934), and Thomas E. Finegan, ed., *Free Schools: A Documentary History of the Free School Movement in New York State* (Albany: University of the State of New York, 1921). Excellent secondary works describing the reduction in and secularization of public services after the Revolution include Robert W. Kelso, *The History of Poor Relief in Massachusetts, 1620–1920* (Montclair, NJ: Patterson Smith, 1969); Walter I. Trattner, *From Poor Law to Welfare State: A History of Social Welfare in America* (New York: Free Press, 1989); Roy M. Brown, *Public Poor Relief in North Carolina* (New York: Arno Press, 1976); Martha Branscombe, *The Courts and the Poor Law in New York State, 1784–1929* (Chicago: University of Chicago Press, 1943); Charles Lawrence, *History of the Philadelphia Almshouses and Hospitals* (New York: Arno Press, 1976); Lorraine Smith Pangle and Thomas L. Pangle, *The Learning of Liberty: The Educational Ideas of the American Founders* (Lawrence: University of Kansas Press, 1993); Conrad Edick Wright, *The Transformation of Charity in Post-Revolutionary New England* (Boston: Northeast University Press, 1992); T. Laurence Moore, "Bible Reading and Nonsectarian Schooling: The Failure of Religious Instruction in Nineteenth Century Public Education," *Journal of American History* 86(4) (March 2000): 1581–99; Bernard Bailyn, *Education in the Forming of American Society* (New York: Vintage Books, 1960); Newton Edwards and Herman G. Richey, *The School in the American Social Order* (Boston: Houghton Mifflin, 1947); Vera Butler, *Education as Revealed by New England Newspapers Prior to 1850* (Philadelphia: Temple University Press, 1935); Maria Louise Greene, *The Development of Religious Liberty in Connecticut* (reprinted in the Civil Liberties in American History Series), ed. by Leonard W. Levy (New York: De Capo Press, 1970); Ava Harriet Chadburne, *A History of Education in Maine* (Orono, ME: Self-published, 1936); H.G. Good, *A History of American Education* (New York: Macmillan, 1956); Edwin Grant Dexter, *A History of Education in the United States* (New York: Macmillan, 1904); Benjamin Joseph Klebaner, *Public Poor Relief in America, 1790–1860* (New York: Arno Press, 1976); Curtis

D. Johnson, *Islands of Holiness: Rural Religion in Upstate New York, 1790–1860* (Ithaca, NY: Cornell University Press, 1989); John Webb Pratt, *Religion, Politics, and Diversity: The Church-State Theme in New York History* (Ithaca, NY: Cornell University Press, 1967); John Furman Thomason, *The Foundation of the Public Schools of South Carolina* (Columbia, SC: The State Company, 1925).

Historian Linda Kerber, writing in 1980, asserted that the post-Revolutionary idea of "republican motherhood," while inarguably limiting married women to the home, nonetheless provided a distinct means for women, as individuals, to pursue valued political and social functions. Linda Kerber, *Women of the Republic: Intellect and Ideology in Revolutionary America* (New York: W.W. Norton, 1986, 1980). Complementary work has shown that while the dominant social values expressed in such terms as "domesticity," the "cult of true womanhood," and "separate spheres" exercised real influence in male-female relationships, sex roles did not necessarily remain one-dimensional. In daily life, men and women saw themselves as largely equal, especially as partners in marriage. See generally Woody Holton, *Abigail Adams* (New York: Free Press, 2009); Nancy F. Cott, *The Bonds of Womanhood: Women's Sphere in New England, 1780–1835* (New Haven, CT: Yale University Press, 1977); and Mary Beth Morton, *Liberty's Daughters: The Revolutionary Experience of American Women, 1750–1800* (Boston: Little, Brown, 1980). Liberalization of the law shaped personal and family relationships as much as it did business relationships as, during and after the Revolution, women's autonomy and property rights increased. Marylynn Salmon, *Women and the Law of Property in Early America* (Chapel Hill: University of North Carolina Press, 1986), xv–xvi. See also Mark Douglas McGarvie, "Transforming Society through Law: St. George Tucker, Women's Property Rights, and an Active Republican Judiciary," *William and Mary Law Review* 47(4) (February 2006), 1393–1425. Evidence of women's understanding of their own individuality is seen in their assertions of economic independence. In fact, the renunciation of dower interests may have been the most common legal action, next to marriage, taken by women in the early 1800s. Joan Hoff Wilson, "Hidden Riches: Legal Records and Women, 1750–1825," in *Woman's Being, Woman's Place: Female Identity and Vocation in American History*, ed. by Mary Kelley (Boston: G.K. Hall, 1979).

Liberalism encouraged arguments that the denial of the vote to women and the perpetuation of coverture, through which a married woman lost control of her property, were inconsistent with Revolutionary ideals. New Jersey even extended the right to vote to women in its wartime constitution, though it continued property thresholds restricting the franchise. Jeanne Boydston, "Making Gender in the Early Republic: Judith Sargent Murray and the Revolution of 1800," in Horn, Lewis, and Onuf, *The Revolution of 1800*. The new status of women expressed in laws concerning marriage and divorce is well developed in Nancy Cott, "Divorce and the Changing Status of Women in Eighteenth-Century America," in *The American Family in Social Historical Perspective*, ed. by Michael Gordon (New York: St. Martin's Press, 1978); Norma Basch, "From the Bonds of Empire to the Bonds of Matrimony," in *Devising Liberty: Preserving and Creating Freedom in the New American Republic*, ed. by David Konig (Stanford, CA: Stanford University Press, 1995); Hendrik Hartog, *Man and Wife in America: A History* (Cambridge, MA: Harvard University Press, 2000); Michael Grossberg, *Governing the Hearth: Law and Family in Nineteenth-Century America* (Chapel Hill: University of North Carolina Press, 1985); Michael Grossberg, "Citizens and Families: A Jeffersonian Vision of Domestic Relations in Generational Change," in *Thomas Jefferson and the Education of a Citizen*, ed. by James Gabreath (Washington, DC: Library of Congress, 1999), 3–27.

The inherent tension between the old colonial model of a Christian community and a rights-oriented democratic and capitalist republic has been given expression in James A. Henretta, *The Origins of American Capitalism: Collected Essays* (Boston: Northeastern University Press, 1991); Richard Bushman, *From Puritan to Yankee* (Cambridge, MA: Harvard University Press, 1967); and Jack P. Greene, *Pursuits of Happiness* (Chapel Hill: University of North Carolina Press, 1988).

The pervasive cultural embrace of individual autonomy in the Revolutionary era through the early republic has widespread acceptance among historians. Yet, significant works have challenged the prevailing historiographic perspective. William J. Novak, *The People's Welfare: Law and Regulation in Nineteenth-Century America* (Chapel Hill: University of North Carolina Press, 1996); Barry Alan Shain, *The Myth of American Individualism: The Protestant Origins of American Political Thought* (Princeton, NJ: Princeton University Press, 1994);

Oscar Handlin and Mary Flug Handlin, *Commonwealth: A Study of the Role of Government in the American Economy, Massachusetts, 1774–1861* (Cambridge, MA: Harvard University Press, 1947, 1969). Novak's work, however, deals more with the Jacksonian era than what I consider to be the early republic. Some historians also have claimed that the tension between religion and commerce noted in the sermons and social activism of the Second Awakening has been overstated by most historians. Mark Noll, ed., *God and Mammon: Protestantism, Money, and the Market, 1790–1860* (New York: Oxford University Press, 2001); Stewart Davenport, *Friends of the Unrighteous Mammon: Northern Christians and Market Capitalism, 1815–1860* (Chicago: University of Chicago Press, 2008).

B. Religion, Revolution, and Constitutional Meanings

Changes in Revolutionary-era Americans' religious attitudes and beliefs correspond to the cultural prioritization of individual freedom and indicate a growing acceptance of religious diversity and, to a lesser degree, relative morality. John Witte, Jr., and M. Christian Green, "The American Constitutional Experiment in Religious Human Rights: The Perennial Search for Principle," in *Religious Human Rights in Global Perspective*, ed. by Johan D. van der Vyner and John Witte, Jr. (Cambridge, MA: Kluwer Law International, 1996), 516–21; William R. Hutchison, *Religious Pluralism in America: The Contentious History of a Founding Ideal* (New Haven, CT: Yale University Press, 2003); Derek H. Davis, *Religion and the Continental Congress, 1774–1789: Contributions to Original Intent* (New York: Oxford University Press, 2000); Chris Beneke, *Beyond Toleration: The Religious Origins of American Pluralism* (New York: Oxford University Press, 2006). The toleration of religious diversity, even of Catholics, in New England is depicted as a pragmatic rather than a doctrinal accommodation in Charles P. Hanson, *Necessary Virtue: The Pragmatic Origins of Religious Liberty in New England* (Charlottesville: University of Virginia Press, 1998), though Hanson himself notes, on page 22, that "evangelical Christianity was [temporarily] knocked out of the saddle during the Revolution."

The growth of Deism and liberal religion in the early republic, reflected in Jefferson's assertion that "I trust there is not a young man now living in the United States who will not die a Unitarian," is documented in Kerry S. Walters, *The American Deists: Voices of*

Reason and Dissent in the Early Republic (Lawrence: University of Kansas Press, 1992); David L. Holmes, *The Faith of the Founding Fathers* (New York: Oxford University Press, 2006); J.D. Bowers, *Joseph Priestly and English Unitarianism in America* (University Park: Pennsylvania State University Press, 2007); Conrad Edick Wright, *The Beginnings of Unitarianism in America* (Boston: Starr King Press, 1955); Frank Lambert, *The Founding Fathers and the Place of Religion in America* (Princeton, NJ: Princeton University Press, 2003). Chapters on this development are also found in Ahlstrom, *Religious History*, and Corrigan and Hudson, *Religion in America*. The liberalization of doctrine within the Congregational and Presbyterian Churches in the early 1800s is addressed in Robert A. Gross, "Dr. Ripley's Church: Congregational Life in Concord, Massachusetts, 1778–1841," *Journal of Unitarian-Universalist History* xxxiii (2009–2010); Mary Kupiec Clayton, "Who Were the Evangelicals? Conservative and Liberal Identity in the Unitarian Controversy in Boston, 1804–1833," *Journal of Social History* 33(1) (1997): 86–107.

As America, after the Revolution, became a marketplace of ideas as well as a commercial marketplace, churches had to compete for members. Nathan Hatch contends that religion assumed a character of "anarchic pluralism, a sort of free market of religious economy." Nathan O. Hatch, "Evangelicalism as a Democratic Movement," in *Fundamentalism and Evangelicalism* (Modern American Protestantism and Its World Series, Vol. 10), ed. by Martin E. Marty (New York: K.G. Sauer, 1993), 4. See also Chris Beneke, "The Free Market and the Founders' Approach to Church-State Relations," *Journal of Church and State* 52(2) (Spring 2010): 323–52.

While Hatch's theory holds great sway regarding the early republic, the role of religion in the American Revolution has become increasingly contested as historians have enlisted in the most recent culture wars over the importance of religion to American identity and law. While most historians consider the Revolutionary era to be a relatively secular age, there is no disputing that most Americans of the time considered themselves to be Christians and that ministers played a great role in mobilizing people to seek independence in pursuit of both a right to self-governance and God's will. Harry Stout, *The New England Soul: Preaching and Religious Culture in Colonial New England* (New York: Oxford University Press, 1986); Nathan O. Hatch, *The*

Sacred Cause of Liberty: Republican Thought and the Millennium in Revolutionary New England (New Haven, CT: Yale University Press, 1977); Mark Noll, *Christians in the American Revolution* (Vancouver, BC: Regent College Publications, 2006). These ministerial appeals come predominantly from dissenters who saw political freedom as embodying the right to worship God without governmental intrusion. To them, political liberty implied the freedom to do the right thing; religious liberty recognized the free will necessary to worship God and follow his dictates. John A. Ragosta, *Wellspring of Liberty: How Virginia's Religious Dissenters Helped Win the American Revolution and Secured Religious Liberty* (New York: Oxford University Press, 2010); A. Gregg Roeber, "The Limited Horizons of Whig Religious Rights," in *The Nature of Rights of the American Founding and Beyond*, ed. by Barry Alan Shain (Charlottesville: University of Virginia Press, 2007); James H. Hutson, *Religion and the Founding of the American Republic* (Washington, DC: Library of Congress, 1998). An excellent collection of wartime sermons is included in Ellis Sandoz, *Political Sermons of the American Founding Era, 1730–1805*, 2 vols. (Indianapolis, IN: Liberty Fund, 1998).

Two significant scholars have recently offered works asserting that religion played a vital role in building support for the Revolution, thereby disputing the prevailing understanding of the war years as a highly secular time period. Timothy Breen, *American Insurgents, American Patriots: The Revolution of the People* (New York: Hill & Wang, 2010); Thomas S. Kidd, *God of Liberty: A Religious History of the American Revolution* (New York: Basic Books, 2010). However, both look largely to sermons during the 1770s that supported Revolution and not to a set of religious beliefs that fostered Revolutionary sentiment. Jon Butler of Yale, in discussing these books, noted that Enlightenment-era humanism, not religion, produced the ideological arguments causative of the Revolution. Religionists merely offered support to the Revolutionary movement and adapted Christian ideas to do so. The lending of religious support as a means of participation cannot be confused with contributing the ideological basis for the social, legal, and political events of the era. Jon Butler, "When Religion Counts and When It Doesn't: How Historians Know," presented at the Biennial Boston College Conference on the History of Religion, Boston, March 30, 2012.

Historians generally agree on the difficulty of using statistics to determine degrees of religiosity; qualitative assessments accomplish far more than quantitative measures. Nonetheless, historians contend that only about 4 percent of Americans belonged to a church in 1776. Leonard W. Levy, *Blasphemy: Verbal Offense Against the Sacred, from Moses to Salman Rushdie* (New York: Alfred A. Knopf, 1993). See also Jon Butler, "Why Revolutionary America Wasn't a 'Christian Nation'" in *Religion and the New Republic: Faith in the Founding of America*, ed. by James H. Hutson (Lanham, MD: Rowman & Littlefield, 2000), 187–202. On the considerable debate among historians as to whether statistics reflecting church membership and attendance of religious services constitute accurate indicia of religiosity, see Patricia Bonomi and Peter Eisenstadt, "Church Adherence in the Eighteenth-Century British American Colonies," *William and Mary Quarterly*, 3rd series, 39(2) (1982): 247; Rodney Stark and Roger Finke, "American Religion in 1776: A Statistical Portrait," *Sociological Analysis* 49 (1988): 39–51. For the predominance of women among the era's churchgoers, see Elaine Forman Crane, "Religion and Rebellion: Women of Faith in the American War for Independence," in *Religion in a Revolutionary Age*, ed. by Ronald Hoffman and Peter J. Albert (Charlottesville: University Press of Virginia, 1994); Ann Douglas, *The Feminization of American Culture* (New York: Noonday Press/Farrar, Straus, and Giroux, 1977); Peter S. Field, *The Crisis of the Standing Order: Clerical Intellectuals and Cultural Authority in Massachusetts, 1780–1833* (Amherst: University of Massachusetts Press, 1998), 59.

Historians' fascination with the founding era's understandings of church-state relations most likely emanates from the Supreme Court, which itself has turned to history as a means of understanding the First Amendment. A postmodernist rejection of the ideal of objective history has seemingly liberated many scholars from the pursuit of that goal. Many histories of the last forty years have sought to place current political arguments in the mouths of the nation's founders.

A growing literature, no doubt spawned in the culture wars that have raged since the late 1970s, has attempted to depict the nation's founders as devout evangelical Christians. By depicting them in this manner the authors seemingly hope to diminish the idea of strict separation of church and state. The implicit assumption underlying this literature is that if true Christians wrote the Constitution, they never could have intended it to limit Christian beliefs, values, and morals from significant roles in governing. Daniel L. Driesbach, Mark David Hall, and Jeffry H. Morrison, *The Forgotten Founders on Religion and Public Life* (Notre Dame, IN: University of Notre Dame Press, 2009); Steven Waldman, *Founding Faith: How Our Founding Fathers Forged a Radical New Approach to Religious Liberty* (New York: Random House, 2009); Vincent Phillip Muñoz, *God and the Founders: Madison, Washington, and Jefferson* (New York: Cambridge University Press, 2009).

This recent work supports a restricted understanding of the separation of church and state first articulated in highly respected work on the history of disestablishment that stressed the important role of dissenters in this process. The best work on religious dissenters from the colonial era through the early republic is still William G. McLaughlin, *New England Dissent, 1630–1833,* 2 vols. (Cambridge, MA: Harvard University Press, 1971). See also William G. McLaughlin, *Isaac Backus and the American Pietistic Tradition* (Library of American Biography Series), ed. by Oscar Handlin (Boston: Little, Brown, 1967). Subsequent work has largely reiterated McLaughlin's findings that dissenters strove for religious equality while using the language of religious freedom, but have expanded the scope of the history from New England to other colonies or states. Ragosta, *Wellspring of Liberty;* Thomas J. Curry, *The First Freedoms: Church and State in America to the Passage of the First Amendment* (New York: Oxford University Press, 1986); Thomas E. Buckley, *Church and State in Revolutionary Virginia, 1776–1789* (Charlottesville: University of Virginia Press, 1979), and *Establishing Religious Freedom: Jefferson's Statute in Virginia* (Charlottesville: University of Virginia Press, 2013). Buckley's latter work notably builds upon Sidney Mead's thesis as the author notes a counter-revolution led by evangelicals in Virginia against Jeffersonian-Madisonian liberalism in the early 1800s.

Some socially conservative authors have built upon the dissenters' articulated goals in championing disestablishment to argue that the establishment clause of the First Amendment only prohibits government from favoring one Christian denomination over another and actually accommodates a broad-based Christian establishment. Akhil Reed Amar, "The Bill of Rights and the Fourteenth Amendment," *Yale Law Journal* 101 (1992): 1193. Christopher F. Mooney, *Public*

Virtue: Law and the Social Character of Religion (Notre Dame, IN: University of Notre Dame Press, 1986); Richard John Neuhaus, *The Naked Public Square: Religion and Democracy in America* (Grand Rapids, MI: Eerdmans, 1984); Robert L. Cord, *Separation of Church and State: Historical Fact and Current Fiction* (New York: Lambeth Press, 1982); Glenn T. Miller, *Religious Liberty in America: History and Prospects* (Philadelphia: Westminster Press, 1976); John T. Noonan, *The Lustre of Our Country: The American Experience of Religious Freedom* (Berkeley: University of California Press, 1998); Chester James Antieu, Arthur L. Downey, and Edward C. Roberts, *Freedom from Federal Establishment: Formation and Early History of the First Amendment Religious Clauses* (Milwaukee, WI: Bruce Publishing, 1964); Walter Berns, *The First Amendment and the Future of American Democracy* (New York: Basic Books, 1976); Michael J. Malbin, *Religion and Politics, The Intentions of the Authors of the First Amendment* (Washington, DC: American Enterprise Institute for Public Policy Research, 1978). Mark DeWolfe Howe comes to a similar conclusion as these social conservatives but adds an interesting insight that the Court's redefinition of rights in the twentieth century was a conscious decision to combat racism and that redefinition had profound effects on the separation of church and state. Mark DeWolfe Howe, *The Garden and the Wilderness: Religion and Government in American Constitutional History* (Chicago: University of Chicago Press, 1965).

Others from the socially conservative perspective have asserted that the establishment clause is merely structural and protects no individual right of conscience. Carl H. Esbeck, "The Establishment Clause as a Structural Restraint on Governmental Power," *Iowa Law Review* 84 (1998): 1; Carl H. Esbeck, "Dissent and Disestablishment: The Church-State Settlement in the Early American Republic," *Brigham Young University Law Review* (2004): 159; Vincent Phillip Muñoz, "The Original Meaning of the Establishment Clause and the Impossibility of Its Incorporation," *University of Pennsylvania Journal of Constitutional Law* 8 (2006); Steven Smith, *Foreordained Failure: The Quest for a Constitutional Principle of Religious Freedom* (New York: Oxford University Press, 1995); Daniel L. Dreisbach, *Thomas Jefferson and the Wall of Separation between Church and State* (New York: New York University Press, 2002). Donald Drakeman contends that the establishment clause meant only to prohibit the legal assertion of a national religion. Donald C. Drakeman, *Church, State, and Original Intent* (New York: Cambridge University Press, 2010). Also arguing that the states should be free from the establishment clause is A. James Reichley, *Religion in American Public Life* (Washington, DC: Brookings Institution, 1985).

Several authors who desire a societal recognition of their own faiths have struggled to integrate that desire with the legal principles of the country. John Courtney Murray asserted that no government should impose a religion or attempt to shelter or aid religion. Yet, as a Catholic, he believed there to be one truth that emanates from God. How can any society not take notice of that truth? "[R]eligious pluralism is against the will of God." John Courtney Murray, *We Hold These Truths: Catholic Reflections on the American Proposition* (New York: Sheed & Ward, 1960). Steven Waldman, editor in chief of Beliefnet.com, contends that James Madison only desired a strict separation of church and state at the federal level. However, rather than rely on constitutional arguments, he adopts a pragmatic view. As separation has prompted religious vitality, he tentatively endorses it. Steven Waldman, *Founding Faith: Providence, Politics, and the Birth of Religious Freedom in America* (New York: Random House, 2008). Another author noted that uncurtailed governmental protection of the free exercise of religion can create special privileges that act as a limited establishment of religion. Walter Berns, "Ratiocinations," *Harper's* (March, 1973), 36. Using similar reasoning, the Supreme Court has recognized the jurisprudential difficulties of reading the clauses separately: "[T]he Establishment Clause commands a separation of church and state"; but, the Court acknowledges that the establishment and free exercise clauses, if read as absolutes and "expanded to a logical extreme," would be contradictory. *Cutter v. Wilkinson*, 544 US 709, 719 (2005).

In recent decades, a school of thought minimizing the founders' commitment to strict separation has traced the idea to reactionary idealism born in social change during the nineteenth, not the eighteenth, century. Steven K. Green, *The Second Constitution: Church and State in Nineteenth-Century America* (New York: Oxford University Press, 2010); Philip Hamburger, *Separation of Church and State* (Cambridge, MA: Harvard University Press, 2002); Kurt Lash, "The Second Adoption of the Establishment Clause: The Rise of the Non-Establishment Principle," *Arizona State Law Journal* 27 (1995): 1085.

Sidney Mead recognized the tremendous contributions of the dissenters to the process of disestablishment but asserted that they would have failed but for an alliance with the Jeffersonian liberals. The alliance secured disestablishment, but on legal terms much more compatible with the goals of the liberals than the evangelical dissenters. Sidney E. Mead, *The Lively Experiment; The Nation with the Soul of a Church* (New York: Harper & Row, 1975); *The Old Religion in the Brave New World: Reflections on the Relation Between Christendom and the Republic* (Berkeley: University of California Press, 1977). I build upon Mead's thesis in my own work on disestablishment, Mark Douglas McGarvie, *One Nation Under Law: America's Early National Struggles to Separate Church and State* (DeKalb: Northern Illinois University Press, 2004). This work joined a body of literature that recognized freedom of conscience as a legal right predicated upon a liberal understanding of religion as a private matter. Leo Pfeffer, *Church, State and Freedom*, 2nd ed. (Boston: Beacon Press, 1967); Leonard Levy, *The Establishment Clause: Religion and the First Amendment* (New York: Macmillan, 1986); Anson Phelps Stokes, *Church and State in the United States: Historical Development and Contemporary Problems of Religious Freedom under the Constitution*, 3 vols. (New York: Harper & Brothers, 1950); Isaac Kramnick and R. Laurence Moore, *The Godless Constitution: The Case Against Religious Correctness* (New York: W.W. Norton, 1996); Robert S. Alley, ed., *James Madison on Religious Liberty* (Buffalo, NY: Prometheus Books, 1985); Martha Nussbaum, *Liberty of Conscience: In Defense of America's Tradition of Religious Equality* (New York: Basic Books, 2008).

Some excellent histories of disestablishment were published before the current culture wars and avoid many of the political issues in which more recent scholarship seems immersed. Several early scholars minimized the ideological tension between dissenters and liberals by focusing instead on religious diversity and the resulting need for toleration as the roots of religious freedom. William Warren Sweet, *The Story of Religion in America* (New York: Harper & Row, 1950); Anson Phelps Stokes and Leo Pfeffer, *Church and State in the United States* (New York: Harper & Row, 1964); Thomas Hanley,

The American Revolution and Religion (Washington, DC: Catholic University of America Press, 1971); Milton Klein, "New York in the American Colonies: A New Look," *New York History* 53 (April 1972): 132–56; Martin E. Marty, *Righteous Empire: The Protestant Experience in America* (Two Centuries of American Life Series), ed. by Harold Hyman and Leonard Levy (New York: Dial Press, 1970). Marty contends that real innovation occurred not in the early republic's legal disestablishment of the churches but in the seventeenth century when colonies formed without established churches in Rhode Island, Delaware, and Pennsylvania. See also Louis Hartz, *The Liberal Tradition in America* (New York: Harcourt, Brace, Jovanovich, 1991). In minimizing religious diversity relative to liberal ideas as the basis for religious freedom, I concur with Richard B. Bernstein, who, in *Are We to Be a Nation? The Making of the Constitution* (Cambridge, MA: Harvard University Press, 1987), asserts that despite sectarian differences, "most Americans [at the time of the Constitution] shared the common heritage of Protestant Christianity" (9–10). Religious diversity and toleration occurred before the Revolution; disestablishment and true religious liberty, afterward.

Our understanding of church-state relations has benefited tremendously from the recent publication of several excellent texts that explore long periods of American history to come to conclusions about this topic. Two new collections of essays are already classics in the field: Derek H. Davis, *The Oxford Handbook of Church and State in the United States* (New York: Oxford University Press, 2010); and T. Jeremy Gunn and John Witte, Jr., *No Establishment of Religion: America's Original Contribution to Religious Liberty* (New York: Oxford University Press, 2012). Of even greater potential interest are Sarah Barringer Gordon, *The Spirit of the Law: Religious Voices and the Constitution in Modern America* (New York: Oxford University Press, 2011); David Sehat, *The Myth of American Religious Freedom* (New York: Oxford University Press, 2011); and Noah Feldman, *Divided by God: America's Church-State Problem and What We Should Do About It* (New York: Farrar, Straus, and Giroux, 2005). All three of these scholars recognize the tension inherent in a diverse American culture that celebrates religious pluralism while preferencing Christianity. Their nuanced and sophisticated analyses promise greater academic understanding of the complexities of the intersection of law and religion in America. See also Featured Book Review by Mark McGarvie on Sehat, *Myth of American Religious Freedom* in *American Historical Review* (October 2011): 1066–8.

C. Legal History of the Early Republic

The legal history on this era, aside from considerations of religion, asserts that law contributed mightily to the ascendency of liberalism and its endorsement of free-enterprise capitalism and individual autonomy. J. Willard Hurst speaks for nearly all subsequent legal historians of the early republic in writing that contract law produced a huge "release of energy," empowering Americans to pursue their goals through economic means. James Willard Hurst, *Law and the Conditions of Freedom in the Nineteenth-Century United States* (Madison: University of Wisconsin Press, 1956). This legal empowerment of individuals, rooted in an understanding of law's primary purpose being the protection of rights rather than the securement of a social good, necessarily limited law's ability to prescribe religion and morality. Bill Nelson finds that after 1776, law ceased to pay much attention to issues of morality. There was a "shift in law's basic function ... from the preservation of morality to the protection of property." William E. Nelson, "Emerging Notions of Modern Criminal Law in the Revolutionary Era: A Historical Perspective," *New York University Law Review* 42 (1967): 451.

However, no scholarly field is free from debate. By the 1980s, legal scholars of the early republic debated law's role in the cultural changes of the era. Did law act as a tool or instrument in the service of elite interests or semiautonomously in expressing liberal republican ideals? The instrumentalist school of thought grew out of the progressive school of history promulgated by Charles Beard and legal positivism and found law to function as a tool in service to certain social interests. Leading works of this nature include Lawrence M. Friedman, *A History of American Law*, 3rd ed. (New York: Simon & Schuster, 2005); Morton J. Horwitz, *The Transformation of American Law, 1780–1860* (Cambridge, MA: Harvard University Press, 1977); and Kermit L. Hall, *The Magic Mirror: Law in American History* (New York: Oxford University Press, 1989).

Conversely, the relative autonomy school of thought perceives law to function as a force that dictates legal policies and resolutions consistent with its expression of principles, tenets, and ideals. Leading works developing this school of thought include Michael Grossberg, *Governing the Hearth: Law and Family in Nineteenth-Century America* (Chapel Hill: University of North Carolina Press, 1985); Christopher Tomlins, *Law, Labor, and Ideology in the Early American Republic* (New York: Cambridge University Press, 1993); and Holly Brewer, *By Birth or Consent: Children, Law, and the Anglo-American Revolution in Authority* (Chapel Hill: University of North Carolina Press, 2005).

Today, these opposing perspectives have given way to a tremendous complexity and diversity in interpretive approaches and means of analysis. The methodologies of scholars of the relative autonomy school broadened scholarly inquiries to consider a wide range of personal relationships that are ultimately influenced by, and in turn contribute to, American law. Seeing law as integrative with social and political activities has refocused attention on local and state court dockets and private law cases. Accordingly, legal history finds its way into a variety of intellectual, cultural, and political histories, as well as works focused on women, race, and geographic region. Numerous works cited in earlier sections of this essay are important resources in legal history.

Despite the significant emphasis in these works on the importance of private law cases at the state and local levels in reforming American society, a great body of work continues to explore constitutional law as a major force in transforming America. An excellent background in American thinking about the nature of constitutions and their role in splitting from England is provided in John Phillip Reid's three-volume *Constitutional History of the American Revolution* (Madison: University of Wisconsin Press, 1986, 1986, 1991). Also helpful in this regard are Edmund S. Morgan and Helen M. Morgan, *The Stamp Act Crisis: Prologue to Revolution* (Chapel Hill: University of North Carolina Press, 1953); Jack P. Greene, *Peripheries and Center: Constitutional Development in the Extended Politics of the British Empire, 1608–1788* (Athens: University of Georgia Press, 1986); Pauline Maier, *From Resistance to Revolution: Colonial Radicals and the Development of American Opposition to Britain, 1765–1776* (New York: Alfred A. Knopf, 1972); and A.E. Dick Howard, *The Road from Runnymede: Magna Carta and Constitutionalism in America* (Charlottesville: University of Virginia Press, 1968).

A good synopsis of the American adoption of social contract theory is provided in Mark Hulliung, *The Social Contract in America* (Lawrence: University of Kansas Press, 2007). The best treatment of early state constitutions is Willi Paul Adams, *The First American Constitutions: Republican Ideology and the Makings of State Constitutions in the Revolutionary Era* (Chapel Hill: University of North Carolina Press, 1980).

Several old classics remain very readable introductions to the constitutional debates at the Philadelphia Convention. Max Farrand, *The Framing of the Constitution of the United States* (New Haven, CT: Yale University Press, 1913); Clinton Rossiter, *1787: The Grand Convention* (New York: Macmillan, 1966); Catherine Drinker Bowen, *Miracle at Philadelphia: The Story of the Constitutional Convention, May to September 1787* (Boston: Little, Brown, 1966).

The Constitution as an expression of American ideology is developed in Alison LaCroix, *The Ideological Origins of American Federalism* (Cambridge, MA: Harvard University Press, 2010); Forrest McDonald, *Novus Ordo Seclorum: The Intellectual Origins of the Constitution* (Lawrence: University of Kansas Press, 1985); Jack Rakove, *Original Meanings: Politics and Ideas in the Making of the Constitution* (New York: Alfred A. Knopf, 1996); Charles R. Kesler, ed., *Saving the Revolution: The Federalist Papers and the American Founding* (New York: Free Press, 1987); Ralph Ketcham, *Framed for Posterity: The Enduring Philosophy of the Constitution* (Lawrence: University of Kansas Press, 1993); Herman Belz, Ronald Hoffman, and Peter J. Alberts, eds., *To Form a More Perfect Union: The Critical Ideas of the Constitution* (Charlottesville: University of Virginia Press, 1992); Richard Beeman, Stephen Botein, and Edward C. Carter II, eds., *Beyond Confederation: Origins of the Constitution and American National Identity* (Chapel Hill: University of North Carolina Press, 1987); and Michael I. Meyerson, *Liberty's Blueprint: How Madison and Hamilton Wrote the Federalist Papers, Defined the Constitution and Made Democracy Safe for the World* (New York: Basic Books, 2008). Most of this literature sees the Constitution as a fulfillment of republican ideals that developed in the Revolutionary era and coalesced in the nation's primary law.

Yet, more materialistic interpretations of the Constitution understand it as a repudiation of or retreat from democratic republican ideals. The leading work of this nature has long been Charles A. Beard, *An Economic Interpretation of the Constitution of the United States* (New York: Macmillan, 1913). Beard's work has retained its historiographic significance despite the repudiation of many of its factual assertions. Robert E. Brown, *Charles Beard and the Constitution: A Critical Analysis of "An Economic Interpretation of the Constitution"* (Princeton, NJ: Princeton University Press, 1956). In recent years, several scholars have reinvigorated Beard's thesis while adding ideological and cultural history as context. Jennifer Nedelsky, *Private Property and the Limits of American Constitutionalism: The Madisonian Framework and its Legacy* (Chicago: University of Chicago Press, 1990); Woody Holton, *Unruly Americans and the Origins of the Constitution* (New York: Hill & Wang, 2007); Terry Bouton, *Taming Democracy: "The People," the Founders, and the Troubled Ending of the American Revolution* (New York: Oxford University Press, 2007).

Jeffersonian liberals generally mistrusted the courts, believing that democracy required a powerful and active electorate. The tensions between this ideal and Republican Party judges pronouncing common-law doctrines to reform American society is presented in Richard E. Ellis, *The Jeffersonian Crisis: Courts and Politics in the Young Republic* (New York: Oxford University Press, 1971); John Phillip Reid, *Controlling the Law: Legal Politics in Early National New Hampshire* (DeKalb: Northern Illinois University Press, 2004); and Mark Douglas McGarvie, "Transforming Society Through Law: St. George Tucker, Women's Property Rights, and an Active Republican Judiciary," *William and Mary Law Review* 47(4) (February 2006): 1393–1425. This contentious issue continues to be debated by scholars and jurists today.

IV. The Jacksonian Era and Antebellum America

A. *The Second Awakening, Religious Diversity, and Reform*

The growth of religious sentiment and practice between 1820 and 1860 is documented in Sehat, *The Myth of American Religious Freedom*; Richard J. Carwardine, *Evangelicals and Politics in Antebellum America* (Knoxville: University of Tennessee Press, 1997); and Karen Armstrong, *The Battle for God: A History of Fundamentalism* (New York: Random House, 2000). The preceding text separates the Second

Awakening into two phases: an early phase that emphasizes doctrinal
and institutional responses within American Christianity to capitalism,
individual autonomy, and the separation of church and state; and a latter phase characterized by social outreach expressed in the Benevolent
Empire. The doctrinal changes within the mainline and evangelical churches of the era are well developed in Sidney E. Ahlstrom,
A Religious History of the American People (New Haven, CT: Yale
University Press, 1972); Sidney Earl Meade, *Nathaniel William Taylor,
1786–1858: A Connecticut Liberal* (Chicago: Archon Books, 1967,
1942); John Corrigan and Winthrop S. Hudson, *Religion in America*;
Daniel Walker Howe, "Protestantism, Voluntarism, and Personal Identity
in Antebellum America," in *New Directions in American Religious
History*, ed. by Harry S. Stout and D. G. Hart (New York: Oxford
University Press, 1997); George M. Marsden, *Religion and American
Culture* (San Diego, CA: Harcourt, Brace, Jovanovich, 1990); Glenn
Hewitt, *Regeneration and Morality: A Study of Charles Finney, Charles
Hodge, John W. Nevin, and Horace Bushnell* (Brooklyn, NY: Carlson,
1991); and William R. Sutton, "Benevolent Calvinism and the
Moral Government of God: The Influence of Nathaniel W. Taylor
on Revivalism in the Second Awakening," *Religion and American
Culture* 2 (Winter 1992): 23–47. Good regional studies of these same
changes include Paul E. Johnson, *A Shopkeepers' Millennium: Society
and Revivals in Rochester, New York, 1815–1838* (New York: Hill &
Wang, 1978); Christine Heyrman, *Southern Cross: The Beginnings of
the Bible Belt* (New York: Alfred A. Knopf, 1997); Curtis D. Johnson,
Islands of Holiness: Rural Religion in Upstate New York, 1790–1860
(Ithaca, NY: Cornell University Press, 1989); and Mitchell Snay,
Gospel of Disunion: Religion and Separatism in the Antebellum South
(New York: Cambridge University Press, 1993).

The idea of churches competing for members and financial support in a free-market environment is developed in Nathan O. Hatch,
The Democratization of American Christianity (New Haven, CT: Yale
University Press, 1989); "The Second Great Awakening and the Market
Revolution," in *Devising Liberty: Preserving and Creating Freedom in
the New American Republic*, ed. by David Thomas Konig (Stanford,
CA: Stanford University Press, 1995). Christian leaders' recognition,
by 1820, that the new nation was committed to a new form of church
governance is outlined in Mark De Wolfe Howe, *The Garden and the*

Wilderness: Religion and Government in American Constitutional History (Chicago: University of Chicago Press, 1965). The growth of the evangelical sects born in the Great Awakening of the 1730s and 1740s is presented in Russell E. Richey, *Early American Methodism* (Religion in North America Series), ed. by Stephen J. Stein and Catherine L. Albanese (Bloomington: Indiana University Press, 1991).

The great diversity of religious beliefs and practices during this era has been the subject of an interesting and extensive body of literature. Historian Robert Abzug, in considering the 1820s through the 1840s, finds:

The free atmosphere for religious speculation and church formation fostered many free consciences and an almost dizzying degree of spiritual indeterminacy. In a society that tolerated almost unlimited versions of religious certainty, all with the right to be preached and none preordained as more truthful than another, there remained no social anchor of religious truth.

Robert H. Abzug, *Cosmos Crumbling: American Reform and the Religious Imagination* (New York: Oxford University Press, 1994), 31. See also Martin E. Marty, *The Infidel: Freethought in American Religion* (Cleveland, OH: Meridian, 1961). The presence of religious diversity from the early 1800s to the present is developed in William R. Hutchison, *Religious Pluralism in America: The Contentious History of a Founding Ideal* (New Haven, CT: Yale University Press, 2003). The wide variety of utopian societies founded during the Jacksonian era is described in Rosabeth Moss Kanter, *Commitment and Community: Communes and Utopias in Sociological Perspective* (Cambridge, MA: Harvard University Press); Michael Fellman, *The Unbounded Frame: Freedom and Community in Nineteenth-Century American Utopianism* (Westport, CT: Greenwood Press, 1973); Mark Holloway, *Heavens on Earth: Utopian Communities in America* (New York: Dover Books, 1966); Edward K. Spann, *Brotherly Tomorrows: Movements for a Cooperative Society in America, 1820–1920* (New York: Columbia University Press, 1989); Priscilla K. Brewer, *Shaker Communities, Shaker Lives* (Hanover: University of New Hampshire Press, 1986); Maren Lockwood Carden, *Oneida: Utopian Community to Modern Corporation* (Baltimore, MD: Johns Hopkins University Press, 1969); Robert David Thomas, *The Man Who Would Be Perfect: John Humphrey Noyes and the*

Utopian Impulse (Philadelphia: University of Pennsylvania Press, 1977);
Louis Kern, *An Ordered Love: Sex Roles and Sexuality in Victorian
Utopias: The Shakers, The Mormons, and the Oneida Community*
(Chapel Hill: University of North Carolina Press, 1981); Lawrence
Foster, *Women, Family, and Utopia – Communal Experiments of
the Shakers, the Oneida Community, and the Mormons* (Syracuse,
NY: Syracuse University Press, 1991).

On early Catholic immigration as well as the attitudes and beliefs
of the people, see Hamburger, *Separation*; and John T. McGreevy,
Catholicism and American Freedom: A History (New York: W.W.
Norton, 2003), 37. On the early Mormons, see Sarah Barringer Gordon,
*The Mormon Question: Polygamy and Constitutional Conflict in the
Nineteenth Century* (Chapel Hill: University of North Carolina Press,
2002), and D. Michael Quinn, *The Mormon Hierarchy: Origins of
Power* (Salt Lake City, UT: Signature Books, 1994).

Slave religion is addressed in Eugene Genovese, *Roll Jordan
Roll: The World the Slaves Made* (New York: Pantheon Books, 1974),
161–284; Albert Raboteau, *Slave Religion: The Invisible Institution
in the Antebellum South* (New York: Oxford University Press,
1978); and John W. Blassingame, *The Slave Community: Plantation
Life in the Antebellum South* (New York: Oxford University Press,
1979), 130–7.

Garry Wills notes historians' recent inclinations to minimize
Romanticism as an intellectual movement. Wills, *Head and Heart*.
A chestnut that still provides a good introduction to the Romantic
Age is Van Wyck Brooks, *The Flowering of New England, 1815–1865*
(Cleveland, OH: World Publishing, 1946). See also Joel Porte, *The
Romance in America: Studies in Cooper, Poe, Hawthorne, Melville
and James* (Middleton, CT: Wesleyan University Press, 1969).

Some of the best works on the growth and influences of
Transcendentalism raise the issue of whether Transcendentalism
is a religion or a philosophical response to it. Donald N. Koster,
Transcendentalism in America (Boston: Twayne, 1975); William
R. Hutchison, *The Transcendentalist Ministers: Church Reform in the
New England Renaissance* (New Haven, CT: Yale University Press,
1959); Paul F. Boller, Jr., *American Transcendentalism, 1830–1860: An
Intellectual Inquiry* (New York: G.P. Putnam's Sons, 1974). Conversely,
a great work on Transcendentalism as a religious phenomenon is

Catherine L. Albanese, *Corresponding Motion: Transcendentalist Religion and the New America* (Philadelphia: Temple University Press, 1977). Transcendentalism's role in reform movements is discussed in Anne C. Rose, *Transcendentalism as a Social Movement, 1830–1850* (New Haven, CT: Yale University Press, 1981). An older work of historical interest both for its subject and the era in which it was written is Odell Shepard, *Pedlar's Progress: The Life of Bronson Alcott* (Boston: Little, Brown, 1937). Important collections of primary and secondary works include Perry Miller, *The Transcendentalists: An Anthology* (Cambridge, MA: Harvard University Press, 1950); Mary Kelley, ed., *The Portable Margaret Fuller* (New York: Penguin Books, 1994); and Brooks Atkinson, ed., *The Essential Writings of Ralph Waldo Emerson* (New York: Classic Books, 2010). The communitarian values of a segment of the Transcendentalist movement is developed in Charles Crowe, *George Ripley: Transcendentalist and Utopian Socialist* (Athens: University of Georgia Press, 1967); F. Lindsay Swift, *Brook Farm: Its Members, Scholars, and Visitors* (New York: Macmillan, 1900).

The religious impulses within the Benevolent Empire have been well documented. Christian reformers of the time sought nothing less than radical change in American values, attitudes, institutions, and laws. As Reverend James G. Birney said, reform was the means of "purifying governments, and bringing them to a perfect conformity with the principles of Divine government." He added that government could only hope to restrain "human wickedness" by conforming civil law to divine law. Donald Meyer, *The Protestant Search for Political Realism, 1919–1941* (Berkeley: University of California Press, 1960), 92, 93. See also Michael P. Young, "Confessional Protest: The Religious Birth of United States National Social Movements," *American Sociological Review* 67(5) (October 2002): 660; Daniel Walker Howe, *What Hath God Wrought*; Charles I. Foster, *An Errand of Mercy: The Evangelical United Front* (Chapel Hill: University of North Carolina Press, 1960); Clifford S. Griffin, *Their Brothers' Keepers: Moral Stewardship in the United States* (New Brunswick, NJ: Rutgers University Press, 1960); David Paul Nord, "Systematic Benevolence: Religious Publishing and the Marketplace in Early Nineteenth Century America," in *Communication and Change in American Religious History*, ed. by Leonard I. Sweet (Grand Rapids, MI: Eerdmans, 1993).

The integration of religious values with secular dreams in Jacksonian America is beautifully articulated by Harriet Martineau, a visitor to America in the 1830s, who wrote an early sociological study of Americans. She notes a tremendous sensitivity to the suffering of others and a hopefulness in people's ability to alleviate them, factors leading to the growth of private philanthropy. Harriet Martineau, *Society in America*, ed. by Seymour Martin Lipset (Garden City, NY: Doubleday, 1962). The growth of private voluntary associations as a means of voicing dissent to mainstream values and policy and encouraging social change was noted as well by Alexis de Tocqueville in the 1830s. Alexis de Tocqueville, *Democracy in America*, ed. by Richard D. Heffner (New York: Penguin Press, 1956, 1984). Recent historians have elaborated upon their findings, particularly in the growing historiography on American philanthropy. Lawrence J. Friedman and Mark D. McGarvie, *Charity, Philanthropy, and Civility in American History* (New York: Cambridge University Press, 2003); Robert H. Bremner, *American Philanthropy*, 2nd ed. (Chicago: University of Chicago Press, 1988); Kathleen D. McCarthy, *American Creed: Philanthropy and the Rise of Civil Society, 1700–1865* (Chicago: University of Chicago Press, 2003); Conrad Edick Wright, *The Transformation of Charity in Postrevolutionary New England* (Boston: Northeastern University Press, 1992).

The role of these private voluntary associations as expressions of free people seeking social reform in the early republic and Jacksonian era is expertly handled in Johann N. Neem, *Creating A Nation of Joiners: Democracy and Civil Society in Early National Massachusetts* (Cambridge, MA: Harvard University Press, 2008). Excellent works on the same topic but highlighting the religious impulses behind the Benevolent Empire include Ronald G. Walters, *American Reformers, 1815–1860* (New York: Hill & Wang, 1977), and Joshua D. Rothman, ed., *Reforming America, 1815–1860* (New York: W.W. Norton, 2010), which includes primary documents excellent for classroom teaching. See also Steven C. Bullock, *Revolutionary Brotherhood: Freemasonry and the Transformation of the American Social Order, 1730–1840* (Chapel Hill: University of North Carolina Press, 1996).

Various aspects of the reform movement have been the subject of their own extensive historiographies. Ministerial desires to return religion and discipline to the classrooms are noted in Michael B. Katz, *The Irony of Early School Reform: Educational Innovation in*

Mid-Nineteenth Century Massachusetts (New York: Teachers College Press, 2001). The role of religion in spawning the abolitionist movement and in fragmenting it is well developed in Lawrence J. Friedman, *Gregarious Saints: Self and Community in American Abolitionism, 1830–1870* (New York: Cambridge University Press, 1982); Bertram Wyatt-Brown, *Lewis Tappan and the Evangelical War Against Slavery* (Cleveland, OH: University Press of Case Western, 1969); Lewis Perry, *Radical Abolitionism: Anarchy and the Government of God in Antislavery Thought* (Ithaca, NY: Cornell University Press, 1973); and Paul E. Johnson and Sean Wilentz, *The Kingdom of Matthias: A Story of Sex and Salvation in Nineteenth-Century America* (New York: Oxford University Press, 1994).

The involvement of Christian women in social reform movements and their effect on understandings of the separation of church and state is developed in Wendy J. Deichmann Edwards and Carolyn De Swarte Gifford, eds., *Gender and the Social Gospel* (Urbana: University of Illinois Press, 2005), 35–52. Women's important role in the temperance movement and its relationship to Christian calls for a more moral society are noted in Carolyn De Swarte Gifford, "The Woman's Course Is Man's?: Frances Willard and the Social Gospel" in *Gender and the Social Gospel*, 22–34, and Richard F. Hamm, *Shaping the Eighteenth Amendment: Temperance Reform, Legal Culture, and the Policy, 1850–1920* (Chapel Hill: University of North Carolina Press, 1995). The temperance movement also was driven in part by other ethnic fears. The conflation of immigration with immorality and a loss of American values is expressed in Alphonso Alva Hopkins, *Profit and Loss in Man* (New York: Funk & Wagnalls, 1909):

Our boast has been that we are a Christian people, with Morality at the center of our civilization. Foreign control or conquest is rapidly making us un-Christian, with immorality throned in power. Besodden Europe, worse bescouraged than by war, famine and pestilence, sends here her drink-makers, her drunkard-makers, and her drunkards, or her more temperate but habitual drinkers, with all their un-American ideas of morality and government; they are absorbed into our national life, but not assimilated; with no liberty whence they came, they demand unrestricted liberty among us, even to license for the things we loathe; and through the ballot-box, flung wide open to them by foolish statesmanship that covets power, their foreign control or conquest has become largely an appalling fact; they dominate our Sabbath, over large areas of country; they have set up for us their own moral standards, which are grossly immoral; they govern our great cities, until even Reform candidates accept their authority and pledge themselves to obey it; the great cities govern the nation; and foreign control or conquest could gain little more, though secured by foreign armies and fleets.

The place of women in American society received considerable attention in Jacksonian America. Changing attitudes on sex are developed in Kevin White, *Sexual Liberation or Sexual License: The American Revolt Against Victorianism* (Chicago: Ivan R. Dee, 2000), 3–26, and Ellen K. Rothman, *Hands and Hearts: A History of Courtship in America* (New York: Basic Books, 1984). The growth of a distinct southern attitude regarding sex and its integration with cultural attitudes regarding religion and slavery is highlighted in William R. Taylor, *Cavalier and Yankee: The Old South and American National Character* (New York: George Braziller, 1961); Rollin G. Osterweis, *Romanticism and Nationalism in the Old South* (Baton Rouge: Louisiana State University Press, 1967); and Stephanie McCurry, *Masters of Small Worlds: Yeoman Households, Gender Relations, and the Political Culture of the Antebellum South Carolina Low Country* (New York: Oxford University Press, 1995).

The relative decline in sexual freedoms experienced by women in early Victorian America, both North and South, received support from socially conservative Christians. Chancellor James Kent held women to greater moral standards than men. He argued that society required women to raise their children with a full appreciation of morality, and that adultery committed by a husband "is not evidence of such entire depravity, not equally injurious in its effects upon the morals, and good order, and happiness of domestic life," as that committed by a wife. While judges such as Kent left Christian principles implicit in their enforcement of marriage laws, other legal actors did not. In 1845, Edward Mansfield published *The Legal Rights, Liabilities, and Duties of Women*, in which he recognized marriage as a means of fulfilling the Christian invocation of patriarchy: "[marriage is] an institution of God ... begun in the garden of Eden [and] perpetuated by the laws of nature, of religion, and of civil society." Sehat, *Myth of Religious Freedom*, 103–4.

Yet, some women responded by vociferously asserting their rights and by organizing to change their society. Women as reformers are highlighted in Lori D. Ginzberg, *Women and the Work of Benevolence: Morality, Politics, and Class in the 19th Century United States* (New Haven, CT: Yale University Press, 1990); Scott Martin, *Devil of the Domestic Sphere: Temperance, Gender, and Middle-Class Ideology* (DeKalb: Northern Illnois University Press, 2008); Ann Braude, *Radical Spirits: Spiritualism and Women's Rights in Nineteenth Century America*, 2nd ed. (Bloomington: Indiana University Press, 2001); Sally G. McMillen, *Seneca Falls and the Origins of the Women's Rights Movement* (New York: Oxford University Press, 2008); Celia Morris Eckhardt, *Fanny Wright: Rebel in America* (Cambridge, MA: Harvard University Press, 1984); and Nancy Cott, *The Bonds of Womanhood* (New Haven, CT: Yale University Press, 1977).

B. Politics, Popular Culture, and Law

The aforementioned *What Hath God Wrought* by Daniel Walker Howe provides a tremendous overview of the Jacksonian era, though it is completely unfair to view this sophisticated analytical work as merely an introduction to the age. Prior to publication of Howe's book, decent political and cultural overviews were provided as parts of larger works on American history, such as Samuel Eliot Morison and Henry Steele Commager, *The Growth of the American Republic*, vol. 1 (New York: Oxford University Press, 1962).

The identity and meaning of Andrew Jackson have been almost as heated and politicized a historiographic debate as the separation of church and state. Some of the better resources include Robert V. Remini, *Andrew Jackson*, 3 vols. (New York: Harper & Row, 1977); Gerard N. Magliocca, *Andrew Jackson and the Constitution: The Rise and Fall of Generational Regimes* (Lawrence: University Press of Kansas, 2007); Andrew Burstein, *The Passions of Andrew Jackson* (New York: Alfred A. Knopf, 2003); Edward Pessen, *Jacksonian America: Society, Personality, and Politics* (Urbana: University of Illinois Press, 1985); Robert V. Remini, *The Revolutionary Age of Andrew Jackson* (New York: Harper & Row, 1985); Arthur M. Schlesinger, Jr., *The Age of Jackson* (New York: Book Find Club, 1945); Harry L. Watson, *Liberty and Power: The Politics of Jacksonian America* (New York: Hill & Wang, 2006); Alexander Saxton, *The Rise and Fall of the White Republic: Class Politics and Mass Culture in Nineteenth Century America* (New York: Verso, 1990); Michael F. Holt,

The Rise and Fall of the American Whig Party: Jacksonian Politics and the Onset of the Civil War (New York: Oxford University Press, 1999); and Daniel Feller, *Jacksonian Promise: America, 1815–1840* (Baltimore, MD: Johns Hopkins University Press, 1995); "Politics and Society: Toward a Jacksonian Synthesis," *Journal of the Early Republic* 10 (Summer 1990): 135–61. The scaling back of individualistic impulses in Jacksonian America is noted in Joseph F. Kett, *Merit: The History of a Founding ideal from the American Revolution to the Twenty-First Century* (Ithaca, NY: Cornell University Press, 2013).

On the industrial revolution, economic growth, and social conditions, see: Robert F. Dalzell, Jr., *Enterprising Elite: The Boston Associates and the World They Made* (New York: W.W. Norton, 1987); Rowland Berthoff, *An Unsettled People: Social Order and Disorder in American History* (New York: Harper & Row, 1971); John Steele Gordon, *An Empire of Wealth* (New York: Harper Collins, 2004); Stanley Lebergott, *The Americans: An Economic Record* (New York: W.W. Norton, 1984); Scott Reynolds Nelson, *A Nation of Deadbeats: An Uncommon History of America's Financial Disasters* (New York: Alfred A. Knopf, 2012); and Sean Wilentz, *Chants Democratic: New York City and the Rise of the American Working Class, 1788–1850* (New York: Oxford University Press, 1984).

The aforementioned *The People's Welfare* by William Novak provides an excellent account of the growth of statutory regulation in Jacksonian America. However, see also Helen Tangiers, *Public Markets and Civic Culture in Nineteenth-Century America* (Baltimore, MD: Johns Hopkins University Press, 2003). Much of the legal history of the period from 1830 to 1865 concerns itself with this growth in state law, the failures of the Supreme Court to protect the rights of slaves and the coming of the Civil War, and questions concerning presidential powers and protected rights during that war. Yet, legal historians have noted that both federal and state laws during this time provided a conducive environment for the continuation of economic growth. Mark Wilson, "Law and the American State, From the Revolution to the Civil War: Institutional Growth and Structural Change," in *Cambridge History of Law in America*, vol. 2; R. Kent Newmyer, *Supreme Court Justice Joseph Story: Statesman of the Old Republic* (Chapel Hill: North Carolina University Press,

1985); Morton Horowitz, *The Transformation of American Law, 1780–1860* (Cambridge, MA: Harvard University Press, 1977). Considerable work on this era has focused on judges, particularly at the state court level. Peter Karsten, *Heart versus Head: Judge-Made Law in Nineteenth-Century America* (Chapel Hill: University of North Carolina Press, 1997); Jeffrey Steven Kahana, *The Unfolding of American Labor Law: Judges, Workers, and Public Policy Across Two Political Generations, 1780–1850* (El Paso, TX: LFB Scholarly Publishers, 2014); Leonard Levy, *The Law of the Commonwealth and Chief Justice Shaw* (Cambridge, MA: Harvard University Press, 1957); John Theodore Horton, *James Kent: A Study in Conservatism, 1763–1847* (New York: Da Capo, 1969); Harry P. Stumpf, *American Judicial Politics*, 2nd ed. (San Diego, CA: Harcourt, Brace, Jovanovich, 1988); Daniel Blinka, "The Roots of the Modern Trial," in *Journal of the Early Republic* 27 (2007): 293–334. On state law's receptivity to Christian campaigns for legal change, see Winnifred Fallers Sullivan, "The State," in *Themes in Religion and American Culture*, ed. by Philip Goff and Paul Harvey (Chapel Hill: University of North Carolina Press, 2004).

Some interesting work has been done on the government's role in internal improvements. Harry N. Schieber, *Ohio Canal Era: A Case Study of Government and the Economy, 1820–1861* (Athens: Ohio University Press, 1969); John Lauritz Larson, *National Improvements: National Public Works and the Promise of Popular Government in the Early United States* (Chapel Hill: University of North Carolina Press, 2001).

The historiography on Abraham Lincoln is voluminous, but help in understanding his religious sentiments and how they influenced his speaking and decision making is found in the aforementioned Garry Wills, *Head and Heart*; *Lincoln at Gettysburg: The Words that Remade America* (New York: Simon & Schuster, 1992); Mark E. Neely, *The Last Best Hope of Earth: Abraham Lincoln and the Promise of America* (Cambridge, MA: Harvard University Press, 1993); Merrill D. Peterson, *Lincoln in American Memory* (New York: Oxford University Press, 1994); Mark Noll, *America's God: From Jonathan Edwards to Abraham Lincoln* (New York: Oxford University Press, 2002); and David L. Weaver-Zercher, "Theologies" in *Themes in Religion and American Culture*.

V. Late Nineteenth and Early Twentieth Centuries

A. *Cultural Histories*

Robert Wiebe describes Americans' activities from 1877 to 1920 as a "search for order." He contends that during this period, the focus of economic, moral, and political cultures shifted from local to national communities. This transformation occurred amid tremendous changes in American culture resulting from the end of slavery; expanded immigration; unprecedented disparities in wealth and social power; technological and scientific advances; the closing of the frontier and completion of the transcontinental railroad; industrialization; the growth of cities; the proliferation of the radio, national magazines, and mail-order catalogues; and a foreign policy that sought to export American values and culture. But, as Wiebe describes the homogenizing or nationalizing impulses these factors encouraged, he also identifies the divergent reactions to this social change as tending to fragment and even polarize American society. Not everyone celebrated the personal and informal communalism of earlier eras being subsumed by a national culture that valued predictability, expertise, professionalism, efficiency, and national functionalism. This new culture substituted anonymity for personal relationships, formality for informality, and a respect for privacy for communalism. Robert H. Wiebe, *The Search for Order, 1877–1920* (New York: Hill & Wang, 1967).

George Fredrickson also notes the growth of a national culture after the Civil War but attributes it to American longings for a new community built upon discipline, self-denial, and respect for authority. He argues that the pain of the Civil War defeated ideas of anti-institutional individualism, such as Thoreau's embrace of civil disobedience, and encouraged conformity to national values. The reliance upon scientific experts, bureaucracies, and even such national arbiters of taste as magazines or catalogs reflects this new preference for conformity in Victorian America. Even more important, Americans embraced an obedience to institutional authority as protecting their values and beliefs. George M. Fredrickson, *The Inner Civil War: Northern Intellectuals and the Crisis of the Union* (Urbana: University of Illinois Press, 1965).

On Victorian-era culture, see: Louise L. Stevenson, *The Victorian Homefront: American Thought and Culture, 1860–1880* (New

York: Twayne, 1991), and Coleen McDonnell, *The Christian Home in Victorian America, 1840–1900* (Bloomington: Indiana University Press, 1986). On the influence of large corporations on this culture, see Alan Trachtenberg, *The Incorporation of America: Culture and Society in the Gilded Age* (New York: Hill & Wang, 2007). A thoroughly entertaining and enlightening cultural history of the late 1800s is Shelley Fisher Fishkin, *Lighting Out for the Territory: Reflections on Mark Twain and American Culture* (New York: Oxford University Press, 1996). Equally readable and enjoyable are cultural histories of the 1920s and 1930s: Frederick Lewis Allen, *Only Yesterday: An Informal History of the 1920s* (New York: Harper & Row, 1931), and *Since Yesterday: 1929–1939* (New York: Harper & Row, 1939). A classic work of great value remains William E. Leuchtenberg, *The Perils of Prosperity, 1914–1932* (Chicago: University of Chicago Press, 1958). For a good account of Prohibition and its failure to fulfill the aims of its proponents, see Daniel Okrent, *Last Call: The Rise and Fall of Prohibition* (New York: Simon & Schuster, 2010).

Immigration and the accompanying rise in American Catholicism, as well as the tensions between Catholics and Protestants at the time, are addressed in Robert Trevino, "Ethnicity," in *Themes in Religion and American Culture*; Oscar Handlin, *The Uprooted: The Epic Story of the Great Migrations that Made the American People* (Boston: Little, Brown, 1951, 1973); John Higham, *Hanging Together: Unity and Diversity in American Culture* (New Haven, CT: Yale University Press, 1981); John Bodnar, *The Transplanted: A History of Immigrants in Early America* (Bloomington: Indiana University Press, 1985); John T. McGreevy, *Catholicism and American Freedom: A History* (New York: W.W. Norton, 2003); Charles E. Curran, *Catholic Social Teaching, 1891–Present: A Historical, Theological, and Ethical Analysis* (Washington, DC: Georgetown University Press, 2002); Kenneth C. Grasso, Gerard V. Bradley, and Robert P. Hunt, *Catholicism, Liberalism and Communitarianism: The Catholic Intellectual Tradition and the Moral Foundations of Democracy* (Lanham, MD: Rowman & Littlefield, 1995); Barbara Miller Solomon, *Ancestors and Immigrants: A Changing New England Tradition* (Boston: Northeastern University Press, 1980); John C. Jeffries, Jr. and James E. Ryan, "A Political History of the Establishment Clause," *Michigan Law Review* 100 (2001): 279; and Jane Addams, *Twenty Years at Hull*

House, ed. by James Hart (Urbana: University of Illnois Press, 1990). The history of the Blaine Amendment is presented in Thomas C. Berg, "Disestablishment from Blaine to Everson: Federalism, School Wars, and the Emerging Modern State," in *No Establishment of Religion*, 307–40; Feldman, *Divided By God*; Sehat, *Myth of American Religious Freedom*; Hamburger, *Separation*; and Alfred W. Meyer, "The Blaine Amendment and the Bill of Rights," *Harvard Law Review*, 64 (1951): 939–45.

Jewish immigration and issues regarding acculturation during the same period are developed in David J. O'Brien, "The Changing Contours of American Religion," in *Religion and Immigration: Christian, Jewish, and Muslim Experiences in the United States*, ed. by Yvonne Yazbeck Haddad, Jane I. Smith, and John Esposito (Lanham, MD: Rowman & Littlefield, 2003); Martha Nussbaum, "Judaism and the Love of Reason," in *Philosophy, Feminism, and Faith*, ed. by Ruth E. Groenhout and Marya Bower (Bloomington: Indiana University Press, 2003); Stephen Whitfield, "In Defense of Diversity: Jewish Thought from Assimilation to Cultural Pluralism," in *Charity, Philanthropy, and Civility*; Lawrence H. Fuchs, *The American Kaleidoscope: Race, Ethnicity, and the Civic Culture* (Hanover, NH: University Press of New England, 1990); and Werner Sollors, *Beyond Ethnicity: Consent and Descent in American Culture* (New York: Oxford University Press, 1986).

The threats to mainstream American culture perceived to derive from Native American religion are discussed in Raymond J. DeMallie, ed., *The Sixth Grandfather: Black Elk's Teachings Given to John G. Neihardt* (Lincoln: University of Nebraska Press, 1984); Robert M. Utley, *The Lance and the Shield: The Life and Times of Sitting Bull* (New York: Ballantine Books, 1993); Dee Brown, *Bury My Heart at Wounded Knee: An Indian History of the American West* (New York: Holt, Rinehart, and Winston, 1970); Tracy Fessenden, "Race," in *Themes in Religion and American Culture*; and Clyde Holler, *Black Elk's Religion: The Sun Dance and Lakota Catholicism* (Syracuse, NY: Syracuse University Press, 1995). Christian missionaries' roles in the federal government's policies to "civilize the Indians" are presented in Francis Paul Prucha, *The Great Father: The United States Government and the American Indians* (Lincoln: University of Nebraska Press, 1984), 152–64; Robert F. Berkhofer, Jr., *Salvation and the Savage: An Analysis of Protestant Missions and American Indian Response, 1787–1862* (Lexington: University of Kentucky Press, 1965); Stuart Banner, *How the Indians Lost Their Land: Law and Power on the Frontier* (Cambridge, MA: Belknap Press, 2005); and Angie Debo, *And Still the Waters Run: The Betrayal of the Five Civilized Tribes* (Princeton, NJ: Princeton University Press, 1973).

On religious influences upon and justification of the reactionary racism generated in response to the freed slaves and the new immigrants of various ethnicities and religions, see Kelly J. Baker, *Gospel According to the Klan: The KKK's Appeal to Protestant America, 1915–1930* (Lawrence: University Press of Kansas, 2011); Tracy Fessenden, "Race," in *Themes in Religion and American Culture*; Donald Warren, *Radio Priest: Charles Coughlin, the Father of Hate Radio* (New York: Free Press, 1996); James A. Madison, *A Lynching in the Heartland: Race and Memory in America* (New York: St. Martin's Press, 2001); Jane Dailey, *The Age of Jim Crow* (New York: W.W. Norton, 2009); and Kathleen Blee, *Women of the Klan: Racism and Gender in the 1920s* (Berkeley: University of California Press, 1991).

B. Intellectual and Religious Histories

Several books provide excellent understandings of the intellectual currents of late nineteenth- and early twentieth-century America, though the scope of the works is larger. William H. Goetzman, *Beyond the Revolution: A History of American Thought from Paine to Pragmatism* (New York: Basic Books, 2009); Richard Hofstadter, *Anti-Intellectualism in American Life* (New York: Random House, 1962); Louis Hartz, *The Liberal Tradition in America* (San Diego, CA: Harcourt, Brace, Jovanovich, 1955); Michael Kammen, *People of Paradox: An Inquiry Concerning the Origins of American Civilization* (New York: Random House, 1972).

On the literary and artistic culture of the late nineteenth century, see Van Wyck Brooks, *New England: Indian Summer, 1865–1915* (New York: E.P. Dutton, 1940). On social Darwinism, see Richard Hofstadter, *Social Darwinism in American Thought* (Boston: Beacon Press, 1944); Robert C. Bannister, *Social Darwinism: Science and Myth in Anglo-American Social Thought* (Philadelphia: Temple University Press, 1979); and Mike Hawkins, *Social Darwinism in European and American Thought, 1860–1945* (New York: Cambridge University

Press, 1997). In the second half of the nineteenth century, many Americans, as often titularly Christian as atheistic, sought to pursue their professional lives in a completely secular realm – "without the constraint of religious obligations." Hamburger, *Separation*, 262. On the growth of secular rationalism, see James German "Economy," in *Themes in Religion and American Culture*; and William A. Durbin, "Science," in *Themes in Religion and American Culture*. The free-thought movement is addressed in David M. Rabban, *Free Speech in its Forgotten Years* (New York: Cambridge University Press, 1997), and Martin E. Marty, *The Infidel*, and in relation to one of its leading advocates in Oliver Larson, *American Infidel: Robert G. Ingersoll* (Madison, WI: Freedom From Religion Foundation, 1993).

Very good works in intellectual history over the last fifty years have brought greater understanding and appreciation of the writings and ideas of the social critics of the early twentieth century. Casey Nelson Blake, *Beloved Community: The Cultural Criticism of Randolph Bourne, Van Wyck Brooks, Waldo Frank, and Lewis Mumford* (Chapel Hill: University of North Carolina Press, 1990); John L. Thomas, *Alternative America: Henry George, Edward Bellamy, Henry Demarest Lloyd, and the Adversary Tradition* (Cambridge, MA: Harvard University Press, 1983); James T. Kloppenberg, *Uncertain Victory: Social Democracy and Progressivism in European and American Thought, 1890–1920* (New York: Oxford University Press, 1986); Richard H. Pells, *Radical Visions and American Dreams: Culture and Social Thought in the Depression Years* (New York: Harper & Row, 1973); Christopher Lasch, *The New Radicalism in America, 1889–1963: The Intellectual as a Social Type* (New York: W.W. Norton, 1965).

The advent of the feminist movement can be seen as a part of this social criticism. Insights can be drawn from: Rosalind Rosenberg, *Beyond Separate Spheres: Intellectual Roots of Modern Feminism* (New Haven, CT: Yale University Press, 1982), and Wendy J. Deichmann Edwards and Carolyn De Swarte Gifford, *Gender and the Social Gospel* (Urbana: University of Illinois Press, 2003). A good summary of the suffrage movement and its relationship to Christian dissent is provided in Sehat, *Myth of American Religious Freedom*. For more detail, see Barbara Goldsmith, *The Age of Suffrage, Spiritualism, and the Scandalous Victoria Woodhull* (New York: Alfred A. Knopf,

1998), and Mary Gabriel, *The Life of Victoria Woodhull, Uncensored* (Chapel Hill: Algonquin Books, 1998). A book very accessible for students is Myra MacPherson, *The Scarlet Sisters: Sex, Suffrage, and Scandal in the Gilded Age* (New York: Hatchett Book Group, 2014).

The thoughts of the social critics are closely aligned with those of the Social Gospelers and Christian Socialists. Suggested readings in these areas include Martin E. Marty, *Modern American Religion*, Vol. 2: *The Noise of Conflict, 1919–1941* (Chicago: University of Chicago Press, 1986); Gaines M. Foster, *Moral Reconstruction: Christian Lobbyists and the Federal Legislation of Morality, 1865–1920* (Chapel Hill: University of North Carolina Press, 2002); James Dombrowski, *The Early Days of Christian Socialism in America* (New York: Octagon Books, 1966); and Robert T. Handy, *The Social Gospel in America, 1870–1920* (New York: Oxford University Press, 1966). Crucial primary texts exhibiting communitarian critiques of contemporary American culture include Edward A. Ross, *Sin and Society: An Analysis of Latter-Day Iniquity* (Boston: Houghton Mifflin, 1907); Charles Cooley, *Social Organization: A Study of the Larger Mind* (New York: Charles Scribner's Sons, 1909); Samuel Zane Batten, *The Christian State: The State, Democracy, and Christianity* (Philadelphia: Griffin & Rowland, 1909); Walter Rauschenbusch, *Christianity and the Social Crisis*, ed. by Robert D. Cross (New York: Harper & Row, 1964, 1907); and Charles Sheldon, *In His Steps: What Would Jesus Do?* (Nashville, TN: Broadman Press, 1935, 1896).

The civil religion tempered both liberal and conservative religious expressions as it came to dominate American cultural life from the Civil War to World War II. Generations of commentators and historians have tried to capture the idea of the "civil religion"; continued disagreement as to the meaning or relevance of the term testifies to their failure. Still, the idea of a prevailing Protestant ideology rooted in broadly based Christian values, American exceptionalism, and patriotic duty resonates in the historical record, though it was challenged by the very diversity it sought to stymie. Henry May writes: "In 1876 Protestantism presented a massive, almost unbroken front in its defense of the status quo." Henry F. May, *The Protestant Churches and Industrial America* (New York: Octagon Books, 1963, 1949), 4. May is far from alone in noting that Americans of the era generally conceived of their Christian heritage in Protestant terms. But the nature of this Protestantism was as much political and cultural as it was religious. It combined the essential fundamental truth of Protestantism with "mythic, patriotic, and secular" understandings of national identity. Derek H. Davis, *Religion and the Continental Congress, 1774–1789: Contributions to Original Intent* (New York: Oxford University Press, 2000), 218.

The term "civil religion," borrowed from Jean-Jacques Rousseau, was used proudly by Robert Bellah, who contends that without a civil religion, society would lack the requisite moral and spiritual bonds to hold it together. Robert Bellah, "Civil Religion in America," in *Beyond Belief: Essays on Religion in a Post-Traditional World* (New York: Harper & Row, 1970), 170ff. Sidney Mead wrote more disparagingly of a "religion of the republic." Sidney E. Mead, *The Old Religion in the Brave New World; A Nation with the Soul of a Church;* and *The Lively Experiment.* Recently, Noah Feldman has identified a "nonsectarian" moral religion that persists in American culture. Feldman, *Divided by God.* The term "Public Protestantism" has been offered as well. Catherine L. Albanese, *America: Religions and Religion* (Belmont, CA: Wadsworth, 1981), 249. More recently, David Sehat argues that a moral establishment better describes Americans' integration of religious values into public life. Sehat, *Myth of American Religious Freedom.* Each term refers to a similar concept: a religious understanding that lacks expression through a common church and that eschews theology, creation myths, doctrinal creeds, and pretension to unique or absolute truth but is essential to popular understandings of morality as well as of the nation and one's love for and duties to it. See also Michael McConnell, "The Origins and Historical Understandings of Free Exercise of Religion," *Harvard Law Review* 103 (1990): 1409, arguing that the state could not survive without the force of a civil religion to support it. However, Mark A. Noll, *America's God*, argues, on page 9, that a synthesis of "evangelical Protestant religion, republican political ideology, and common sense moral reasoning" existed before the Civil War but broke down afterward. The civil religion tended to moderate the prophetic nature of Christianity and its compulsion to act on behalf of others. Ardent religionists on the right and left sought a different form of religious expression.

The communal aspects of Christianity and its imposition of social duty during the Victorian era are discussed in Winthrop S. Hudson,

The Great Tradition of the American Churches (New York: Harper & Row, 1953), and Martin E. Marty, *The One and the Many: America's Struggle for the Common Good* (Cambridge, MA: Harvard University Press, 1997). Catholicism's embrace of communitarian goals preceded the Protestant Social Gospel movement. Mary J. Oates, "Faith and Good Works: Catholic Giving and Taking," in *Charity, Philanthropy, and Civility*, and Charles J. Tull, *Father Coughlin and the New Deal* (Syracuse, NY: Syracuse University Press, 1965). Coughlin's radio show ran from 1926 to 1942. He became known as the "Radio Messiah," calling for a return to traditional Christian values as "an authentic voice of the America majority." Warren, *Radio Priest*, 1, 2. However, a highly respected historian disagrees that Father Coughlin advocated collectivism. He contends that both Huey Long and Coughlin developed their perspectives "from similar political traditions and espouse[d] similar ideologies" in an attempt to redefine individualism in a changing society. To him, Coughlin and Long offered a chance for working-class Americans to retain control of their lives by making power more accessible and wealth more evenly distributed. Alan Brinkley, *Voices of Protest: Huey Long, Father Coughlin, and the Great Depression* (New York: Alfred A. Knopf, 1982), ix.

Protestant churches during this period experienced tremendous divisions over both the privatization of social duties and the means of fulfilling them as fundamentalism clashed with various forms of Christian liberalism and the Social Gospel. The development of liberal Christianity served as both a precursor and antagonist to fundamentalism. Good synopses are provided once again in Ahlstrom, *Religious History of the American People*; Hutchison, *Religious Pluralism*; and Martin E. Marty, *Modern American Religion*, Vol. 1: *The Irony of It All, 1893–1919* (Chicago: University of Chicago Press, 1986). Marty notes the irony of a time known as "liberal and modern and progressive" giving rise to "thriving conservative movements" that persist to this day. See also William R. Hutchison, *Between the Times: The Travails of the Protestant Establishment in America, 1900–1960* (New York: Cambridge University Press, 1989).

The development of fundamentalism is traced in Donald B. Meyer, *The Protestant Search for Political Realism, 1919–1941* (Berkeley: University of California Press, 1960); George M. Marsden, *Fundamentalism and*

American Culture: The Shaping of Twentieth-Century Evangelicalism, 1870–1925 (New York: Oxford University Press, 190); Michael Lienesch, *In the Beginning: Fundamentalism, the Scopes Trial, and the Making of the Anti-Evolution Movement* (Chapel Hill: University of North Carolina Press, 2007); and Armstrong, *The Battle for God.* George Marsden integrates the fundamentalist and evangelical movements in his analysis of the theology espoused at Princeton at the turn of the century. He approvingly quotes Grant Walker to define evangelicalism as a belief that "[t]he sole authority in religion is the Bible and the sole means of salvation is a life-transforming experience wrought by the Holy Spirit through faith in Jesus Christ." George M. Marsden, "Evangelicals and the Scientific Culture: An Overview," in *Religion and Twentieth-Century American Intellectual Life*, ed. by Michael J. Lacey (New York: Cambridge University Press, 1991), 25. See also George M. Marsden, *Fundamentalism and American Culture*, and Paul Harvey, "Proselytization," in *Themes in Religion and American Culture.* Richard Hofstadter links Christian fundamentalism to intellectual persecutions and social intolerance in Richard Hofstadter, William Miller, and Daniel Aaron, *The United States: The History of the Republic* (Englewood Cliffs, NJ: Prentice-Hall, 1957). See also Richard Hofstadter, *Anti-Intellectualism in American Life.*

The growth of southern evangelicalism during this period is explained in Charles Reagan Wilson, "The Religion of the Lost Cause: Ritual and Organization of the Southern Civil Religion, 1865–1920," *Journal of Southern History*, 42(2) (May 1980), 219–38; Edward J. Blum and W. Scott Poole, *Vale of Tears: New Essays on Religion and Reconstruction* (Macon, GA: Mercer University Press, 2005).

Yet, as significant as the religious changes, especially the development of fundamentalism, have proven to be, perhaps the intellectual movement from this era of greatest long-lasting significance is Pragmatism. The ideas of Marx, Freud, and Levi-Strauss served as necessary prerequisites for the changing worldview that produced Pragmatism. The role of these three intellectual movements in shaping Western thought is explored in the context of the Jewish Diaspora from nineteenth-century ghettos. John Murray Cuddihy, *The Ordeal of Civility: Freud, Marx, Levi-Strauss, and the Jewish Struggle with Modernity* (New York: Basic Books, 1974). The secondary literature on Pragmatism is nearly exhaustive, but of particular value in this project are the essays in Robert Hollinger and David DePew, *Pragmatism: From Progressivism to Postmodernism* (Westport, CT: Praeger Press, 1995); Robert J. Lacey, *American Pragmatism and Democratic Faith* (DeKalb: Northern Illinois University Press, 2008); and Richard Rorty, *Philosophy and the Mirror of Nature* (Princeton, NJ: Princeton University Press, 1979).

C. Legal History

The aforementioned Sehat, *Myth of Religious Freedom*; Gordon, *Spirit of the Law*; and Feldman, *Divided by God*, provide excellent analyses of the major legal developments and cases of the era concerning religion. Broader legal summaries are available in Sarah Barringer Gordon, "Law and Religion, 1790–1920"; William E. Forbath, "Politics, State-Building, and the Courts, 1870–1920"; and Laura Edwards, "The Civil War and Reconstruction," in *Cambridge History of Law in America*, Vol. 2. A recently published text by a political scientist John W. Compton, *The Evangelical Origins of the Living Constitution* (Cambridge, MA: Harvard University Press, 2014), traces the evangelical contributions to moral regulation from the Benevolent Empire to the New Deal. Compton's work develops the argument noted here, that after ratification of the Constitution and the election of Jefferson in 1800, evangelicals sought to undo the liberal changes in society and reprioritized morality over property.

The best work on the *Scopes* trial is Edward J. Larson, *Summer for the Gods: The Scopes Trial and America's Continuing Debate over Science and Religion* (New York: Basic Books, 1997). As a teaching tool, none is better than Jeffrey P. Moran, *The Scopes Trial: A Brief History with Documents* (Boston: Bedford/St. Martin's, 2002). However, recourse also should be had to Michael Kazin, *A Godly Hero: The Life of William Jennings Bryan* (New York: Alfred A. Knopf, 2006); Ferenc M. Szasz, "William Jennings Bryan, Evolution, and the Fundamentalist-Modernist Controversy," in *Modern American Protestantism and Its World*, Vols. 10 (Munich, Germany: K.G. Saur, 1993); C. Allyn Russell, "William Jennings Bryan: Statesman-Fundamentalist," in *Modern American Protestantism*, Vol. 10, 75; and Lienesch, *In the Beginning*.

The best synopses and analyses of the *Reynolds* case are in the works of Sarah Gordon. See Sarah B. Gordon, *The Mormon Question*, and "Law and Religion, 1790–1920," in *Cambridge History of Law in America*, Vol. 2, 432–3.

Discussions of the Christian attempts to amend the Constitution can be found in Richard B. Bernstein, *Amending America: If We Love the Constitution So Much, Why Do We Keep Trying to Change It?* (New York: Times Books, 1993), 188, and David E. Kyvig, *Explicit and Authentic Acts: Amending the U.S. Constitution, 1776–1995* (Lawrence: University of Kansas Press, 1996), 189–90.

VI. 1930s to the Present

A. *Legal History*

On the decline of the contract clause and the Supreme Court's ultimate endorsement of the New Deal, see G. Edward White, *The Constitution and the New Deal* (Cambridge, MA: Harvard University Press, 2000); Jeff Shesol, *Supreme Power: Franklin Roosevelt vs. the Supreme Court* (New York: W.W. Norton, 2010); Barry Friedman, *The Will of the People*; Bernard Schwartz, *A History of the Supreme Court* (New York: Oxford University Press, 1993); Peter Charles Hoffer, Williamjames Hoffer, and N.E.H. Hull, *The Supreme Court: An Essential History* (Lawrence: University of Kansas Press, 2007); John A. Fliter and Derek S. Hoff, *Fighting Foreclosure: The Blaisdell Case, the Contract Clause, and the Great Depression* (Lawrence: University of Kansas Press, 2007); and Barry Cushman, "The Great Depression and the New Deal," in *Cambridge History of Law in America*, Vol. III, 268–318. The religious influences upon the New Deal are described in Ronald Isetti, "The Moneychangers of the Temple: FDR, American Civil Religion, and the New Deal," *Presidential Studies Quarterly* 26 (1966): 678–93.

On Pragmatism's influence upon law, leading to the growth of legal positivism, legal historian Mark Tushnet writes:

The pragmatic philosophers, led by John Dewey, developed a jurisprudence, sometimes described as sociological jurisprudence, that placed the idea of rights under real pressure. To pragmatists, social policy – and constitutional law – rested in the end on a careful balancing of interests. Yet, the very point of identifying something as a constitutional right was to block consideration of some social interests. Pragmatism weakened the distinction between rights and mere social policy, at a time when legal pragmatists were insisting that courts had given inadequate attention to social policy by erecting strong and pragmatically indefensible barriers to legislation in the name of rights.

Mark Tushnet, *The Rights Revolution in the Twentieth Century* (Washington, DC: American Historical Association, 2009), 11. Bruce Kuklick identifies both the thought of Dewey and that of popular Christianity in New Deal politics. Bruce Kuklick, "John Dewey, American Theology, and Scientific Politics" in *Religion and Intellectual Life*, 78–93. The ability of legal positivism to address moral issues as well as to express a scientific understanding of law is documented in Robert P. George, ed., *The Autonomy of Law: Essays on Legal Positivism* (New York: Oxford University Press, 1996).

Interesting scholarship exists from vastly different perspectives on the legal history of First Amendment rights and the nature of the separation of church and state in the late twentieth and twenty-first centuries. Some of the better works are Philip B. Kurland, "Of Church and State and the Supreme Court," *University of Chicago Law Review*, 29(1) (1961), 96; John C. Jeffries and James E. Ryan, "A Political History of the Establishment Clause," *Michigan Law Review* 100 (2001): 279–309; Ronald Dworkin, *Taking Rights Seriously* (London: Duckworth, 1977); Linda Przybyszewski, *Religion, Morality, and the Constitutional Order* (Washington, DC: American Historical Association, 2011); John Witte, Jr., *Religion and the American Constitutional Experiment*, 2nd ed. (Boulder, CO: Westview Press, 2005); Rousas John Rushdoony, *Law and Liberty* (Vallecito, CA: Ross House, 1984); Robert N. Bork, *Tradition and Morality in Constitutional Law* (Washington, DC: American Enterprise Institute for Public Policy Research, 1984); and Christopher Eisgruber and Lawrence G. Sager, *Religious Freedom and the Constitution* (Cambridge, MA: Harvard University Press, 2007). Kurland asserts the argument reprised in this text, that the establishment and free exercise clauses must be read together to make sense. James Madison made this argument implicitly when he argued that any establishment of religion "violated the free exercise of religion." Quoted in Martin E. Marty, "Getting Beyond the Myth of Christian America," in *No Establishment of Religion*, 376. The risk of subjecting religious tolerance to political debate and resolution is developed in Andrew R. Murphy, *Prodigal*

Nation: Moral Decline and Divine Punishment from New England to 9/11 (New York: Oxford University Press, 2009).

The earliest freedom of religion cases arising under the First Amendment are discussed in Gordon, *Spirit of the Law*, and David Manwaring, *Render Unto Caesar: The Flag Waving Controversy* (University of Chicago Press, 1962). The argument that the *Cantwell* decision, as well as the religion clause cases that followed it, were rooted in the application of rights to specific minority religious groups is convincingly presented in Van der Veyver and Witte, *Religious Human Rights in a Global Perspective*.

The diminution of individual rights as a result of collectivist policies and the assertion of group rights is intelligently argued in Richard Epstein, *Takings: Private Property and the Power of Eminent Domain* (Cambridge, MA: Harvard University Press, 1985), and Tushnet, *The Rights Revolution in the Twentieth Century*. See also Christine Sistare, Larry May, and Leslie Francis, eds., *Groups and Group Rights* (Lawrence: University Press of Kansas, 2001), and Axel R. Schäfer, *Piety and Public Funding: Evangelicals and the State in Modern America* (Philadelphia: University of Pennsylvania Press, 2012). The latter text offers an excellent analysis of religious communitarianism's interaction with the welfare state and the growth of big government. Schäfer uses the term "subsidiarity" in lieu of the term "allocative state," which is attributable to Peter Dobkin Hall, "Philanthropy, the Welfare State, and the Transformation of American Public and Private Institutions, 1945–2000," *Working Paper 5* (Cambridge, MA: Hauser Center for Non-Profit Organizations, Harvard University, 2000).

The idea that the Supreme Court can rely on principles consistent with and supportive of constitutional text is a subject of significant debate but convincingly developed in case law and legal commentary:

In expounding the Constitution, the Court's role is to discern "principles sufficiently absolute to give them roots throughout the community and continuity over significant periods of time, and to lift them above the level of the pragmatic political judgments of a particular time and place.

Archibald Cox, *The Role of the Supreme Court in American Government* (New York: Oxford University Press, 1976), 114. See also William E. Nelson, "The Eighteenth-Century Constitution as a Basis for Protecting Personal Liberty," in *Liberty and Community: Constitution and Rights in the Early American Republic*, ed. by William E. Nelson and Robert C. Palmer (New York: Oceana Publications, 1987); William E. Nelson, *Marbury v. Madison: The Origins and Legacy of Judicial Review* (Lawrence: University of Kansas Press, 2000); and James R. Stoner, Jr., *Common Law and Liberal Theory: Coke, Hobbes, and the Origins of American Constitutionalism* (Lawrence: University Press of Kansas, 1992). The historiography on judicial review has been strongly influenced of late by works asserting "popular constitutionalism." Asserting a malleable or living Constitution governed by political processes are Larry D. Kramer, *The People Themselves: Popular Constitutionalism and Judicial Review* (New York: Oxford University Press, 2004); Barry Friedman, *The Will of the People: How Public Opinion Has Influenced the Supreme Court and Shaped the Meaning of the Constitution* (New York: Farrar, Straus, and Giroux, 2009); and Ariela Gross, "Beyond Black and White: Cultural Approaches to Race and Slavery," *Columbia Law Review* 101 (April 2001): 640–90. Conversely, some assert the Constitution to be a fixed body of rules expressing ideological precepts that can only be altered by amendment. Gary L. McDowell, *The Language of Law and the Foundations of American Constitutionalism* (New York: Cambridge University Press, 2010). For a brief synopsis of how these positions have played out in recent debates over judicial review, see Mark McGarvie, "That Elusive Consensus: The Historiographic Significance of William E. Nelson's Works on Judicial Review," *Chicago-Kent Law Review* 89(3) (2014): 957–96.

Christian values have long been the justification for limiting law's prioritization of personal liberties. Kenneth L. Grasso, Gerard V. Bradley, and Robert P. Hunt, *Catholicism, Liberalism and Communitarianism: The Catholic Intellectual Tradition and the Moral Foundations of Democracy* (Lanham, MD: Rowman & Littlefield, 1995). The authors of this book are Catholic conservatives espousing Catholicism as a means of purging society of its rampant individualism in order to save democracy. A southern variant of communalism, with roots in a near-feudalistic conception of society justifying slavery in the early 1800s but redefined through evangelicalism in the twentieth century, also eschews strict rights protections for the social good. Gaines M. Foster, "The End of Slavery and the Origins of the Bible Belt," in *Vale of Tears*, 147–63. By the 1930s and 1940s, other groups of socially conscious Christians openly questioned Americans' devotion to economic and social liberty. The Niebuhrs and Paul Tillich led a neo-orthodox rejection of liberal individualism. Hutchison, *Religious Pluralism in America*, and Marty, *Modern American Religion*, Vol. 2, 323–30. The rights revolution of the 1960s enhanced the ability of evangelicals to marshal support for socially conservative movements. Garry Wills, *Head and Heart*; James Davison Hunter, *American Evangelicalism: Conservative Religion and the Quandary of Modernity* (New Brunswick, NJ: Rutgers University Press, 1983); Michael Lienesch, *Redeeming America: Piety and Politics in the New Christian Right* (Chapel Hill: University of North Carolina Press, 1993); Eugene F. Provenzo, *Religious Fundamentalism and American Education: The Battle for the Public Schools* (Albany: State University of New York Press, 1990).

Rights-oriented liberals generally underestimated the political power of evangelical social conservatives. "In the middle of the twentieth century, it was generally taken for granted that secularism was an irreversible trend." Karen Armstrong, *The Battle for God*, xi–xii. A legalistic protection of rights has clashed with political interests rooted in Christian communitarianism in several specific arenas, each well documented in historical literature. Excellent analyses and commentaries regarding state funding for religiously oriented schools and the *Everson* decision can be found in Feldman, *Divided by Law*, 171–7; Gordon, *Spirit of the Law*, 60–72; Hamburger, *Separation*, 454–78; Witte, *Religion and the American Constitutional Experiment*, 138–9; and Sehat, *Myth of American Religious Freedom*, 235–8. The battle over public school teachers leading students in prayer during class is wonderfully portrayed in Bruce J. Dierenfield, *The Battle over School Prayer: How* Engel v. Vitale *Changed America* (Lawrence: University of Kansas Press, 2007).

The issue of teaching evolution versus creationism has been addressed in Wendell R. Bird, "Freedom from Establishment and Unneutrality in Public School Instruction and Religious School Regulation," *Harvard Journal of Law and Public Policy* 2 (1970); 124–216, and Robert Rubin, "Defining Religion by Its Function: Christian-Conservative Use of the Establishment Clause to Purge Classrooms of the 'Religion' of Secular Humanism," American Society for Legal History Annual Conference, Philadelphia, November 18–20, 2010.

The abortion issue has been the subject of voluminous literature. No less a supporter of civil rights than legal scholar Ronald Dworkin has recognized the complexity of the issue. While arguing in support of a woman's right to abort her fetus, he asserts that the Christian argument that each life has intrinsic value is a "contestable value," and that the freedom of religion requires law to respect religiously derived contestable values. Ronald Dworkin, "What Is Sacred," in *Life's Dominion: An Argument about Abortion, Euthanasia, and Individual Freedom* (New York: Alfred A. Knopf, 1993), 68–101.

On the legal issues concerning religion, sex, and marriage, see Nancy Cott, *Public Vows: A History of Marriage and the Nation* (Cambridge, MA: Harvard University Press, 2000); Alan Sears and Craig Osten, *The Homosexual Agenda: Exposing the Principle Threat to Religious Freedom Today* (Nashville, TN: Broadman & Holman, 2003); Douglas Laycock, Anthony Picarello, and Robin Fretwell Wilson, eds., *Same-Sex Marriage and Religious Liberty: Emerging Conflicts* (Lanham, MD: Rowman & Litlefield, 2008); Gordon, *Spirit of the Law*, 169–207; Fay Botham, *Almighty God Created the Races: Christianity, Interracial Marriage, and American Law* (Chapel Hill: University of North Carolina Press, 2009); Margo Canaday, "Heterosexuality as a Legal Regime," in *Cambridge History*, Vol. 3, 442–71; Dale Carpenter, *Flagrant Conduct: The Story of* Lawrence v. Texas*: How a Bedroom Arrest Decriminalized Gay Americans* (New York: W.W. Norton, 2011); and Erik J. Krueger, "God versus Government: Understanding State Authority in the Context of the Same-Sex Marriage Movement," *Liberty University Law Review* 235 (2013).

The accommodation doctrine and the confusion it has created have been criticized by legal scholars on the left and the right. John Witte writes that the "Supreme Court, which has directed the American experiment" in religious liberty since the 1940s, "no longer inspires confidence," and as a result, religious liberty appears to be "wandering without any regular system of operations." Witte, *Religion and the Constitutional Experiment*, xx. Mary Ann Glendon and Paul Yanes similarly contend that "[r]eligious clause jurisprudence has been described on all sides, and even by Justices themselves, as unprincipled, incoherent, and unworkable." Mary Ann Glendon and Paul F. Yanes, "Structured Free Exercise," *Michigan Law Review* 90 (1991): 477,

478. In 2009, NYU Law Professor Barry Friedman wrote: "[F]or the first time in American history, the Supreme Court's power of judicial review has come under siege simultaneously from both sides of the ideological spectrum." Barry Friedman, *The Will of the People: How Public Opinion Has Influenced the Supreme Court and Shaped the Meaning of the Constitution* (New York: Farrar, Straus, and Giroux, 2009), 7.

B. Culture and Religion

In the postwar era, "any lingering sense of Protestant hegemony gave way to recognition of pluralism as the American cultural reality." John F. Wilson and Donald L. Drakeman, eds., *Church and State in American History: Key Documents, Decisions, and Commentary from the Past Three Centuries*, 3rd ed. (Cambridge, MA: Westview Press, 2003), 219. Ahlstrom discusses the new expression and meanings of religion after 1945. Ahlstrom, *A Religious History of the American People*, 949–64, 1037–96. The liberalization of the mainline churches in the 1960s and the resulting exodus of conservatives to nondenominational evangelical churches are described in Donald Drakeman, "The Churches on Church and State," in *The Church's Public Role: Retrospect and Prospect*, ed. by Dieter T. Hessel (Grand Rapids, MI: William B. Eerdmans, 1992), and Feldman, *Divided by God*, 186–219. During the 1960s, the public image of the Nation of Islam benefited from two charismatic leaders, Malcolm X and Cassius Clay, who changed his name to Muhammad Ali out of respect for his faith. Yet, control of the Nation of Islam remained with Elijah Muhammad until his death in 1974. Claude Clegg, *Original Man: The Life and Times of Elijah Muhammad* (New York: St. Martin's Press, 1997). Ali's refusal to join the military further raised awareness of the organization. The Selective Service of the United States denied him an exemption, finding that Ali was inconsistent in explaining his reasons, a decision upheld by the Fifth Circuit. Ali was stripped of his championship, fined, and, as a convicted felon, prevented from fighting. In 1971, the Supreme Court overturned the Appellate Court decision. *Clay v. United States*, 403 US 698 (1971).

On the increasingly conservative political and social culture in the United States since the early 1970s, see William C. Berman, *America's Right Turn: From Nixon to Bush* (Baltimore, MD: Johns

Hopkins University Press, 1994); H.W. Brands, *The Strange Death of American Liberalism* (New Haven, CT: Yale University Press, 2001); and Steve Fraser and Gary Gerstle, *The Rise and Fall of the New Deal Order, 1930–1980* (Princeton, NJ: Princeton University Press, 1989). See also Wills, *Head and Heart,* and Sean Wilentz, *The Age of Reagan, 1974–2008* (New York: HarperCollins, 2008). A burgeoning literature on the use of private-sector organizations to perform public responsibilities is highlighted by David Harvey, *A Brief History of Neoliberalism* (New York: Oxford University Press, 2005), and Manfred B. Steger and Ravi K. Roy, *Neoliberalism: A Very Short Introduction* (New York: Oxford University Press, 2010). The historic reality of a public/private distinction is attacked by an author who asserts that government has generally catered to and supported private businesses. Mike O'Connor, *A Commercial Republic: America's Enduring Debate over Democratic Capitalism* (Lawrence: University Press of Kansas, 2014).

The private voluntary associations of the Religious Right since the 1980s have behaved much like those of the early 1800s under the encouragement of Beecher and Finney; they have targeted liberal ideas and social behaviors as causes for concern that would spur true believers to action. Perhaps because the Religious Right had its founding in attacking the Equal Rights Amendment, many of its early crusades concerned sex and gender. Its advocacy of sexual abstinence among high school and college students began in the 1970s. Abortion continued to be a rallying call through the 1970s, 1980s, 1990s, and even into the twenty-first century. Pornography, too, came under attack from the Religious Right. One Christian author argued that the growth of pornography in the 1970s was the product of a plot by enemies of Christianity and America intended "to create such an obsession with sex among young people that they have no time or interest in spiritual pursuits." James R. Parsons, *The Assault on the Family* (Melbourne, FL, 1978), 10. Also, as the positions taken by Schlafly and LaHaye in the ERA debate indicate, women's roles in society became topics of debate. Christian women faced a conundrum of how to pursue their faith, their new social, economic, and sexual freedoms, and their philosophical or feminist interests simultaneously. By being true to conservative Christian expressions of women's duties, women seemingly would have to renounce their social and intellectual lives, and to behave conversely seemed to promise both alienation from the church and God's damnation. As women's issues became the focal point of the culture wars, women especially had to choose a side. Groenhout and Bower, *Philosophy, Feminism, and Faith*.

Criticism of rights as diminishing morality and societal integrity has been presented in Robert H. Bork, *Slouching Towards Gomorrah: Modern Liberalism and American Decline* (New York: Regan Books, 1996); William J. Bennett, *The Broken Hearth: Reversing the Moral Collapse of the American Family* (New York: Doubleday, 2001); and Gertrude Himmelfarb, *The De-Moralization of Society: From Victorian Virtues to Modern Values* (New York: Alfred A. Knopf, 1995). The communitarian character of Christianity, both historically and as expressed in contemporary conservative movements, is developed in the works of James Davison Hunter. In particular, see James Davison Hunter, *Culture Wars: The Struggle to Define America* (New York: Basic Books, 1991).

A primary focus on the Religious Right has been legal protection for Christian morals and values. In 1984, the National Council of Churches of Christ issued guidelines concerning what it described as the "controversy over religion and politics." It included the following statement:

[As] one of the purposes of law is to define and punish unacceptable behavior [and] determining what behavior is unacceptable is the promise of morality [and] religion is one important source of morality, all voices urging the embodiment of morality in law [should] be subject to debate and criticism, religion no less than any other.

Wilson and Drakeman, *Church and State in American History*, 269. On conservative ecumenism, see also Charles E. Curran, *Catholic Social Teaching*, and Michael P. Hornsby-Smith, *An Introduction to Catholic Social Thought* (New York: Cambridge University Press, 2006). However, long-time Republican Senator and Ambassador John Danforth explains that the moralism of the Religious Right betrays both the ideals of the Republican Party and the principles of Christian faith. John Danforth, *Faith and Politics* (New York: Viking Press, 2006).

The scholarly search for a greater sense of community since the 1980s has contributed to a decline in the relevance of the distinction between public and private sectors. Representative is Robert

Wuthnow, *Christianity and Civil Society: The Contemporary Debate* (Valley Forge, PA: Trinity Press International, 1996); Robert Putnam, *Bowling Alone: The Collapse and Revival of American Community* (New York: Simon & Schuster, 2000); and Mary Ann Glendon, *Rights Talk: The Impoverishment of Political Discourse* (New York: Free Press, 1991). Some assert that a legal reliance on rights "encourages a strident, self-interested individualism" detrimental to the social good. Austin Sarat and Thomas R. Kearns, eds., *Identities, Politics, and Rights* (Ann Arbor: University of Michigan Press, 1995), 7, referencing Richard Morgan, *Disabling America: The "Rights Industry" in Our Time* (New York: Basic Books, 1984). Harvard Professor Anna Greenberg argues that religious institutions in general, and churches in particular, serve a vital role in building community, but to do so they must act as political institutions supporting "grassroots democracy." Anna Greenberg, "The Church and the Revitalization of Politics and Community," *Political Science Quarterly* 115 (Fall 2000), 377–94. See also Douglas A. Hicks, *With God on All Sides: Leadership in a Devout and Diverse America* (New York: Oxford University Press, 2009).

Index